Indonesia   *Resources and their Technological Development*

A Publication of the CENTER FOR DEVELOPMENTAL CHANGE, University of Kentucky

Indonesia

Resources and their Technological Development

EDITED BY HOWARD W. BEERS

The University Press of Kentucky   *Lexington*

Standard Book Number 8131–5118–X
Library of Congress Catalog Card Number 78–111503

Copyright © 1970 by The University Press of Kentucky

A statewide cooperative scholarly publishing agency
serving Berea College, Centre College of Kentucky,
Eastern Kentucky University, Kentucky State College,
Morehead State University, Murray State University,
University of Kentucky, University of Louisville,
and Western Kentucky University.

Editorial and Sales Offices: Lexington, Kentucky 40506

Contents

CHAPTER I

Howard W. Beers **Introduction**

Since 1964, Indonesia has experienced one of the most drastic political and economic reversals to be observed in modern history. Former President Sukarno had demanded of his people a "stir benteng,"[1] a sharp turn to the political left. The results were frequently regrettable and need not be recapitulated here. Perhaps the most unfortunate one, certainly the most germane to our discussion, was the virtual wreckage of the Indonesian economy, to which destruction governmental neglect and mismanagement abundantly contributed. It was a period of slogans and fantasies, of expensive, nonproductive projects, and of unbridled monetary inflation.

A corrective change was demanded and achieved by the Army and the new patriots of the "generasi 66,"[2] and in a brief agony of political convulsion, Indonesia wrested guidance from the pilots of political romanticism, placing it instead with the designers of a new economic realism.

Under the policies of Sukarno's successor, President Suharto, there is room for hope in Indonesia, and even for optimism. The Suharto government has succeeded in slowing inflation and in 1968 the government managed to balance its budget for the first time in the twenty-three-year history of the Republic of Indonesia. The priorities of the new government are realistic, showing a strong concern for the elemental need for food and clothing. Under the new regime, most of the expropriated properties of foreign-based firms have been returned, and the economic climate is favorable to investment of foreign capital.[3]

The results have been well-nigh dramatic. Between 1967 and 1968, the production of rice increased by nearly a million tons, and for 1974 (the last year of the current five-year plan) the government has set a goal of 15 million tons, as against the 10.16 million tons produced in 1968. Within the past two years, over 200 foreign companies, almost half of them American, have entered proposals for investment. Both foreign and Indonesian investors are planning to exploit such agricultural resources as timber, rubber, and sugar, and there is a rapidly growing exploitation and exploration of such mineral resources as oil, bauxite, tin, and copper. The government has marked off areas of oil exploration for over twenty Western and Japanese oil companies. After years of stagnation, the economy is reviving.

There is, to be sure, a race against time. Indonesia's problems are great and pressing, and politically, the government needs quick and easily visible improvements in the popular level of living. To speed national development, the application of modern science and technology may well be the magical ingredient. Recognizing this, many Indonesians and foreign friends of Indonesia have begun to "pick up the pieces," to inventory available knowledge, and to ponder how more of the data for development might quickly be made accessible.

This book is a 1967 product of the new mood. The main body of the book is a set of papers which were read and discussed in a seminar. Organized by the Center for Developmental Change at the University of Kentucky, and held in Lexington, May 21–27, 1967, the Seminar on Science and Technology in Indonesian Development marked the end of a decade of the University's involvement in Indonesian education (at Bandung and Bogor) and expressed the University's continuing interest.

The participants in the seminar advanced many interesting views and suggestions, some of which can be summarized. As a basis for realistic and achievable strategy toward Indonesian development, the contributors emphasized the importance of economic planning, in which agricultural development should have first priority to assure food supply, raw materials, and an export market to earn foreign exchange. In agriculture, a number of new trends seem promising: the intensification of production, the selective opening of new land areas (mainly through improved irrigation), the acceptance of petrochemicals as new sources of clothing materials, and the reorganization of production for export. Other promising trends include stress on vocational agricultural education, the introduction of regional experiment stations and testing programs, a further strengthening and development of the Agricultural University and its affiliated faculties, feasibility studies for rural development, and further application of the "mass guidance" (BIMAS)[4] techniques in tropical agriculture, in rural development, and in research and graduate study of the agricultural and biological sciences.

The seminar emphasized the need for vigorous further exploration and development of marine resources in the seas around the islands. There is also need for widening exploration of mineral reserves, especially of oil, but including sources of phosphates for fertilizer. It is important that the scientific data resulting from such explorations be accumulated, preserved, and shared.

The seminar, recognizing the serious lack in Indonesia of data and records essential to economic planning, urged that the Indonesian government and other agencies, as a matter of high priority, establish records of economic activity.

In relation to the need for intensified research in many fields, the seminar participants discussed the relative needs for basic versus applied research and concluded that Indonesian development currently requires "oriented research" on topics of vital importance to Indonesian growth and applicable to the improvement of technology and the solution of developmental problems.

Economic research, in particular, could be made more practical. There is need for a better inventory of existing information and of improved utilization of data already collected. Research projects should be chosen carefully and, to insure coordination with national policy, should be discussed in advance with the men who make that policy. To be of practical value, the research should be based on something more than professional interest, though the research itself should be a thoroughly professional and unprejudiced analysis. Projects should have sufficient duration and continuity to provide at least preliminary reports as pilot projects. They should also be kept to a scale that can be coped with in present-day conditions. Nationwide surveys of ambitious scope can be deferred; projects which can exert an early influence in the making of policy will be a greater contribution to economic advancement.

Seminar opinion favored the principle of joint scientific and technical activity by Indonesian and foreign scholars and research workers, as offering a more useful relationship than the conventional technical assistance arrangements in earlier years. In the long run, the foreigner who comes to Indonesia as a visiting scientist and works with Indonesian colleagues at operational levels performs a more effective educational service than the one who comes specifically to give instruction or to do "hit and run" research.

Oriented research was discussed also as a guiding principle for the various institutes, especially the National Biological Institute and its sister organizations, which require support not only in the context of national development but also as participants in world science. Indonesia, through its research institutes, its marine science establishments, and biological field stations, is moving into a position of capability to make important contributions to world science, from which it deserves and requires corresponding support. In organizing its participation in national development, in world science, and in Southeast Asian regional development, Indonesia requires the utmost cooperation, intercommunication, and mutual support among its own institutes, faculties, and professional personnel, including joint participation in research, technical cooperation, and projects for national development. Indonesia must work toward the development of its own scientists, by developing Indonesianized methods of science education extending eventually from the elementary through graduate levels.

As indicated above, the seminar took a favorable (though possibly overoptimistic) view of the BIMAS project, in which students have lived among villagers while instructing, advising, and encouraging them to use better farming (rice production) methods. The BIMAS principle can also be applied to other kinds of food production, health education, and nutrition education. Graduates and civic volunteers, as well as students, should be included in BIMAS projects. Obviously, these students and volunteers must be supplied with technical information, and they will require some supervision by technically competent superiors. Administrative controls, however, should not be heavyhanded; BIMAS projects, by their very nature, are most effective when least bureaucratized.

The discussion of BIMAS drew the seminar's attention to broad questions of motivation and incentives—because the enthusiasm of students has been a key ingredient to the early success of the program. This led the seminar to conclude that attention to incentives must be a part of all developmental planning, if popular cooperation is required. The pattern of incentives may vary, but the profit motive should never be ignored.

Seminar discussions also touched on several problems of health, nutrition, and medical science and technology. The most urgent nutrition problem in Indonesia is that of preschool children, for whom food deficiency has lifelong effects. Mothers must supplement breast feeding before babies are six months old. In addition to rice, protein must be increased by use, among various sources, of beans, greens, fish, and sweet potatoes. Other nutrition problems are also serious, but the need of the preschool children in Indonesia is of an emergency character, not only to reduce infant mortality, but to assure a future population of healthy and productive adults. A high infant death rate is not an acceptable means of population control. In this connection, the seminar accepted the conclusion that population limitation by family planning and birth control require immediate large-scale support and implementation as a central feature of national policy. Food production can catch up with population increase only if the rate of population increase is reduced.

It is necessary for Indonesia to take up again the establishment of health programs and services and the training of medical and paramedical personnel, a situation which deserves the attention of international bodies. In the field of public health, the needs of Indonesia are current and urgent: provision of some training abroad (which will be necessary for several years to come); collaborative research by Indonesian and foreign specialists; and special programs in public health, rodent control, immunization, sanitation, health education, insect control, hospital administration, and tuberculosis prevention and control. The quality of medical education in the twelve or more medical schools also requires improvement.

The seminar was particularly interested in several aspects of getting and supplying the information vital to all the processes of development.

One aspect of this is research. But, to put urgently needed technical information in the possession of those who must use it for developmental changes—in agriculture, as well as in other fields—systems are needed for preparing and regularly distributing usable, easily read, and readily comprehensible summaries, digests, and interpretations of currently important technical knowledge. Institutions and persons concerned with promoting development should undertake projects of this nature to make technical information available to the extension agents, supervisers, administrators, and even the policy-makers.

The book's home is a library. Indonesia's storehouse of the world's culture, and its working library of knowledge which can aid development, requires the establishment of a national library system with strong centers for the acquisition, accumulation, and maintenance of materials, and with affiliated specialized subcenters in provincial libraries, institutes, and schools. Implementation of plans for such a national system is urgently important to Indonesia's development.

There is need for a national law to require the copyright-deposit of every book or journal published in Indonesia. Because of the lack of such a law, there is no comprehensive or inclusive national bibliography. This is a great handicap to students and all persons who must consult written materials, and the situation could be set straight by the enactment and enforcement of a simple law on the subject.

A major suggestion for Indonesia's reservoir of technical and scientific knowledge is that international provision should be made for continuous microfilm and microcard reproduction of essential books and scientific journals, and for their regular placement in an Indonesian national library and documentation system, with equipment for further reproduction and distribution within the nation.

As can be observed, the range of our seminar discussion, though wide, is by no means comprehensive, even within the limits of its general subject, for the selection of papers was limited to topics for which specialists with recent research experience in Indonesia could be commissioned. The value of these discussions is much enhanced, however, by the competence and diverse professional backgrounds of the participants. The forty members of the seminar who presented papers or took part in the discussion came to Lexington from the Institute of Agricultural Sciences in Bogor, the Institute of Technology in Bandung, the National Academy of Sciences (U.S.A.), the Economic Development Institute of the International Bank for Reconstruction and Development, the Indonesian Embassy in Washington, the Provisional Parliament in Indonesia, the Office of International Scientific and Technological Affairs in the U.S. Department of State, the Agency for International Development, the Agricultural Development Council, Inc., the Ford Foundation, the Universities of

California, Berkeley and Los Angeles, the University of the Philippines, and the Universities of Oregon, Hawaii, Illinois, Pennsylvania, Western Michigan, Yale, Chicago, Florida, and Valparaiso (Indiana). In addition, there were observer participants from the former University of Kentucky–AID contract teams at Bandung and Bogor, from the University of Kentucky Faculty Committee on Indonesia, and from the staff of the Center for Developmental Change.

Members of the seminar were unanimous in their hopes for Indonesia's success in achieving development and in their confidence that science and technology will be effectively applied in the fuller utilization of the nation's vast natural resources and human talent.

After the seminar, several authors revised their papers to take into account some of the discussion which had occurred during the meetings, and some additional materials were prepared. Dr. Leon Mears was invited to contribute his paper on rice production because of its timeliness and relevance to the discussions on agriculture. Dr. Vincent Nelson broadened the coverage of Koesoemadinata's paper, which dealt initially only with petroleum resources. Dr. Karl Pelzer participated in the seminar as a discussant. Because of a prior commitment, Dr. Murray Thomas was unable to accept an invitation to participate in the seminar, but he later prepared the chapter on science education which is included in this volume.

Initially it was not intended that discussion would be included with the published papers. Study of the taped record, however, indicated that discussants had offered some additional material from which selected condensations are here included.

---

[1] *Stir benteng:* literally "buffalo turn," a corrective swerve to be enforced with the ferocity of the wild buffalo, a traditional symbol of ethnic power.

[2] *Generasi '66:* A term applied to the students and youths who exerted pressure on the Army to hasten Sukarno's denigration.

[3] According to the *Far Eastern Economic Review* of March 13, 1969, the Foreign Investment Board reports that foreign investments since 1967 have totaled US$ 475 million, mostly in oil, mining, and forestry.

[4] *Bimas* S.S.B.M., *Bimbingan Massal Swa Semboda Bahan Makanan.* Mass guidance toward self-sufficiency in food production.

Part I **Land, Man, Determination**

CHAPTER 2

Suwito Kusumowidagdo **Land, Man, and His Determination to Work**

Indonesia is a land of vast problems and great opportunities. It is a nation which, since its very beginning, has been in continuous struggle, first for national liberation and then for a new and respectable identity in the community of nations. Only recently has it emerged from a period of civil disorders and threats to its national unity.

It is in such a political atmosphere that free Indonesia has entered its third decade of national existence and has embarked upon a political and economic stabilization program. Stabilization should not be interpreted, however, as a rejection of change. On the contrary, it is aimed at accelerating a progressive development based on a consolidated set of principles and along a steady course of an independent but active foreign policy. Indonesia's *Pantjasila* constitute the basic principles on which the people want to build a society of justice and prosperity. Indonesia's constitution defines the course of our state policies. Our activities in Indonesia's development will be consistently guided by whatever our people decide in the People's *Madjelis* (or Congress) and Parliament through democratic procedures. The Rule of Law instead of Law of Rulers, rationalism in place of emotionalism, and pragmatism instead of sterile idealism—such is the spirit of Indonesia's new order. Whatever we do, we do so primarily in the spirit of serving our people's interest, and of putting our country's household in proper order. To foreign nations, we offer our sincere friendship and cooperation, based on mutual understanding and respect, common interest, and mutual benefit.

Indonesian development, interpreted broadly, has many aspects, covering the whole range of nation-building. Indonesia's two decades of free and sovereign nationhood is just one-tenth of the nearly two centuries-long history of development of the United States. Your stage of development is almost beyond comprehension. In 1967, I am informed, it resulted in a GNP of $789,663 million. This equals the combined GNP of all NATO countries and Japan; twice that of the Soviet Union; ten times that of mainland China; ten times that of all Latin America; and, I don't know how many times that of Indonesia.

In comparison, Indonesia (with an average GNP per capita of below $100), is one of the twenty-five Asian countries with an average GNP per capita of below $300 and belongs therefore to the group of economically underdeveloped countries.

For a rough idea of the kinds of problems involved in Indonesian development, let us remember that Indonesia is an archipelago republic, consisting of over three thousand inhabited but by-and-large still virgin islands. Those islands are spread out over an area nearly as large as the United States of America, with about 60 to 70 percent of that area consisting of water. It is one of the few sea-locked republics in the world.

We have an unevenly distributed population of about 116 million, increasing at an annual rate of 2.5 percent, with Java the most highly cultivated but most heavily populated island, having only about 4 percent forest land. In view of recent political developments it may be of interest to note in passing that there are at present about three million overseas Chinese in Indonesia, about half of whom have adopted Indonesian nationality. The remainder are either legally stateless persons or citizens of Communist China. Most of them are economically active—retail dealers in many villages in Java, fishermen in coastal areas of northeast Sumatra, and agricultural workers in heavily Chinese-populated West Kalimantan.

Despite such geographic and demographic problems as these many bright areas of hope for the future of Indonesian economic development exist. Indonesia does have the basic prerequisites for its economic development: land, man, and his determination to work. The economic resources by which Indonesia's islands are richly endowed by nature have been only 5 percent subterraneously explored, exploited, and translated into actual wealth. The vast resources of fish in the interinsular seas have contributed only 10 percent of their hidden wealth to the development of our economy. Various kinds of high-quality woods, rubber, and other forest products from the virgin forests in Sumatra, Kalimantan, and West Irian could supply materials for various types of industries. Many areas of those forests could be laid open for new rice plantations to achieve self-sufficiency in food. At the same time, these could provide new areas of settlement to relieve heavily populated islands and cities from population pressures, especially on the island of Java.

Mountain lakes, such as Toba in North Sumatra, and the big and lengthy rivers in Sumatra, Kalimantan, and Java, are potential sources for hydroelectric power, needed for modern industrial development. The islands of Sumatra, Kalimantan, West Irian, and Java offer potential areas of still untapped oil resources, besides those already under exploitation. Offshore oil mining along the east coast of South Sumatra and offshore tin mining around the Bangka island group, are potential new resources for industrial wealth. Resources of gold, iron, coal, and bauxite in Java and Sumatra, diamonds in Kalimantan, nickel and silver in Sulawesi, copper in West Irian are still underexploited, or even unexplored.

This is only a rough picture of the vast resources still untapped in our archipelago, and the many and various possibilities in Indonesian economic development. This is Indonesian natural capital. In natural resources, Indonesia is listed as the sixth richest country in the world.

In manpower, Indonesia now ranks fifth in the world after China, India, the Soviet Union, and the United States. It is certainly the most populous nation in Southeast Asia. Centuries-long colonial subjugation, however, prevented the full development of our people's skills and capabilities. The Netherlands Indies colonial education was limited in purpose, mainly the creation of a corps of colonial civil servants, useful to the Dutch colonial administration. Even then, the educational system did not offer sufficient opportunities to bring forth the latent talents and skills available among the teeming millions of our people. The low standards of living of the great majority of parents prevented them from giving their children the highest possible degree of education. Private schools and other vocational training institutions set up by nationalistic organizations suffered not only from lack of adequate financing and teaching facilities but also from colonial restricting ordinances.

An interesting phenomenon in free Indonesia is, therefore, the accelerated growth in number and variety of schools and other educational institutions, government as well as private, from primary up to university level. And yet, population growth and the flood of graduates from the lower levels of educational institutions mean that still not all students can be adequately absorbed into the next higher level. This could cause potential talents and skills of the younger generation to be lost or to remain underdeveloped merely by a lack of opportunities for continued training. This would be detrimental to the cause of a developing nation such as Indonesia. Increasing the number of educational institutions; enlarging their capacities to absorb all eager-to-learn students; improvement of teaching methods and educational equipment; a wider diversification of vocational, professional, and managerial training; graduate and specialized training abroad through bilateral or multilateral cooperation, regional as well as international—these are the logical ways to bring forth all possible talents and skills of our 116 million people and use them to maximum capacity for Indonesia's development.

Our younger generation are eager, even impatient, to learn all the new things in science and technology which can accelerate their country's development, realizing as they do that Indonesia lags far behind even the minimum standard befitting a country which is the fifth largest in population and the sixth richest in natural resources. Supporting them are the Indonesian parents, who fought for Indonesia's independence and worked to secure it for the present and future generations, and who are still making the sacrifices necessary to achieve the creation of a just and prosperous society for Indonesia. This readiness and determination of both the young and the old to work hard for that ideal is our human capital.

These are valuable resources indeed, but more is required to convert them into a creative and productive force for accelerated Indonesian development. A sound and well-planned policy in the use of natural and human resources, efficient organization and administration, and honest and effective leadership in management, assisted by a devoted staff of professionals and skillful technicians—these are needed in all branches of government and private endeavors for the Indonesian economic development. For long-term development, the teaching of science and technology in all branches and levels of education should gain more and more emphasis. Under the present conditions of scientific and technological progress in the world, it must even be considered as a necessity and as a possibility to start science teaching and training in technical skills at the earliest possible stage of education in Indonesia. The daily life of present-day Indonesian children is surrounded by all kinds of products of modern technology, and they hear and read about, or see and even deal with, things which can only be understood through this sort of study. An early, though gradual, introduction into the world of science and technology during the formative growth of the young generation could create the habit of rational approach to the various problems of modern life.

Educational policies in Indonesia should be adapted to its need for development, laying more emphasis on digging out talents rather than pumping in doctrines, producing more creative, pioneering, and skillful people for managerial, professional, and vocational jobs rather than would-be politicians—practitioners rather than philosophers.

For that purpose, the teaching staff could be increased. Its mission might well be broadened not only to give our trainees or students abroad a mastery of certain branches of science and technology for themselves but also to train them to teach what they have learned to their countrymen when they return home. Indonesian and American university affiliations could be revived. Such affiliation could comprise the exchange not only of professors, students, and libraries but also of teaching equipment or teaching materials.

In the urgent problem of Indonesia's economic rehabilitation, technology and science can and must play a constructive role. Only thus can Indonesia ever hope to solve its complex problem of underdevelopment and to bridge the deep gulf that separates Indonesia, and developing countries in general, from the industrialized countries of the world. It is a matter of some urgency. One of the dangerous risks of our time is a growing polarization between the world's areas of metropolitan wealth and its rural areas of deprivation. It is a potential which can be exploited by unscrupulous demagogues and political theorists.

Scientists and technologists the world over should pool their wisdom and join their skills to face the challenge. There is indeed the challenge posed by the mysteries of outer space, but there is also a real and vital challenge upon their own planet.

In meeting this challenge, as it pertains to economic underdevelopment in Indonesia, this seminar may play a pioneering part, for there is a need of useful and practicable suggestions. Several come readily to mind: scientific surveys to collect adequate statistical data for developmental planning of the 95 percent wholly or partially unexplored natural riches of Indonesia; research in the possibility of more diversified uses of our abundant raw materials; research and experimentation to produce new varieties of rice and other food products in greater quantity and quality; adaptation of traditional popular medicine for employment of our rich tropical herbarium; and research and experimentation in the use of domestic materials for various small industries to provide our people with daily household necessities and to supply building and clothing materials. These are just a few pointers, among many others, which indicate where science can play its guiding role and could eventually lead to new discoveries and new inventions. When young Indonesian scientists can be drawn more to those challenging scientific adventures than to the world of white collars, new horizons will gradually but certainly open up for Indonesian development.

When we now shift to the question of conversion of our natural and human resources into actual wealth, the problems of technical know-how and financial capital come to the fore. These are indispensable ingredients for development, ingredients with which Indonesia is unfortunately not yet richly endowed. Since our freedom has been regained, there has, however, never been a lack of self-confidence among our people, nor a surrender to pessimism. We do realize the seriousness of these inadequacies, but we are confident that technical know-how can be acquired through relentless learning and practice, whenever our people are given the opportunities to acquire it. National capital can be accumulated gradually through hard work to produce those commodities we can sell to the world market; this, by healthy administration and efficient use, can advance national development. Our goals are economically healthful. A balanced state budget is to be achieved and maintained with the greatest possible discipline. We need a credit policy that is tight against waste but flexible for productive purposes, thereby selecting priorities for whatever can help us earn or save foreign currencies and which are of quick-yielding nature. A more intensified, well-administrated collection of state revenues and taxes belongs to the normal state functions that ought to be exercised.

In addition to those domestic main channels for national capital accumulation, our recently enacted law on foreign investment opens new avenues for the participation of foreign capital, in cooperation with our own private or government capital, to wage and win the peaceful war against economic underdevelopment in Indonesia. Besides those joint enterprises, the law provides wide opportunities for straight capital investment with reasonable length of tax holidays, besides profits transfer and security guarantees for the investor.

Through such international cooperation and partnership, based on mutual respect and mutual benefit and replacing the old style of colonial economic exploitation, Indonesia is hoping to introduce modern working methods and technology to increase speedily its productivity. In pursuit of this goal we shall, of course, require an increased use of modern equipment to achieve greater effectiveness with lower production costs. This should, however, be balanced with labor-consuming investment projects to widen employment opportunities. Diversification of investment projects and sound distribution of their sites over the entire archipelago could promote a better distribution of population and create more varied employment opportunities for the people. This would in turn induce a higher eagerness to adopt new vocations and acquire new skills, so that the annual stream of school graduates to white-collar jobs could gradually be redirected to the widening horizons of development.

For this purpose, investors are requested by our law on foreign investment to include in their investment projects training programs and facilities to train Indonesian personnel for the undertaking. Such programs, in addition to improvement of operational efficiency, will promote a spirit of cooperation and partnership in Indonesian development among our people and secure their support for such development through their active participation.

Underlying all developmental possibilities is a great and basic problem of transport and communication. There are still numerous mountain-locked and forest-locked village communities, and to integrate them, with their by-and-large static economic life, into the dynamic economy of the whole country, the road system in various islands has to be increased, however modest the improvement may be. This will at least facilitate speedy transportation of local products to coastal localities in exchange for the supply of other necessities. Areas producing export commodities especially deserve improved road and transport facilities to the seaports, so that their products can be loaded in time by our interisland shipping, which still operates with limited frequency.

Our interisland merchant fleet still needs enlargement to increase the volume of trade among the many islands, some of them tiny and remote, with different kinds of products and different levels of productivity. A more stimulated flow in the interisland exchange of goods will not only prevent certain products from wasting and perhaps rotting in one island, while badly needed in another, but may to some extent also help in equalizing price levels of certain daily necessities. At the initial stages of development of our shipping industry, more wharfs for interisland trade could be built on a modest basis by using high quality woods as basic material, before commencing modern shipbuilding. Our virgin forests in Sumatra and Kalimantan offer possibilities for multipurpose projects, such as winning new lands for food production, for new settlements of interisland migration, and new industries for housing and shipbuilding. Financing such a project could probably be achieved through joint enterprises, the Indonesian share of which could be produced by the export of quality wood.

Indonesian economic development could be enhanced greatly by improved facilities for business travel by land, sea, and air. The great distances in the Indonesian archipelago make interisland aviation a technical necessity to save much of our valuable time, otherwise lost in the travel between islands, and even between various cities in jungle-infested islands. Short-distance helicopter services will bring greater efficiency in the administration of various regions in Sumatra, Kalimantan, Sulawesi, and West Irian. Much more could be said about the problems and opportunities of domestic transport and communication, including their relationship to the rapidly increasing number of foreign tourists in Indonesia.

The various fields in which the aid of modern technology is required are still infinitely wide. With the present speed of scientific and technological progress in other parts of the world, Indonesia, and many other developing countries, constituting the majority of mankind, should be given the benefit of such progress, by not necessarily having to undergo all the phases in the long road of development along which the present industrialized countries have grown to their present maturity. The centuries-long sufferings of those nations under colonial subjugation, thereby contributing a great deal to the wealth of many of those countries at the cost of their own national development, justify a more generous aid policy toward developing countries. Aid policies should not be frustrated by fear of future industrial competition from these developing nations; the chance is practically negligible because of the existing great development-gaps between developing and industrialized countries. A too-great and prolonged disharmony in the economic development of the world, however, harbors greater dangers. What is at stake ultimately is not the millions of dollars spent in foreign aid or foreign investments, but rather the future of teeming millions of peoples in developing countries surrounding a minority group of industrialized countries. Under the present unstable political conditions in the world, such a state of affairs cannot be without serious consequences and effect on world peace. Poverty mixed with frustration could be a source of unpredictable international developments.

If science and technology are God's blessings to mankind, they should also give their services to the creation of more harmony in the economic development of the world. It is not only a problem of moral and humanitarian obligation of scientists toward God and their fellow men but also toward the further development of science itself.

Those then are my remarks on the problems of Indonesian development. I have been trying to give you an overall sketch of the political atmosphere in my country, the basic policies of my government, the spirit of my people, their concern of today, and also their hope for the future in their present battle to win political and economic stabilization for Indonesia. I hope that such a sketch may serve as the spiritual and political frame within which the great importance and meaning of your deliberations in this seminar will gain a rightful emphasis.

Now it is your turn. I have brought before you the problem of Indonesia's development—as though on a surgery table. Switch on your scientific light in your surgery room, which is this seminar. Take up your sharp, clean knives and scissors to dissect and analyze it with skillful hands. I shall await your findings with the greatest of expectation.

Here is a chance for you and the University of Kentucky to make with this seminar a piece of history in Indonesian development, by showing us the way to go ahead on the long march toward the secured and sustained development of one of your western neighbors in Asia.

Part II   **Land: Natural Capital**

CHAPTER 3

Tojib Hadiwidjaja New Trends in Agricultural Development Programs in Indonesia

Indonesia is an agrarian country. Seventy-two percent of the population live from agriculture, broadly defined to include smallholder farming, estate agriculture, forestry, animal husbandry, and inland fisheries. Fifty percent derive their total income from these agriculturally related pursuits; the remaining 22 percent have, besides farming, additional employment. More than 50 percent of the value of exports is in agricultural products such as rubber, tobacco, palm oil, copra, tea, coffee, quinine, spices, forest products, and cattle.

Nevertheless, Indonesia has never been able to be self-sufficient in food. During the prewar period of colonial rule, 1921–1940, an average of 460 thousand tons of rice had to be imported annually. Rice imports after independence were even greater, rising to 763 thousand tons in 1956, and this accounted for 13 percent of the total cost of imports. The rice yield between 1940 and 1965 increased 150 percent, but the population increased simultaneously in at least the same proportion.

Income from the export of agricultural products shows an ever-declining trend since 1955. The reasons are very complicated and they include decline in quantity, quality, and prices. Rubber prices (RSS 1 grade) in 1955 and 1965 were respectively 39.14 and 25.69 U.S. cents per pound, and by April 1967 less than 15 cents per pound, in response to many factors, some political and some economic.

Plans to overcome these problems of food supply and income from export were included in Indonesia's eight-year Overall Development Plan, adopted in 1960, the nation's first formal attempt at total planning since achieving independence. The fields of agricultural development and education were not overlooked, as experience would soon reveal.

After the abortive Communist coup d'état on October 1, 1965, and especially after the action of the Provisional Peoples' Congress (MPRS, *Madjelis Permusjawaratan Rakjat Sementera*) in June 1966, new ideas and principles in development programs came to the fore. This paper deals with some failures, achievements, and problems experienced during the years 1960–1966 in the fields of agriculture and higher education, and with some of the new and more realistic and rational trends in agricultural development in Indonesia.

THE OVERALL NATIONAL DEVELOPMENT PLAN, 1960

The outlines of a development plan produced by the National Planning Board (DEPERNAS, *Departemen Perentjanaan Nasional*) were accepted on December 3, 1960, by the Congress as a basic and official overall eight-year National Development Plan, which was intended to control Indonesian development through 1969. This plan established goals and provided for development toward them in the following fields: intellectual, religious, and spiritual affairs; welfare; government and matters of security and defense; production; distribution and commmunication; finance and financing.

Plans relevant to agriculture included specifications for the food and clothing program (*sandang pangan*), which was to receive national and urgent attention.

Targets in agricultural production called for early achievement (within two years, 1960–1962) of an increase in rice production from 93 kg. to 100 kg. per capita per year. Also expected within the first two years was an increase in production of corn and other carbohydrate sources to an equivalent of 60 kg. of rice per capita per year. The increase of rice production was to be accomplished both by intensification of farming practices and expansion of cultivated areas. The first was expected to be achieved through mass intensification and through the so-called paddy centers (*padi sentra*) established for the purpose. The plan also called for continued expansion of irrigation and for systems of mechanized rice farming. The planners were, of course, too optimistic, or at least unrealistic; they expected Indonesia to be self-supporting by 1962, but the targets were not reached. The Overall Plan provided similarly for increases in the areas and yields of beans, other vegetables, and fruits.

Targets were set also for the provision of animal protein (meat, eggs, and milk). It was proposed that there be 60 grams of protein made available per capita per day. Forty-five grams were to be derived from vegetable and 15 grams from animal sources; of the latter, 7.5 grams were to be provided through the stimulation of animal husbandry on farms. For 1967 the target was put at 271 thousand tons of animal protein, but actual production that year only reached 134 thousand tons. This is a shortfall of more than 50 percent. This target was to have been met from two sources: an increase of poultry production from an average of 1.5 to 3 chickens per capita, and an increase of milk production. Long-range plans included the improvement of cattle, feed, and cattle breeding and a better geographical distribution of cattle.

The remaining 7.5 grams per capita of protein from animal sources were to have been derived from sea and inland fisheries. Fish production in 1959 totaled 700 thousand tons, and the target was to be at least twice that quantity. To reach this target, production of sea fisheries (employing 500,000 men) was expected to be doubled from 850 to 1,760 kg. of fish per man per year in 1967. The plan prescribed a number of measures to improve the yield of inland fisheries (on lakes, rivers, swamps, fish ponds, in rice paddies) and to assure adequate production of salt.

Raw materials for clothing were to be derived from cotton, *rami* (china grass), and rayon. The area target for cotton was 900,000 hectares, even though only 450,000 hectares can really be considered suitable for cotton growing. This target also was too ambitious.

Agricultural products to be exported according to the plan comprised sugarcane, rubber, palm oil, tea, tobacco, coffee, quinine, and cacao. The actual plans were as follows:

—Sugar: Expansion of sugar areas in Atjeh, South Sumatra, and South Celebes, and the rehabilitation of old sugar factories on Java.
—Rubber: Rejuvenation of 260 thousand hectares of native rubber, and 180 thousand hectares of estate rubber plantations were put into the development plan.
—Tobacco: Enlargement of the acreage in Sumatra (Deli tobacco); improvement of the yield in Java through intensified crop rotation and other practices; opening of new areas for Virginia tobacco in South Sulawesi and Nusatenggara.
—Palm Oil: Increase of the yield of existing plantations.
—Tea and Coffee: Increased production by rehabilitation of estates which were closed or abandoned during the war.

No specific targets were set for cacao and quinine production. Some data about the above export crops are shown in Table 3:1.

TABLE 3:1   Actual and Planned Production: Selected Export Crops
(in thousands of tons)

Crop	Actual Production			Planned Production	
	1957	1958	1959	1960	1961
Cane sugar	829	775	851	857	900
Rubber	646	569	650	700	720
Tobacco		117	135	148	158
Deli		21	27	35	40
Besuki		30	31	31	31
Vorstenlands		6	7	7	7
Native		60	70	75	80
Palm oil	160	147	—	—	—
Palm kernels	40	35	—	—	—
Tea	48	46	—	—	—

Some Failures and Achievements

The plan to make Indonesia self-supporting in rice by 1962 was not fulfilled; during the period of 1961–1964 more than one million tons of rice were imported annually. In 1965, only 186 thousand tons were imported, but in 1966 the amount was larger again (+ 275,000 tons).

Nor were plans realized for cloth production. In 1967, textile mills in West Java were able to operate at only approximately 10–20 percent of their capacity, because raw materials were not available.

In export crops, except for palm oil, there has been a constant decline in quantity, quality, and also prices in the world market, resulting in a decline of earned foreign exchange from $620 million (U.S.) in 1960 to $485 million in 1966.

In addition to the failures, however, there were achievements which offer encouragement that plans for the future may be fulfilled more successfully. An example is provided by the data on rising rice yields. There has been some increase in the acreage harvested and the total yield, as is shown in Table 3:2.

The results achieved through the BIMAS (mass counseling) projects pioneered by the Faculty of Agriculture, Bogor, were even more heartening, as shown in Tables 3:3 and 3:4.

Progress has also been made in the growing of corn. Recent yields have increased from 1 ton per hectare to 4–5 tons per hectare, following the use of high-yielding varieties and fertilizers, the control of pests and diseases, and improvement in cultural methods and irrigation.

Considerations Relevant to Agricultural Education

The development of higher education in the agricultural sciences and technologies was—and must continue to be—a part of the overall program in agricultural development. It is thus important to review the fate of education in the overall plan years, against the general rapid growth of education in the first two decades of Indonesian independence. Probably Indonesia's greatest achievements after the Proclamation of

TABLE 3:2 Development of Paddy Yields in Indonesia: 1950–1965

Year	Area harvested (millions of hectares)	Paddy yield (millions of metric tons)	Average yield (quintals per hectare of paddy)	Paddy yield (kilogram per capita for year)
1950	5.7	11.6	20.3	149.9
1955	6.6	15.1	22.8	180.0
1960	7.3	16.9	23.1	186.2
1961	6.9	15.9	23.2	163.2
1962	7.3	17.1	23.5	171.8
1963	6.7	15.3	22.7	149.8
1964	7.0	16.3	23.1	155.9
1965	7.3	19.4	26.4	181.1

TABLE 3:3 Development of Paddy Yields Through BIMAS
Projects: Krawang Area, Indonesia[1]

Year	Area of BIMAS projects (hectares)	Average yield (quintals per hectare)	
		within projects	outside projects
1963–1964	103	64.5	31.0
1964–1965	11,000	68.0	31.1
1965–1966	157,820	55.0	31.6

TABLE 3:4 Maximum and Minimum Yields in Quintals per Hectare within and outside the Projects[1]

Year	Maximum Yield		Minimum Yield	
	within BIMAS	outside BIMAS	within BIMAS	outside BIMAS
1963–1964	68.9	43.7	62.2	24.4
1964–1965	175.0	36.0	29.0	15.0
1965–1966	83.44	34.45	26.1	15.61

[1] Source: Djatijanto Kretosastro, 1967.

Independence were in the field of education. Illiteracy, which was over 90 percent in 1942, has been greatly reduced. The number of students in the elementary schools increased from 2.5 million in 1942 to nearly 7.5 million in 1959 and over 15 million in 1966, a sixfold increase in twenty-four years.

The program for higher education included the establishment of state universities and colleges in the regions including the outer islands, according to regional requirements. (In 1959 there were five universities on Java, two on Sumatra, and one on Celebes.) Special attention was directed to developing colleges in technological and exact sciences, and a Ministry of Higher Education and Sciences was established in the national cabinet. The statistics of this development are shown in Tables 3:5, 3:6, and 3:7.

The number of agriculturists and foresters employed in Indonesia in 1941–1942 totaled 430 and 170 respectively, of whom only a dozen were Indonesians. They were practically all graduates of Wageningen Agricultural University, Holland.

TABLE 3:5 Development of Universities in Indonesia: 1942, 1961, and 1965[2]

Institutions and Enrollment	1942	1961	1965
Number of Institutions for Higher Education			
State universities/institutes	0	14	39
Colleges, academies sponsored by other ministries	0	55	88
Private universities/colleges	0	112	228
Student Enrollment			
State universities/institutes	800[1]	65,000	158,000
Colleges, academies sponsored by other ministries	0	17,000	38,000
Private universities/colleges	0	27,000	82,000

[1] In 1942, these were, strictly speaking, not "state universities," but Dutch institutes.
[2] Source: Bachtiar Rifai *et al.*, 1965.

TABLE 3:6 Development of Higher Education in the Agricultural Sciences and Technologies: Number of Faculties

Faculties	1942	1959	1965
Agriculture	1	5	17
Veterinary Medicine	0	2	5
Forestry	0	0	3
Animal Husbandry	0	0	5
Fisheries	0	0	1
Agricultural Technology and Agricultural Engineering	0	0	2

The establishment of the Institut Pertanian Bogor in September 1963 was a landmark in the development of higher agricultural education. The development of this institution, which combined two existing faculties with three that were newly organized, was facilitated by affiliation with the University of Kentucky.

The tremendous growth of enrollment in the elementary and secondary schools from 2.5 million in 1942 to over 15 million in 1966, occurred in a complex of financial, technical, and psychological factors which have posed several developmental problems.

Traditions from the colonial era persisted. People everywhere continued to prefer white-collar jobs to manual labor. Parents were eager to have their children enrolled in universities, which during colonial days were limited to the privileged few. Because of the colonial tradition, and with the added factor that vocational schools require much capital investment, the number of junior and senior high schools surpassed that of vocational schools.

As a result, senior high school graduates in ever-increasing numbers (1962–1964, respectively, 60, 70, and 80 thousand) sought admission to universities, but only about 60 percent of them could be enrolled at state universities and academies. This stimulated the establishment of new private universities, of which over 90 percent offer work in the social and political sciences. There has been excess production of graduates in some areas, and deficiency in others. It has been predicted that during 1967–1971, demand would exceed supply, especially in scientific and technical fields. Possibility of unemployment or underemployment in certain other categories of educational facilities must be faced from now on.

TABLE 3:7 Graduates in Higher Agricultural Education

Faculties	Before 1942	During 24 years 1942–1966	Estimated 1967–1971
Agriculture	0	1,000	1,300
Veterinary Medicine	0	200	200
Forestry	0	250	500
Animal Husbandry	0	0	225
Fisheries	0	45	200
Agricultural Technology and Agricultural Engineering	0	10	120

NEW APPROACHES IN AGRICULTURAL
DEVELOPMENT PROGRAMS

Especially after the AMPERA (*Amanat Penderitaan Rakjat:* "The message of the suffering of the people") Cabinet was installed in July 1966, awareness prevailed that deterioration of the economic situation had resulted, at least in part, from a lack of harmony between political and economic interests. New trends appeared in development programs, some applicable to agriculture.

Priorities in the Economic Development Programs

Policies on economic, monetary, and developmental matters were expressed in a short-term program to stop inflation and to rehabilitate production with the following scale of priorities: to stop inflation, to acquire self-sufficiency in food, to rehabilitate communications, to promote export activities, and to acquire self-sufficiency in clothing.

Investment priorities for the long-term program were stated by the new government in a scale of priorities placing agriculture first, followed by communications, and then by industry, mining, and oil. In industry, the announced sequence of priorities began with home industry, then listed small industry, basic industry, and eventually heavy industry.

The New Trends in Agricultural Development Programs

Self-sufficiency in food was now to be approached primarily through intensification programs making use of "mass guidance" (BIMAS). Opening of new rice areas would be on a selective basis, primarily by improvement of irrigation. Mechanized rice-farming would be undertaken on a pioneering basis and not on a large scale, as before.

At the time that this manuscript was prepared, the Ministry of Agriculture was drafting a five-year plan (1969–1974). A national seminar, attended by representatives from the fields of extension, research, and education, revised the draft plan and it was incorporated into the nation's development plan in 1969. The 1960 plan for clothing (materials) was greatly changed. Rayon, for example, is now regarded as less efficient than petrochemical products (fully synthetic fibers), and large-scale experiments in the use of cotton had had disappointing results. The program on export crops was revised through a thorough study of world markets and the taking of steps to acquire marketing facilities. More attention was given to vocational agricultural education and the establishing of training centers to produce skilled farmers. A new goal was to arouse a pioneering spirit in both teachers and students, including university students, motivating them to produce enterprising and independent farmers rather than merely prospective officials and seekers of white-collar jobs. Our government officials adopted several new ideas for agricultural research. These include, for example: (a) regional experiment stations to fulfill the needs of regional extension services; (b) intensive feasibility studies for rural development, primarily on overpopulated Java, to improve the well-being of present subsistence farmers by means of intensive farming systems, interisland migration, and the establishment of home and small industries; and (c) steps toward the establishment of an agricultural economics institute.

The principles of extension used in BIMAS S.S.B.M. are to be applied and expanded to other fields of agriculture, such as poultry-breeding, fish production, and forestry. Programs in family planning will be undertaken in response to a new awareness of need which has started to prevail, even among Indonesian agriculturists.

An additional new approach in agricultural development and education lies in regional cooperation through membership in the South East Asian Ministers of Education Council (SEAMEC), which Indonesia joined in November 1966. Initial proposals from Indonesia to SEAMEC related to regional institutes for education and research in tropical agriculture, for agricultural and rural development, and for research, training, and graduate study in agricultural and biological sciences. The availability of regional resources will further facilitate Indonesian progress in these phases of development.

REFERENCES

Bachtiar Rifai *et al. Perguruan Tinggi di Indonesia.* Djakarta: Departemen Perguruan Tinggi dan Ilmu Pengetahuan, 1965.

Djatijanto Kretosastro. *Bimas S. S. B. M. Bimbingan Masal Swa Sembada Bahan Makanan.* Djakarta: Direktorat Pertanian Rakjat, 1967.

Madjelis Permusjawaratan Rakjat Sementara, 1960. (a) *Ketetapan Madjelis Permusjawaratan Rakjat Sementara R. I.* No. II, MPRS, 1960. (b) id. Vol. V, p. 1087, etc. (c) id. Vol. VI, p. 1302 etc. (d) id. Vol. VII pp. 3989-4638.

———, 1966. *Hasil-hasil Sidang Umum MPRS ke IV Tahun 1966.*

Sadikin Sumintawikarta. Beberapa masalah tentang organisasi dan program penelitian dalam lingkungan Direktorat Djendral Pertanian. Working paper, Conference on Agr. Research, Bogor, Feb. 1967.

Tojib Hadiwidjaja. Sistim Perguruan Tinggi Pertanian untuk Indonesia. Seminar, Bogor, Dec. 1956.

———. Quelques aspects du developpement de l'agriculture indigene en Indonesie. *Revue de la Soc. d'Etudes et d'Expansion,* No. 219, 166: 31-41 (Brussels).

———. Perkembangan academic man-power di Indonesia. Seminar Perguruan Tinggi, Tugu, March 1967.

Ralph H. Allee **Comments**

An explanation of why Asia had to import 30 million tons of grain during 1966 is not simple, but some of the salient factors are now discernible and can be taken as points of departure. These factors relate to the correction of *a priori* notions about the strategy of development and to certain misconceptions concerning the social technology involved in development, as follows:

1. Since prices of manufactured goods tend to increase faster than prices of raw materials, it often has been assumed that industrial production should have priority over agriculture. But neglect of agriculture has produced inadequate food supply, shortage of agriculturally produced raw materials for industry, insufficient market for industrial production, and diminished foreign exchange earnings at a stage in development when agriculture is the main source of foreign exchange.

2. There has been an overemphasis on raising national incomes, without due concern for a parallel and direct attack on the bases of physical poverty. As a result, most of the potential producers in rural areas have tended to remain close to a subsistence level and unable to contribute to development.

3. Cities have too often been viewed as the loci for prestige buildings, deluxe residential suburbs, and ostentatious cultural centers, rather than as places for the exchange of goods and ideas.

4. Too much importance has been placed on overgeneralized and outdated ideologies and too little on skills, knowledge, and values pertinent to successful behavior.

5. Too much energy has been expended on the minor improvements which can be fostered in traditional farming and too little energy expended on obtaining major gains from the production, adaptation, and application of new technology.

6. Leadership, group dynamics, and other methods of promoting change have been taught to extension agents, but too little importance has been placed on technical adequacy and technical appropriateness, both of the practices recommended and of the extension agents. The result has been a resistance of farmers, not to change but to inept agents of change and unfeasible practices.

7. The "grass roots" fallacy has brought about the isolation of extension agents in villages and failure to note the essential town-centered nature of rural development.

8. Since trade schools have successfully trained carpenters and mechanics in cities, it has been assumed that specialized secondary schools

can train future farmers. The result too often has been a system of overly expensive schools which prepare farm youth for higher education or white-collar employment.

The Indonesian agricultural program now in evolution emphasizes changes which are obviously necessary to agricultural production. The initial point of concentration is rice, with corn and beans (including soy beans) next in line. When these three basic elements in the tropical diet are assured, the food problem will be well on the way to solution. Also, when a volume of these crops becomes available, it becomes feasible to promote market efficiency and to conduct other activities in support of modernizing farming. The projected step-by-step approach in Indonesia takes advantage of the experience gained in the BIMAS program. This effort increased production through the action of student volunteers. The students were coached, mainly at the Agricultural University in Bogor (IPB), in the factors of production and in the choice of areas with outstanding production potential—particularly with respect to irrigation, drainage, and transport. They spent the entire crop season working with farmers, from the time of soil preparation to time of harvest. An effort was made to supply the BIMAS areas with improved seed varieties and with fertilizers and pesticides.

The "systematized BIMAS" now being initiated includes six months of intensive training of selected staff who will work in the promotion of food-crop production. This training will be carried out in Bogor under cooperation between IPB and the central Food Crops Research Institute of the Ministry of Agriculture, from which certain staff members are being sent with AID financing to the International Rice Research Institute, Los Banos, Philippines. These trainees will bring to the Bogor center some of the features in the "breakthrough" achieved at IRRI during the past three years in the training of rice-production specialists.

A first group of thirty such specialists will be trained at Bogor during the crop season which begins in December 1967. During the second crop season, in 1968, the specialists will be established in about sixty centers in the prime rice areas for simple adaptation testing, demonstration, and training under technical supervision of the Bogor staff. They will test rice varieties for local adaptation and determine optimum fertilizer and pest control practices, including insect and rat control. They will choose cooperating farmers, assist them in establishing demonstrations, and help them to influence other producers. They will give apprentice training to selected extension agents. Volunteer students from agricultural colleges will continue to be used both directly and in cooperation with these crop-producing centers. The process will be continued to cover, initially, the prime rice area of about 600 thousand hectares (about 1,500,000 acres).

It must be emphasized that significantly improved technology is now available. The essential problem, and this too should be borne in mind, is the diffusion of this knowledge. By concentration of areas, the fertilizer and pesticide supply problem is simplified, and competent staff can be prepared as the program advances.

In the new Indonesian program, it is recognized that increase in production is only the start, but it is the start to everything. Unless real help can be given to the farmer in increasing production, it is better to leave him to his own devices. Indonesian farmers have been producing about 12 quintals (one quintal equals 220.46 pounds) per hectare of rice. Recently, however, at the Food Crops Experiment Station in Bogor, one of the new rice varieties being tested produced 6 tons, not of paddy (unhulled rice), but of rice. In other words, there were 12 tons of paddy in that test. It would not be realistic to expect all farmers to produce at that level, but this establishes a ceiling toward which production can move, and new varieties are available which make this possible.

The variety situation in Indonesia is an interesting example of agricultural progress and also of international cooperation. Sixty percent of all the rice grown in the Philippines is from Indonesian varieties. They are prominent, also, in Thailand, Burma, and wherever rice is grown in the tropics. Formerly, they were the best varieties available, or they would not have spread throughout the region. For this, a salute is due to the genius of Siregar, long-time director, and his colleagues, at the Cereals Experiment Station in Bogor. But those varieties were bred to produce without fertilizer, and the current need is for response to the use of fertilizer. Hence, at the International Rice Research Institute at Los Banos, the Indonesian varieties were further developed to breed into them the necessary present-day features. Today Indonesia has Peta No. 8 and Peta No. 5, greatly improved strains which quite properly are given Indonesian names because they spring from the great Indonesian variety Peta. This is one of the varieties which yielded six tons per hectare in the recent tests at Bogor. There is also in Indonesia an outstanding Philippine variety, BPI No. 76, and there are four varieties which are somewhat less adapted for response to fertilizer. These are suitable as improvements over the traditional variety for planting in the areas peripheral to the prime rice areas.

It is important, also, that in considering its nine or more million hectares of rice-producing land, Indonesia singled out 400 thousand hectares which are the prime producing areas in terms of water supply (quality and control), runoff, drainage, and safety from flooding. This selected area was later increased to include about 600 thousand hectares where first emphasis will be put on production of rice. It is reasonable to expect more rapid increases in production here than in outlying areas.

Shortly after the intensified effort to increase rice production, the focus of attention will be turned to the production of corn and beans, for which modern varieties also are available and for which gradual expansion in area is feasible.

This approach involves starting out within the broader range of strategic possibilities that may be undertaken later, to do things that are known and feasible in order that experience can be applied in later steps. Beyond doubt, there is developing in Indonesia a new concept of public services to farming and rural communities on the basis of their needs rather than on bureaucratic criteria for the allocation of personnel to programs and places. Personnel to work on marketing, for example, will find it necessary to be *en rapport* with merchants. The merchant will be identified as performing a vital function which must be carried out efficiently. A similar principle holds for extension education. Extension personnel must understand the essence of farming and features of modernization of farms, in addition to their understanding and skill in group dynamics and related fields.

If production increases, a wider range of problems can be tackled, perhaps making use of the adaptive-testing centers, and including markets, price incentives, credit, supply services, transport and communications, group action, and extension education. Sometimes the attack in these areas may have been premature, in that the increased production necessary to their success has not yet occurred. When, for example, the production of rice, corn, and beans (including soy beans) occurs in adequate volume, there will be a new basis for dealing with production credit needs. Programs to extend production credit have been unsuccessful in many countries because the possible margin of increase over subsistence was so small that the peasant was actually being bribed to undertake practices that better judgment told him would not be to his personal benefit. In such programs, the farmers were not able to repay, and what was intended to be production credit was found to be actually another kind of program. Similarly, the attention to marketing can be intensified when there is enough volume of production to require bigger and better markets.

What is being considered in Indonesia, thus, is a gradual assumption of responsibility for support to modernizing a rural community. Once the complex of services in a town-centered work area has become a functioning unit in a few areas, the problems of broader organization with intermediate and central agencies can be worked out pragmatically. Local units can be integrated eventually into a national system and contribute to comprehensive national planning. In organizing the new attacks on agricultural production and modernization of farming, Indonesia proposes to establish the *ketjamatan* (similar to a county) as the local work area (*daerah kerdja*). The *tjamat* (county representative of the Indonesian government) is at the local end of the civil service chain, when measured in administrative distance from the national center. Within the work areas, there are the villagers over which the *lurahs* (village heads) preside. There are about 3,000 of these *ketjamatan* work areas in Indonesia; the average *ketjamatan* includes about fifteen villages with population of 1,600 people each. The rice is grown in these areas: as one of the officials said in Djakarta not long ago, "Unfortunately, no rice is grown on the pavements in Djakarta." In such an organizational framework, personnel working to promote increased production, to improve markets, to solve problems of supply, and to conduct extension education can join in effective relationship with intermediate and central supervisors, service people, and consultants toward a rational nationwide integration of an agricultural program, beginning with concentrated attention to increased production on farms.

While the Indonesian process is evolving, there is a strategic role for the university-level training and research institution to play. IPB and the other agricultural institutions, as they grow into competence, can supply the creative research, the versatility, and continuity of effort required as they contribute to the national process and learn from it. They can train functional staff and can predict the features of a modernizing farm business, an expanding market, patterns of investment, and town-centered development. Patterns of investment become increasingly important. Where should liquid spending power be applied? To roads, to other items of infrastructure, to rural development, or more exclusively, to other kinds of investments? To anticipate such questions, the agricultural university at Bogor is initiating what Dr. Tojib has called feasibility studies. Efforts are being undertaken in a nearby laboratory *ketjamatan* (work area) to determine what actually is involved in supporting a modernizing rural community in Indonesia. One notable achievement has been the cooperation of the faculty of the agricultural university itself and the technicians in the Ministry of Agriculture with its units, with the local governments, and with rural people. The former agricultural academy near Bogor, at Tjiawi, which provided a three-year training in agriculture, has been converted to become the center of an upgrading program for the staff in the Ministry of Agriculture, a program in which the ministry and the university will have joint responsibility, involving also the other agricultural institutions in the country.

Discussion

Additional points on agricultural development in Indonesia (enough if fully expanded to generate several other papers) were presented by members of the seminar in the discussion stimulated by Rector Tojib's proposals. Among the most important supplemental topics were rice disease, markets, land reform, alternatives to rice, stimulation of "pioneer spirit," employment of college graduates, simultaneous promotion of agriculture and industry, rice-mechanization, rat control, fertilizer, the inevitability of absorbing workers in agriculture, interisland migration—and last in order, though first along with food production in importance—population control through family planning.

A precautionary warning against oversanguine expectations from the immediate use of new high-yielding rice in Indonesia was presented in the form of a suspicion that high-yielding varieties may be susceptible to certain diseases, more in Indonesia than in other countries, a difficult problem, but one not impossible to surmount.

Although it had been suggested that attention to marketing might be deferred, pending efforts to increase production, it was reported that BIMAS stimulation of production in South Celebes had been successful but that farmers there were hesitant to harvest the rice because they had no assurance that it would be bought. In this instance, it was argued, attention to marketing was as important a first concern as attention to production.

Would land reform be relevant to programs for increasing production? Legal provision for land reform was actually made in Indonesia in 1961–1962, with the intention that each farmer would have a maximum of five or ten hectares, depending on regional location, but the size of holdings was somewhat arbitrarily determined. Land reform has never really been implemented, although it was an object of excited political discussion during the years before the attempted takeover of government in late 1965. Some land had indeed been taken away from former owners, but it is reported that in general there was widespread disinterest in the implementation of land reform regulations. There is question whether land reform is an urgent nationwide problem in Indonesia, and the whole topic will no doubt get thorough reconsideration in the development of the plan for agriculture.

Would not sugarcane be a suitable alternative for the production of rice, because it yields about ten times as much as rice? Would it not be more advantageous for Indonesia to export sugar and import rice? Sugarcane production, however, uses the land for sixteen or eighteen months; if rice yields increase and three crops are grown, rice calls for less investment than sugar, and rice production is argued to be preferable. It is cheaper to import sugar than rice, and it is by no means certain that the world market for sugar could sustain any large Indonesian export of that commodity. From a nutritional viewpoint, rice production would be the more important. Rice provides both carbohydrates and protein. Processing takes all the protein out of sugar, and unprocessed sugar is not desired by Indonesians.

Dr. Tojib's insistence that a new spirit of pioneering is necessary for agricultural development occasioned a question as to whether Peace Corps programs would be useful. It was recalled that Indonesia hosted a few U.S. Peace Corps members in sports, but not in agriculture or education, before the withdrawal of American programs in 1965. The presence of a pioneering spirit among Indonesian youth, especially students, has been identified, but "will they be the Peace Corps type?" It was concluded that Indonesian students indeed have been pioneering in social control or political change. It is not yet clear whether they will pioneer also in economic activity. A question for Indonesian leadership now is how the vigor of Indonesian youth may be redirected from political to economic ends.

In the ensuing discussion of surplus college graduates in fields where no employment could be expected, it was noted that many private universities had sprung up in response to the popular demand for educational opportunity. Promoters of the private universities have argued that if youth were not trained, they would be "cross-boys." But the question was then asked whether high school or college graduate "cross-boys" would be preferable. A proposed attack on this problem was that technical training for a year or so be organized for college graduates in an effort to make them entrepreneurs.

Does Indonesia have to begin with agricultural development and postpone industrial development, or might agricultural and industrial development be put together according to certain "agro-industry" patterns? Could not agricultural products be converted to consumer goods, thus introducing a rural-industry component in the overall pattern of agricultural development? The objective would be industrial production for local use and not for export. Cassava was mentioned as an illustrative case: export to Europe of cassava chopped and dried required payment of a 6 percent tax; export of cassava powdered, a 15 percent tax. Export of cane sugar would require payment of an 80 percent tax. Production for local consumption seems to be a better objective in this case.

A reason for deferring mechanization in the production of rice is asserted to be cost. The estimated cost of mechanization was reported by one study to be 24 cents per kilo because of the cost of importing machines, spare parts, fertilizer, and pesticides, whereas the rice price in the world market at the same time was 14–18 cents per kilo. Traditional rice growing, on the other hand, costs only 8–10 cents per kilo, and rice thus produced would be sufficiently under the international market price to make it profitable. On the point of developing industry, it was argued that Indonesia must begin to develop household or cottage industry, then small-scale industry, and finally "basic industry."

The depredations of rats were mentioned as a threat to grain production, and rat control was acknowledged as a serious problem, more so in some years than in others. Chemical control will probably be the method used. Phosphorus was formerly used, but now there are new chemicals. The control of other pests is also very important.

Can Indonesia be self-sufficient in fertilizer? There is now one large plant at Palembang, producing 100 thousand tons a year. Other plants will become productive in Java, where natural gas is an available resource. Phosphate deposits are limited and scattered and transport is difficult, but there may be sufficient deposits for the next ten to twenty years. In this case, it is suggested that Indonesia may have to negotiate with Australia for phosphate from Christmas Island. Geologists may be encouraged to explore for other deposits.

Studies show that even enormous rates of growth of industry and manufacturing would not begin to absorb all the people who are going to be looking for jobs in Indonesia. Many must be absorbed in agriculture and household industry. The infrastructure is lacking (roads, markets, transportation, institutions)—otherwise a "Marshall Plan" might be considered (Europe had infrastructure; Indonesia does not). Thus, there is some point to the suggestion that first emphasis must be on agricultural production in the local work-area. Furthermore, for incentive to produce there must be a market and a stable money system. The pioneer spirit in the United States was fostered by homesteading. Could this occur also in Indonesia, resulting in migration for example, from Java to Sumatra? The experienced farmer of middle age or over and with a family is not aware of a need to migrate. Younger, inexperienced people might be more willing to move, but working in the new area baffles them. Spontaneous migration (voluntary, at personal initiative) of experienced farmers succeeds better than governmentally planned migration. The government has tried to pretrain migrants, but only about 100 thousand families have been moved in recent years, and Java's growth is two million persons annually. Except under conditions of bare subsistence, there is no longer room for these new people. This circumstance is a newly effective push-from-Java factor that has not operated historically. The government pays transportation and pays for food for the firxt six months; perhaps this will be changed to one year in order to provide subsistence to migrants until the first crop is harvested. The government provides some housing subsidy and pays wages for work done at the migration project site. These are some of the incentives. In South Kalimantan, peat soils have been reclaimed by paid laborers who may get up to five hectares (12.5 acres) per family. It is doubtful, however, that a paid labor system would be feasible for hand tillage or even cattle-raising. Consideration is being given to providing these settlers with small tractors such as are used in Japan.

There have been pilot projects for settlement of veterans; one has been conducted successfully in South Banten. The army helped make roads; the government helped clear forest. It is planned to give agricultural training to soldiers before demobilization, and some of them will be diverted to transmigration centers. The progam for resettlement of veterans has been argued to be one of the worst-managed in Indonesia. Veterans were lured to South Sumatra 40 or 50 kilometers beyond the last point which could be reached by car, in areas where they had to carry everything in and out. A road had been put through but there was no bridge. "You can't move across rough country by bicycle unless you have bridges." It was reported that the money allocated for the bridges had disappeared. In 1956 there was actually a return of veterans from South Sumatra to Java. There are, however, great possibilities in working with veterans in land settlement, as has been seen in other parts of the world—for example, Australia. But very careful planning is needed, and this is why breakdowns tend to occur in the first few years. For example, in South Sumatra, projects started in the early 1950s and mid-1950s had not been adequately surveyed. Local political leaders had been transferred or made available to the transmigration service. There was land in which the local people were not interested, but the leader was interested in getting the contract for land clearing. He was making his money, clearing land for Javanese settlers who had to move out at the end of the second year because they couldn't make ends meet. The one obvious shortcoming here was the lack of careful preparation, including lack of soil surveys. The other difficulty which developed in the early 1950s was that the Department of Public Works fell behind on the irrigation system. Mechanized equipment was being used for bulldozing the forest when it might better have been used for construction of all-weather roads and for irrigation systems. In comment on these difficulties, it was acknowledged that Indonesia has had "some bad experiences in the past," that some of the migrations due to political pressures were done too quickly, and migrants were actually put on soil with no potential for farming. "Now, we hope not to make the same mistake again."

But migration enough to keep Javanese population from further increase would require unavailable facilities: "a whole fleet" of interisland vessels and a "very sophisticated organization." Migration cannot solve the problem, and family planning must be promoted vigorously. An association for family planning has been established, but there are many problems: it is observed that even with governmental backing in India, only a small percentage of the population is affected—and Indonesia will surely face similar difficulties. The Pill can be used by people "with some education," but it is not the answer for the masses.

Leon A. Mears   **Suggestions for an Agricultural Strategy**

No explanation is necessary as to why this paper concentrates heavily on the problem of increasing rice production in Indonesia in the short run and over the Five-Year Plan period.[1] This would be true even if the government had not placed a major emphasis on the need for increasing food production during the present stabilization and rehabilitation period. Rice is the basic food of most of the population, and its import to satisfy consumption requirements has frequently consumed over 10 percent of the scarce foreign exchange which is generated by exports and critically needed to finance capital for rehabilitation and economic growth.[2]

Analysis of the role of environmental, technological, and institutional factors in explaining the growth of rice production and the high yields per hectare in Taiwan and Japan gives guidance for strategy to increase production and yields of rice in Indonesia and other Asian countries. Lessons gained from these experiences will be discussed first. Then, in light of these strategy guidelines, consideration will be given to the short and longer run potentialities for rice production. Finally, strategy guidelines are developed and summarized in the conclusion.

I

A major lesson learned from the development experiences in Taiwan and Japan is that yield increases resulting from the adoption of improved technology were associated with simultaneous improvement over a period of at least half a century of applied technological research, infrastructure, and institutional innovations. Total production did increase, as has also been true in Indonesia, from the expansion of land area. However, the larger yield increases—which have not been evident elsewhere in Southeast Asia—required and were associated with complementary development in applied technology, infrastructure, and institutions.[3] To facilitate discussion, this package of requirements can be detailed as follows.[4]

A. Applied Technological Research
   1. Improvement of seed varieties
   2. Fertilizer experiments
   3. Insecticide and pesticide experiments
B. Improvement in Infrastructure
   1. Irrigation
   2. Drainage
   3. Flood control
   4. Transportation
C. Institutional Innovations
   1. Education, including extension service
   2. Organization appropriate for marketing and finance, including cooperatives
   3. Land reform

Experience has shown that because of the complementary nature of the elements of this package, yield increases of any consequence will be realized only when improvement takes place concurrently in all these aspects. The problem for any developing country is how to achieve these complementary investments. Applied technological research is necessary to produce the high-yielding, fertilizer-responsive, and disease-resistant varieties suitable for the particular conditions existing in a given country. Fertilizer experiments are required to determine the economical application of fertilizer under existing soil conditions. If large investment is to be made in fertilizers and other inputs, preventative chemicals must be developed and available for use to minimize loss from pests and disease. Pest control is of particular importance, since pests seem to be attracted to the most productive fields. As with fertilizers, economical application must be determined through field experiments.

A physical infrastructure of irrigation, drainage, flood control, and transportation is needed to achieve the potential productivity inherent in the results of research. Yield response to fertilizer can be reduced materially by the lack of water control made possible by regulated irrigation, a fact that has undoubtedly had a strong influence in minimizing the use of fertilizer on rainfed hectarage in Southeast Asia—even when fertilizer has been available.[5] Drainage is necessary in many situations to facilitate water control, while flood control is essential to reduce the risk of crop loss, especially if a high investment is at stake. Economical transportation is also required if the product is to be marketed profitably.

Institutional innovations are essential to extend the results of the research to the farmer in the village, to finance the distribution and use of essentials such as fertilizer and chemicals, and to collect and market the production. Land reform, aside from its social value, gives the farmer a chance to make a profit, and thus increases his willingness to invest in agricultural improvements.

Until recently, few people had fully appreciated the great amount of investment necessary to realize the production potential generated by applied research (which itself requires considerable investment). Large investments must be made in drainage, flood control, and transport. Where these are already adequate, continued investment is required for maintenance. Investment must be made to insure a supply of fertilizer and chemicals, either by construction of production facilities or by import from abroad. There must be an effective marketing organization to bring these supplies to the farm when they are needed, and at reasonable prices to the farmer. Heavy investment must also be made in the development of trained manpower. This includes not only the training of farmers to use the new technology effectively but also the training of extension workers, of experts in marketing, management, and finance, and of engineers and scientists to build and maintain the infrastructure and to carry on the applied research.

Some of this investment—such as in major irrigation projects, applied research, roads, and flood control—must necessarily be made by government. However, governmental performance, especially in marketing activities, seems to vary widely throughout Asia, raising doubts as to where emphasis should be placed. If the potential productivity is raised through government investment in research and infrastructure, it is possible that this could increasingly provide private producers with the incentive to invest in local irrigation works and trained manpower as well as the purchase of seeds, fertilizer, and chemicals. In the Philippines, after the development of the "miracle rice seed," farmers and other entrepreneurs have been increasingly assuming this investment responsibility.

The strategy suggested by this approach places emphasis on investment in highly expensive infrastructure, accompanied by complementary investment in research that will create new production potentials. We must recognize, however, that the real production potential is realized in rice-producing areas of South and Southeast Asia only when accompanied by institutional innovations that induce the farmer to combine these new facilities with fertilizer and pest control.[6] This is quite in contrast to policy recommendations that place initial emphasis on innovations not requiring large increases in the use of purchased inputs.[7] It is unfortunate but true that investment in research has not opened up such a low-cost route to rapid increase in yields in this region.

II

Short-Run Potentials

In contrast with the experience in Taiwan and Japan, the complementary elements in the package of applied technological research, infrastructure, and institutional innovations have not been developing simultaneously in Indonesia. Before Indonesian independence, progress already was being made in such things as seed development, fertilizer experimentation, irrigation, and transport, but complementary activity lagged in other sectors such as flood control, insecticide testing, and institutional improvement. Selective improvement continued after the revolution, but in recent years infrastructure maintenance and expansion has been minimized, while government emphasis on other activities resulted in reduced support to research and to improvement of agricultural institutions.

For example, while improved varieties of seed have recently been developed, potential yields from these seeds are still far below those currently obtained in Japan and Taiwan and from the new "miracle" seed in the Philippines. Fertilizer and pest control experiments have been continued but on a reduced scale, and with but little expansion to islands outside Java. Lack of maintenance has drastically reduced the effectiveness of irrigation works that once served approximately one and a half million hectares on Java, thus limiting the area where farmers dare risk heavy investment. Barely a start has been made to restore the denuded watersheds in order to minimize the annual flood damage to crops.

Institutional innovations have probably been the least successful and, at least until the advent of the BIMAS program, have continued to be a major limitation in the package of requirements to induce adoption of available technology. The government has invested heavily in developing an extension service with a staff of over 3,000 technically trained personnel. Their effectiveness in working with the farmer to induce adaptation of known technological improvements still leaves much to be desired. In part this may stem from an imperfect recognition that the skills needed to improve rice production must be learned in the paddy and that the extension service must work closely with both farmers and researchers.

Marketing organizations are also deficient, with high costs and inefficiency in distribution of both farm supplies and farm products.[8] Institutions have not been developed to serve effectively the small farmer's need for production credits. Some of these difficulties might have been overcome if the attempts to develop efficient cooperatives had met with more success. Even the existing land reform legislation has not been implemented effectively.

In one respect, the picture given above is far too negative, for the country's outstanding organizational innovation, the BIMAS program, has not been adequately emphasized. This program was a short-run tactic to capture the production potential of existing improved seed by concentrating available resources where infrastructure was best suited and to the extent complementary resources could be provided through government innovations.

After a successful pilot project in 1963, and within the constraints resulting from insufficient research and inadequacy of infrastructure, the BIMAS organization has substituted for inadequate organization elsewhere to the extent that yield increases of about one ton of rice per hectare are reported to have been realized on almost 500 thousand hectares of paddy land during the 1966–1967 wet-season crop.[9]

The following aspects of the BIMAS program have been of particular importance to its success. A corps of agriculture students, together with extension staff, worked with the farmers in paddy fields to help transmit the skills associated with improved practices and use of capital intensive inputs. The students, particularly, were ready to bypass bureaucratic channels of communication to insure that necessary supplies reached the farmers when required. In this way they compensated to a degree for inadequate institutional development and helped to provide the farmer with sufficient security so that he would be less inclined to discount the future income to be gained from new technology. In the absence of effective credit institutions, procedures were developed to provide the credit in kind, with repayment by paddy from the increased harvest. The area to which this program could be extended is limited in the short run by the constraints of effective water control, transport facilities, student manpower, and the government's budget. Also, production increase was limited by the potential yield of the available seed.

The BIMAS program was started on a trial basis during the rainy season of 1963–1964, with yield increases averaging 1.2 tons of milled rice per hectare on the small trial area of 105 hectares (see Table 3:8). Benefiting the following year from earlier experience, average yield increases of 2 tons per hectare were realized on 11,006 hectares. As the program was expanded in the next two years, the effectiveness of student participation was diluted by limitations of supplies. Foreign exchange constraints made it necessary to reduce the use of fertilizer, and organizational constraints interfered with the supply of improved seed and fertilizer. In spite of these difficulties, and compared to non-BIMAS areas, average yield increase was 1.3 tons per hectare in 1965–1966 on 157,795 hectares and approximately 0.9 tons per hectare on 845 thousand hectares in 1966–1967.

Original plans were to expand the total BIMAS program in 1967–1968 to more than 900 thousand hectares. This expansion was considered possible, given budget constraints, only by limiting to not over 300 thousand hectares the granting of credit in kind. Student participation was to be limited to this portion of the total program. In the other 625

TABLE 3:8 BIMAS Program Hectarage and Yield, 1963-1964—1967-1968

Year and Season	Actual and/or planned (*) hectarage	BIMAS area	Control area outside BIMAS	In tons of stalk paddy per hectare	In tons of milled rice per hectare
				Yield in quintals of stalk Paddy/ha.[7]	Yield Increase BIMAS Area over Control
1963–1964 wet	105	66.4	43.0	2.34	1.23
1964–1965 wet	11,006	72.3	33.1	3.92	2.04
1965–1966 wet	157,795	55.7	31.6	2.41	1.35
1966 dry	46,493	45.3	25.0	2.03	1.07
1966–1967 wet	485,000[1]				0.9[5]
1967 dry	15,000[2]				
1967–1968 wet Original Plan	(300,000* Regular[6] (625,000* IM[3] (75,000* Sulawesi[4]				
Alternative being considered	(600,000 Regular[6] (170,000 IM[3] (75,000 Sulawesi[4]				

Source: Directorat Pertanian Rakjat, Government of Indonesia.

[1] Final figure may be 5 to 15,000 higher.

[2] Final figure may be slightly different.

[3] IM BIMAS differs from regular BIMAS in that supervision is less intensive and farmer must purchase inputs for cash (while on regular BIMAS, farmer is given inputs for credit and repays in stalk paddy).

[4] Special program with management assistance and may include insecticide only and not fertilizer, although this decision still not final.

[5] Preliminary estimate.

[6] 241,000 ha. in Java, balance in Sumatra (20,000), Bali (14,000), Nusa Tenggara Barat (10,000), and South Sulawesi (15,000).

[7] 1 quintal = 100 kg. Stalk paddy is unthreshed rice in the husk, harvested with part of the stalk, converted to rice equivalent at 1 quintal stalk paddy = 52 kg. milled rice.

thousand hectares, distinguished from the regular program by being called IM BIMAS (*intensificasi masal* or massive intensification), the farmers would have to find their own source of credit and pay for inputs with cash. Even though the government has considered providing credit facilities where necessary to this latter group through the state bank, rice mills, and cooperatives, it is questionable how well these institutions are organized and located to perform this task effectively. Other private sources of credit, where they remained at all under the restrictive conditions existing in the country, could not be expected to provide funds at rates under 10 percent a month, which rate was frequently exceeded.[10]

Another difficulty has also arisen as the relative prices of inputs (fertilizer and other chemicals) and outputs (rice) have changed along with the gradual rationalization toward a free market economy. Fertilizer prices have risen to world market levels plus high internal transport and distribution costs, while rice prices have been held considerably below world market levels. Thus, many of the farmers who must purchase inputs for cash will no longer see sufficient inducement to use the production-increasing inputs even if they can obtain the necessary credit. This situation will exist even though the government plans to provide a 25 percent subsidy to reduce the cost of fertilizer to the cash buyer.

The basis for this last conclusion is illustrated in Chart 3:1. Benefit/cost relationships are shown separately for landlords who receive all the harvest and for tenants who have to divide the harvest with the landlord but may have to pay for all the fertilizer and chemical inputs themselves. This latter situation reportedly exists in at least part of the area to be covered by the cash-payment BIMAS program. To determine which benefit/cost ratio applies to a particular group of farmers, it is necessary to know how they make their production plans. Farmers in Indonesia and elsewhere have generally been found to base their planning on an expectation that the price they will receive for next year's harvest will be the same as received for the prior year's harvest.[11] They might make some allowance for inflation, but with the rate of inflation declining in 1967, it is unlikely that much allowance would be made for this factor at planting time in October 1967.

Thus, based on prices received for the 1967 harvest, it is unlikely that the farmer will anticipate a price above Rp. 10/kg. of milled rice.[12] In areas such as Southern Sulawesi (Southern Celebes) and Atjeh, with prices in July 1967 between Rp. 4 and 5 per kg. of milled rice, the anticipation would be for an even lower price. Also, the farmer would be unlikely to invest in high cost inputs unless some percentage of profit seemed assured to allow for the risks he faces. On this basis, an anticipated benefit/cost ratio of at least 1.25, allowing for a 25 percent benefit from the additional inputs, would be a probable lower limit that would

CHART 3:1 *Benefit/Cost Ratios at Alternative Rice Prices (1968) for Farmers Buying BIMAS Inputs for Cash in the Market**

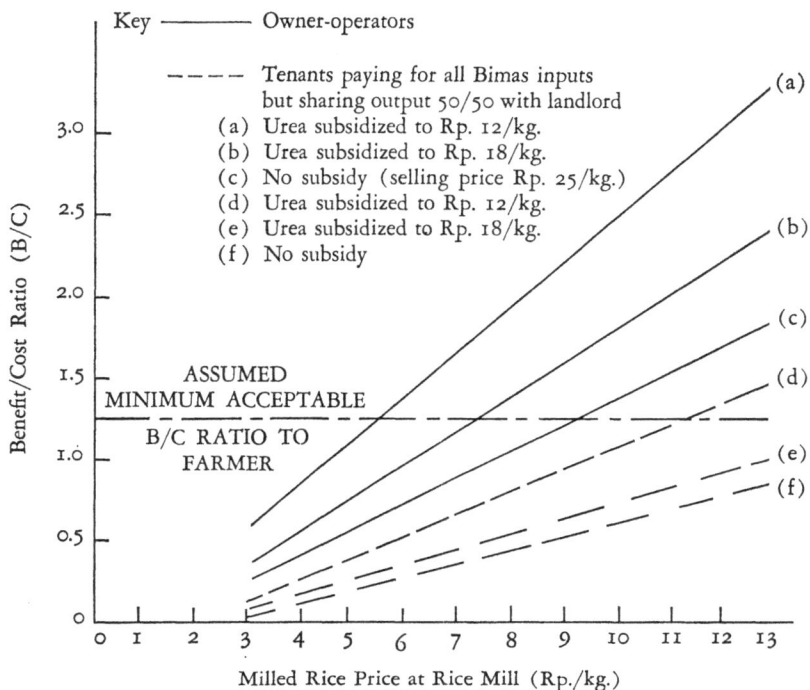

Key ——————— Owner-operators

– – – – Tenants paying for all Bimas inputs but sharing output 50/50 with landlord
(a) Urea subsidized to Rp. 12/kg.
(b) Urea subsidized to Rp. 18/kg.
(c) No subsidy (selling price Rp. 25/kg.)
(d) Urea subsidized to Rp. 12/kg.
(e) Urea subsidized to Rp. 18/kg.
(f) No subsidy

ASSUMED MINIMUM ACCEPTABLE B/C RATIO TO FARMER

Milled Rice Price at Rice Mill (Rp./kg.)

* Assumes: Bawon = 20% (payment in kind to harvesters) of Harvest
Interest rate 4%/month and credit *is* available
Farmers can obtain high quality seed
No special assessments at lower political levels.
Where these exist, B/C ratios will decline accordingly.

induce the farmer to use fertilizer and other chemicals if he had to pay cash for them, even if he were familiar with the new technology.

By referring to Chart 3:1, and using the assumptions indicated above, it will be seen that while the landlord could anticipate a benefit/cost ratio of approximately 1.8 (with urea subsidized to Rp. 18/kg.) and so would be likely to use the subsidized inputs, the tenant farmer premised would anticipate a benefit/cost ratio of less than 1, and so would not use fertilizer and chemicals. If, it is suggested, the percentage of tenant farmers in the BIMAS areas may be as high as 60 percent of the total, this would mean that farmers would not participate in the program on more than 250,000 hectares of the 625,000 hectares where BIMAS cooperators are expected to pay cash for inputs.

On the basis of this discouraging possibility, and keeping in mind budgetary and other constraints, alternative programs have been evaluated. This has been done with the objective of insuring greater participation in the 1967–1968 rainy season BIMAS and to insure increased production on BIMAS areas over that of the past year. This increased production would make possible the reduction of expenditure of scarce foreign exchange on rice imports. A further objective has been to insure expansion of the production on BIMAS areas to maintain the confidence and participation of farmers who have already used fertilizer and chemicals in earlier programs.

Table 3:9 summarizes the net benefits that might be forthcoming from alternative program combinations, as compared with the original program (indicated as alternative 1). Alternative 2 holds the regular BIMAS participation (inputs received in kind for repayment in paddy) to 300 thousand hectares as in the original program. However, allowance is taken of the reality that participation in the IM BIMAS (those paying cash for inputs) would be unlikely to exceed 250,000 hectares. This alternative creates the least strain on credit facilities of the government, providing no credit for fertilizer and chemicals where IM BIMAS cooperators cannot be expected to participate.[13]

Alternatives 3 and 4 provide greater assured participation by increasing the regular BIMAS program to 500 thousand and 600 thousand hectares respectively. Alternative 4 appears to provide the greatest overall benefits, remains well below the credit requirements of the original program, and puts a minimum additional strain on the manpower resources required for supervision, as it provides for only a 20 percent increase in regular BIMAS over the 1966–1967 program. As shown in Table 3:10, fertilizer import requirements for the alternative, compared with alternative 1, show a reduction of almost 20,000 tons for urea and 10,000 tons for D. S. P. (double super-phosphate). With concurrent reductions of insecticide, immediate foreign exchange requirements will be reduced by $3.6 million. In addition, while the subsidy is increased in the short run, the overall net benefit to the government, taking into account the reduced rice import requirements in 1968, will be at least Rp. 1 billion higher than for the original program. Considering that the farmer will also benefit from the increased quantity of rice he retains for consumption, the net benefit to the economy as a whole will be approximately Rp. 3 billion.[14] And, while outstanding credits at the end of 1967 are almost Rp. 3 billion, these reverse to a net benefit to the government of over Rp. 5 billion by mid-1968.[15]

This analysis of alternatives is merely an example of the continuous process of reanalysis that must be performed as relative prices change with closer approach to a free market economy and as new constraints

TABLE 3:9 Credit Requirements and Net Benefits to Indonesia from Alternate BIMAS Program Combinations for 1967–1968 Rainy Season[1] (in millions of rupiahs)

Specified Requirements and Net Benefits	Alternate BIMAS Program Combinations			
	1	2	3	4
1. Program Hectarage[2]				
a. Regular BIMAS (in 1000 ha.)	300.00	300.00	500.00	600.00
b. IM BIMAS (in 1000 ha.)	625.00	250.00	170.00	130.00
2. Credit Required for all BIMAS Inputs[3]	4,268.75	2,562.50	3,148.50	3,441.50
3. Cash Sales in 1967 to IM BIMAS Farmers	909.50	909.50	618.00	462.75
4. Net BIMAS Credit Outstanding 12/31/67 (line 2—line 3)	3,359.25	1,653.00	2,530.50	2,978.75
5. 1968 Proceeds from Regular BIMAS Repayment 2½ qt. rice per ha. @ Rp. 1,000 per qt.	750.00	750.00	1,250.00	1,500.00
6. Investment in stock on hand 1968—not sold (fertilizers and insecticides)[4]	1,706.25			
7. Net Subsidy after 1968 Repayment in kind (line 4—lines 5 and 6)	903.00	903.00	1,280.50	1,478.75
8. Benefits to Indonesia in terms of Imports @ Rp. 20,250 per ton[5]	10,024.00	10,024.00	12,200.00	13,300.00
9. Gross Benefits to Indonesia from 1967/68 BIMAS Program (line 8—line 7)	9,121.00	9,121.00	10,919.50	11,821.25
10. Estimate value of maximum portion of increased production that might be retained and consumed by the farmers[6]	5,012.00	5,012.00	6,100.00	6,650.00
11. Net Benefits to Government from 1967/68 BIMAS Program (line 9—line 10)	4,109.00	4,109.00	4,819.50	5,171.25

Notes for Table 3:9

[1] Assumptions: (1) Average price anticipated by farmers and actually existing at rice mills for milled rice during 1968 harvest = Rp. 10/kg. (2) Rp. 135 = U.S. $1.00. This price would be valid from the country's viewpoint even though fertilizer imports granted subsidized exchange rate of Rp. 100 = U.S. $1.00. (3) Fertilizer subsidized on the market with urea subsidized to Rp. 18/kg. and D.S.P. to Rp. 15.75/kg.

[2] "Regular BIMAS" refers to portion of program providing inputs (fertilizer and other chemicals, sprayers, management and irrigation repair costs) to farmer on credit to be repaid by 5 quintals of stalk paddy (unthreshed rice in the husk, harvested with part of the stalk) at harvest time. "IM BIMAS" refers to portion of program where farmers must purchase all inputs for cash on the market. Alternative programs assume participation by only those IM BIMAS farmers for whom anticipated relative prices of outputs and inputs will result in an expected B/C ratio of 1.25 or more. It is also assumed that these farmers can obtain credit from the market, a somewhat questionable assumption in many cases.

[3] Includes fertilizer (100 kg. urea and 50 kg. D.S.P. per hectare), insecticides, and sprayer for IM BIMAS, plus management fee and irrigation repair for Regular BIMAS.

[4] Stocks remaining result from lower purchases than planned by IM BIMAS farmer because of lack of incentive, given assumed price structure; i.e., in alternative 1, it could be expected that 40%—only farmers on 250,000 ha.—would be landlords, the balance would be tenants for whom benefits would not warrant participation; see Chart 1.

[5] Increased production on BIMAS acreage estimated to be at least 0.9 ton/ha.

[6] Assuming the farmers' income elasticity of demand for rice = 0.5.

TABLE 3:10   Import of Fertilizers and Insecticides—Alternative BIMAS Programs, Rainy Season 1967–1968*

	Alternative BIMAS Program Combinations			
	1	2	3	4
1. Program Hectarage				
a. Regular BIMAS (in 1000 ha.)	300	300	500	600
b. IM BIMAS (in 1000 ha.)	625	250	170	130
2. Tons required—Urea	92,500	55,000	67,000	73,000
—D.S.P.	46,250	27,500	33,500	36,500
3. Cost (000 $)				
@ $90/ton Urea	8,375	4,950	6,025	6,570
@ $78/ton D.S.P.	3,605	2,145	2,580	2,810
@ $5/ha. insecticides, etc.	4,625	2,750	3,355	3,650
4. Total Import Cost—$ (000)	16,605	9,845	11,960	13,030
—Rp. (mill.)	2,240	1,330	1,620	1,760
5. Savings in imports vs. alternative 1—Rp. (millions)		910	620	480

* See Table 3:9 for assumptions and notes.

arise when the program is expanded further or replaced. Consideration of expansion of the use of these capital intensive inputs raises questions of priority to be considered in formulating the Five-Year Plan.

III

The Longer-Run Picture

The innovations in Indonesia have shown promise of bringing this one aspect of the total package of complementary factors up to the level of the other factors in a limited area of the country. To the extent that these new institutions can fill the gap, advances can be made in the short run to realize the potential productivity of available higher yielding seeds. Looking at the possibility of expanding this program, areas for strategic concentration in the longer run soon become apparent.

Increased yields could be obtained even with the existing level of the BIMAS program if the potential productivity of the available seed approached that in the Philippines, Taiwan, and Japan. The ecology of the monsoon tropics generally rules out the effective transfer of these high fertilizer responsive varieties. What can be transferred to assist in the development of improved varieties is the skill and method of organizing scientific manpower that has, for example, been learned at the International Rice Research Institute in the Philippines from having solved similar problems. At the same time, it might be possible to overcome the shortage of student supervisors by organizing the extension services in concentrated coordinated groups at the farm level, as is now being tried in the Philippines.[16] Other Philippine innovations offer suggestions for improving organizational deficiencies. These include the successful rural banks, which capitalize on the effectiveness of the family-type organization in Southeast Asia, the provision of incentives to attract private enterprise to establish a widespread network of fertilizer dealers and to multiply and distribute the high-yielding seed varieties, and the provision by businessmen of management services to groups of farmers willing to share increased yields in return for help in adopting new technology.

Lack of irrigation is not an immediate bottleneck to the use of high-yielding inputs, as a large portion of the irrigated land still is not being used with the available technology. However, given large benefit/cost ratios (from the national viewpoint), there is strong reason to expand both the limits to which the capital-intensive inputs can be spread and the area where larger yields can be obtained through irrigation alone. Increased farm incomes can provide an important increase in the market for industrial goods, while the increment in rice production can be expected to find a profitable market, given the rapidly growing internal and external demand. (Improved marketing practices and an expanded marketing organization will be required if surpluses arise to permit exporting.) Irrigation can be expanded rapidly and at relatively little cost by rehabilitation of older existing systems. Ground water surveys will indicate where pump irrigation can be utilized safely to augment inadequate river flow in the dry season and to supply full irrigation needs where surface water is not available. At the same time, increased attention should be paid to drainage and flood control to minimize losses from those sources.

Other actions that may be of less urgency at the moment include the need for improving farm-to-market transport in outlying areas and for expanded fertilizer and pest control tests. Both of these will help increase the profitability of adopting new technology. Land reform could help accomplish the same goal, but the institutional problems may take longer to solve on a large scale. Thus, while land reform should not be forgotten, other action would seem to be of more strategic importance, given the need for rapid growth in output and the limited resources available. In Indonesia, where increased efficiency in distribution of the rice from the farm to the market assumes a much higher priority than in a country such as the Philippines, permission for rice-millers to reenter the private distribution network should bring major improvement, but much still needs to be done to reduce the transport bottlenecks that add to costs and reduce efficiency at every level.

It must also be remembered that the present BIMAS organization has been an innovation to overcome problems arising where regular institutions had not developed sufficiently to meet the need. The question must be asked, "Are the institutions involved in BIMAS the most efficient and effective for the longer run?" Competitive private enterprise might be more efficient and so reduce costs of fertilizer distribution, but then effective credit institutions must be assured to meet the farmers' need to pay cash. Also, the effectiveness of the extension service must be improved if it is adequately to serve the farmer in introducing new technology and then in giving help to the farmer in overcoming problems raised by the adoption of that technology.

In developing a strategy for the improvement of organization, benefit can be gained by studying the change in organization that is facilitating the adoption of new technology outside of BIMAS. In Indonesia, suggestions might be obtained from watching the effectiveness of institutions being tested in Sulawesi, where a "private-sector BIMAS" is being tried out to increase rice yields, or in Karawang, where planters are also employing a BIMAS variation to increase corn yields.

IV

The BIMAS principle is already being tested in the attempt to induce the use of a new technology in corn production in Indonesia. For crops other than corn or rice, the same impediments as those discussed above stand in the way of rapid adoption of technological change that can increase yields and incomes of the farmer. In some situations, particularly in areas where year-round irrigation is not now available, peanuts or soya beans might be grown where other less profitable crops, or no crops at all, are now being raised in the dry season. Careful study must be given to the need for research on these and other crops, as well as the means to improve the institutions necessary to serve them, particularly in marketing.

The question of plantation crops places emphasis on different factors in the package. Space does not permit their detailed discussion in this paper, but it is well to remember that the plantation organization, frequently with consolidated management for a group of plantations, is just another way of trying to solve the institutional organization problem. To the extent that private management can be rapidly improved, it may have special capabilities to utilize technological research for increased agricultural yields. Also, these larger organizations may find less difficulty in obtaining finance for agricultural supplies, but they will not be willing to invest in such supplies unless a profit is apparent.

V

To summarize, it has been argued that farmers can be induced to adopt improved technology in the production of food grains in Indonesia only to the extent that profitable production can be expected after considering the entire package of applied technological research, infrastructure, and institutions. Since the elements of this package have not all developed evenly in Indonesia to provide the incentive necessary to induce rapid technological change, special innovations can be advantageous, at least temporarily. But, for continuous advance over the coming decade, special programs will need continued review to conform more effectively to the changing environment and to admit expansion of the new technology. Immediate emphasis should be placed on increasing the potential productivity of rice varieties and on reducing the constraints that limit the growth-effectiveness of the BIMAS innovation. Also, Indonesia can increase inducements that will lead private capital to play a greater part in providing adequate credit, seed multiplication, production and distribution of farm supplies, and localized pump irrigation, thus releasing limited government revenues and scarce foreign exchange for infrastructure improvement, especially in irrigation and farm-to-market roads. At the same time, price policies must be maintained that assure adequate inducement to the farmers to adopt and continue using the highly fertilizer-responsive varieties of plants and the more expensive fertilizers and insecticides they require.

[1] Preliminary draft originally presented for discussion at the Seminar on the Five-Year Agricultural Development Plan, Jogjakarta, Indonesia, July 1, 1967. The author wishes to acknowledge the assistance in obtaining current information used in this paper given by Mr. Amien Tjokrosoeseno, Secretary General, Ministry of Agriculture, and Mr. Soegandhi Soerjo Amidharmo, *Direktorat Pertanian Rakjat.*

[2] For example, in 1965 over 11 percent of the foreign exchange earned from exports was required to finance rice imports into Indonesia; Central Bureau of Statistics, Djakarta.

[3] In Indonesia, while average yields on Java increased from 1.19 tons per hectare to 1.43 tons per hectare from 1956–1958 to 1964–1966, average yields outside Java did not increase at all during this period; Indonesian Agricultural Extension Service records, unpublished. For discussion of environment associated with growth of yields in Taiwan, see S. C. Hseih and T. H. Lee, *Agricultural Development and Its Contribution to Economic Growth in Taiwan,* Joint Commission on Rural Reconstruction, Taipei, April 1966. The Japanese aspect is discussed in B. F. Johnson, "Agricultural Development and Economic Transformation: A Comparative Study of the Japanese Experience," *Food Research Institute Studies* (November 1962): 223–76, and A. M. Tang, "Research and Education in Japanese Agricultural Development, 1880–1938," *The Economic Studies Quarterly* (February and May 1963): 27–41, 91–99.

[4] This listing is restricted to give emphasis to major yield-increasing inputs. Further yield improvement can of course occur from such things as optimal spacing, intensive weed control, and deeper plowing as may be possible with improved plows or tractor-power. Also, tractor-power may permit more total output per year by shortening time required for cultivation.

[5] See H. R. von Uexkuell, "Obstacles to Using Fertilizers for Rice in Southeast Asia," *World Crops* (March 1964): 70–75.

[6] This relates to overcoming the "subsistence mindedness" and to there being sufficient inducement to invest to compensate for the "large subjective discounts," as discussed in this seminar by David H. Penny and J. Price Gittinger in "Economics and Indonesian Agricultural Development."

[7] For example, see B. F. Johnson and G. S. Tolley, "Strategy for Agriculture in Development," *Journal of Farm Economics* (May 1965): 365–79. These authorities give priority to such things as "the development and introduction of innovations such as high-yielding varieties, improved crop rotations, optimum spacing and time of planting, and a better seasonal distribution of the work load."

[8] For example, see Leon Mears, *Rice Marketing in the Republic of Indonesia* (Djakarta: Pembangunan Press, 1961).

[9] Preliminary estimates by *Direktorat Pertanian Rakjat,* July 1967.

[10] If funds had been supplied under competitive conditions, the interest rate of 10 percent a month might not have been far from an equilibrium rate,

considering the high commercial bank rate (4 to 6 percent a month) plus servicing costs and risks connected with loans to near-subsistence farmers. D. H. Penny suggests that a large percentage of farmers may be able to provide their own capital, "Farm Credit Policy in the Early States of Agricultural Development," *Australian Journal of Agricultural Economics* (December 1967).

[11] For example, see Mubyarto and Lehman B. Fletcher, *The Marketable Surplus of Rice in Indonesia: A Study in Java-Madura,* Monograph No. 4, Department of Economics, Iowa State University, October 1966, and Mahar Mangahas, *The Response of Philippine Rice Farmers to Price* (M.A. Thesis, University of the Philippines, Diliman, 1965). This conclusion was evident in Mangahas's findings, even though he employed a distributed lag approach to the measurement of an expected price, i.e., that this period's expected price is a weighted average of all past prices, the weights decreasing systematically for prices going further back in time.

[12] At the rate of exchange existing in Indonesia in mid-1967 of Rp. 135 per U.S. dollar, this price is equal to $0.074 per kg.

[13] Provision of inputs in kind strains the domestic rupiah budget and also uses scarce foreign exchange, as most of the fertilizer and chemicals must be imported. Increased production will reduce foreign exchange requirements for rice imports in 1968 but gives no help to the tight 1967 foreign exchange position.

[14] Assumes an income elasticity of demand for rice by the rice farmers of 0.5.

[15] Even though none of the credits were ever repaid, the net gain to the government would be over Rp. 2.0 billion. However, the repayment record was 100 percent in 1964–1965, 95.3 percent in 1965–1966, and 66 percent in the dry season of 1966 when major crop damage resulted; *Direktorat Pertanian Rakjat,* letter dated June 21, 1967.

[16] For details, see *Four-Year Rice and Corn Self-Sufficiency Program,* 1966–1970, Philippine Department of Agriculture and Natural Resources, Office of the Rice and Corn Production Coordinating Council, July 21, 1966 (mimeographed).

CHAPTER 4

Otto Soemarwoto **Development of the National Biological Institute**

HISTORICAL INTRODUCTION

C. G. Reinwardt founded the Botanic Gardens at Bogor (then Buitenzorg) on May 18, 1817. The installation at that time was called *s'Lands Plantentuin*. From this installation grew the Bibliotheca Bogoriensis in 1842, the Herbarium Bogoriense in 1844, and the Botanical Laboratory (better known as the Treub Laboratory) in 1884, the Museum Zoologicum Bogoriense in 1894, and finally the Marine Research Laboratory in 1904. To the Botanic Gardens in Bogor was added the mountain garden division in Tjibodas in 1860. In 1940 another garden was established at Purwodadi, near Malang, and another one on the eastern slope of the Ardjuno mountain (Gunung Ardjuno), both in East Java. These latter gardens are intended as dry-climate gardens, thus serving as complements to the Bogor and Tjibodas gardens, which are located in high rainfall areas. Actually other branches of the gardens exist, i.e., at Sibolangit on the slope of the Sibajak volcano on Sumatra's East Coast near Medan, which was started in 1914, the "Setya-Mulia" Garden on Sumatra's West Coast near Padang, established in 1955, and the "Eka-Karja" Garden in Bali, founded in 1959. At present these three gardens are temporarily entrusted to the Forestry Service.

The need for the protection of nature was also felt. In 1912 Dr. S. H. Koorders took the initiative to organize the Society for Nature Protection. Later, in 1935 a special officer for nature protection was appointed at the Director's Office of the Botanic Gardens. In 1948 the Game Laws and Nature Protection was established as an independent division of the Botanic Gardens.

The foundation of the Botanic Gardens also had a far-reaching effect on the economic development of the country. In 1876 the Economic Gardens were established in Bogor as a branch of the Botanic Gardens. Before and after the foundation of the Economic Gardens, the Botanic Gardens introduced many important economic plants, notably the cinchona, the oil-palm, vanilla, getah, and others. Two of the oil-palm trees, which were introduced in 1848, and which became the ancestors of the high grade oil-palms now cultivated in Sumatra and Malaya, are still living in the Gardens in Bogor. Almost all the state research stations in Bogor originated from the Botanic Gardens, e.g., the Laboratory for Chemical Research, the Phytopathological Institute, and other institutes of the General Agricultural Experiment Station. We might also say that the private experiment stations for the plantations in Bogor found their origin in the Botanic Gardens, either directly or indirectly.

When the independence of Indonesia was recognized by the Dutch in 1949, the name *s'Lands Plantentuin* was changed to *Lembaga Pusat Penjelidikan Alam* (Central Institute for Nature Research), under the Ministry of Agriculture. The divisions of this institute were respectively the Botanic Gardens, the Bibliotheca Bogoriensis, the Herbarium Bogoriense, the "Treub" Botanical Laboratory, the Museum Zoologicum Bogoriense, the Marine Research Laboratory, and the Nature Conservatory. When in 1961 the Ministry of Agriculture reorganized structurally the research institutes, the Central Institute for Nature Research was dissolved. The divisions became independent institutes and, together with the other agricultural research institutes, were administered by the Office of Research of the Ministry of Agriculture.

According to the First Overall National Development Plan, the *Madjelis Ilmu Pengetahuan Indonesia* (Council for Sciences of Indonesia), better known under the abbreviated name of MIPI, was entrusted with the task of developing national research institutes. Accordingly, in 1962 the Botanic Gardens, the Herbarium Bogoriense, the Botanical Laboratory, the Museum Zoologicum Bogoriense, and the Marine Research Laboratory were transferred to MIPI and became the National Biological Institute (NBI). The Bibliotheca Bogoriensis came under joint management of MIPI and the Ministry of Agriculture, while the Division of Nature Protection continues to be under the Forestry Service. Recently the Bibliotheca Bogoriensis came under the jurisdiction of the Ministry of Agriculture.

BASIC CONSIDERATIONS

In developing the NBI the first question was whether the divisions should be developed into separate institutions or whether they should be nurtured as a unit. After the independence of Indonesia, when the Central Institute of Nature Research was organized, the divisions were called *"lembaga"* or institutes. This indicated that the divisions were more or less independent and that the Central Institute served as a coordinating body. When in 1961 the Central Institute was dissolved, the divisions became fully independent. Thus the fragmentation process was complete.

The unification of the five institutions, i.e., the Botanic Gardens, the Herbarium, the Botanical Laboratory, the Zoological Museum, and the Marine Research Laboratory, into the National Biological Institute should be interpreted as an effort to reverse this fragmentation. Otherwise the foundation of the NBI would be meaningless. This reversal is not an easy task, primarily due to psychological effects. The general feeling was that this unification meant a degradation of the institutes concerned into divisions of lower level.

Beyond question, this unification has its merits, including the synergistic effect of cooperative research and teamwork among the institutes, less expenditure for administration and other nonscientific duties, and less scientists involved in administration. The Doty team (Doty 1964a) also favors the unification of the institutes.

To achieve this goal, the Doty team recommended that a master plan be drawn up for the development of the NBI. Laboratories of the NBI should be built in an integrated group. Its buildings should include facilities for visiting groups of schoolchildren, with a cafeteria, museum, and lecture hall facilities for them and semihotel facilities for housing professional, scientific, or teacher groups meeting for seminars on Indonesian biological problems or school material. The team suggested that the facilities should be built at a quality level which Indonesia would desire to become the standard of the country. Thus, groups who had visited the NBI would bring home an ideal of what they would like to build in their own communities.

This recommendation was warmly received by the president of MIPI, and a tract of land was procured east of the Botanic Gardens for the future of the NBI campus. An architect was assigned to work out the master plan. At one time he was aided by an American architect who was invited by AID for this purpose. Unfortunately, the economic situation of the country quickly deteriorated, and, as of now, little hope exists that this plan will ever materialize unless financial aid from the outside can be secured.

Realizing this difficulty, I have tried to formulate an NBI program by which the institutes could realize the interdependency and interrelationships of their work. In broad terms this program consists of (1) the inventory of the biological resources of the country, terrestrial as well as marine, and identification of the elements of the resources, their distribution, and seasonal variations, (2) study of the processes leading toward the formation of these resources, and (3) transmission of the acquired knowledge to the scientific community, students, and the general public. These three programs follow each other logically. However, at the present stage of development several aspects of the three programs are being carried out simultaneously.

The inventory of the biological resources falls under the jurisdiction of the Botanic Gardens, the Herbarium, the Zoological Museum, and the Marine Research Laboratory. It is planned that combined expeditions will be organized. With the endless floral and faunal richness of the Indonesian archipelago, this work is of prime importance. The results of these studies will supply invaluable data about the geographic distribution and estimated value of these resources. From the scientific as well as the economic point of view, this forms the first step in our operation. It is easy to understand that without knowledge of what we have and the locality of the natural resources, we are not in a position to exploit them for the welfare of the country.

The next step is to study the processes leading to the formation of the biological resources and the mode of action of the environmental factors on these resources. All kinds of studies of ecological, phenological, and physiological nature can be classified in this group. The Treub Laboratory is entrusted with these investigations as far as the terrestrial communities are concerned, while the Institute of Marine Research does similar work in the marine environment. It should be mentioned here that the duties of the Treub Laboratory have recently been expanded to include nontaxonomical zoology as well. The data thus assembled will supply basic information for the development of rational methods for the economic exploitation and management of biological resources. Further efforts for increasing the yield of the resources will also be based on these data. It is of course of utmost importance that, although the yield should be increased to satisfy the needs of the country due to the increase of population and higher living standards, the resources themselves should not be destroyed.

No clear distinction between the two phases of our program can be made. Overlappings and diffusions here and there will occur, but these will accentuate the interdependency and interrelationship of the work of the several departments. We should, of course, beware of unnecessary duplications.

The final step in this sequence of operations is the reporting of the findings to the scientific community as well as to the general public. More will be said about this public service later.

Difficulties are still being encountered in the integration of the activities of the several departments of the NBI. However, it is evident that the spirit of interdepartment cooperation is improving. For example, many problems, although the subject of frequently heated debate, are being solved during the informal coffee hours. Perhaps the cooperation will become more prominent when the activities at the biological stations in Udjung Kulon and Tjibodas have come into full swing.

Another important question, which has been debated at length, is whether the NBI should engage in fundamental or applied research. In a country which is close to economic bankruptcy, the need for quick-yielding research is very pressing. On the other hand, Indonesia already has research institutes which are assigned to carry out specialized applied research. These institutes belong to several ministries, among which are the Ministries of Agriculture, Industry, and Plantation. If the NBI should move into applied research, it could result in duplication of efforts and confusion. Van Raalte (1965) has commented: "The two types of research are supplementary to each other. Many results of applied research have stimulated fundamental research and vice versa. The question is whether applied research should be given higher priority than fundamental research."

In economically developed countries the people are convinced that fundamental research is a must for the welfare of the people. However, this thesis is difficult to prove. In 1937 the Director of Economic Affairs (of the Dutch East Indies) asked the advice of two professors for the improvement of the results of the experiment station in Indonesia; they advised him that the fundamental research at the Botanic Gardens should be strengthened. They regarded fundamental research as essential for applied research and were aware how essential it is that there be in our country a group of research workers who continuously have to adapt their techniques and researches to the advances of science and who have a broad knowledge of the current scientific literature. These persons, as a group, form a standard for the quality of all research in the country. Their work is based mostly on accumulated experience and tradition. If their work were discontinued, it would take many years of research to regain the high standards formerly achieved.

Therefore I advise that the NBI should not carry out applied research, even temporarily, but should maintain a high quality of fundamental research. However, it would be wise to choose, as much as possible, problems of research which could supply background information for applied research, with the understanding that the researchers should be given the freedom to make their own choice of the problems.

It would be appropriate to mention here that when the Director of Economic Affairs asked for this advice, it was at a time when the Dutch East Indies was in economic difficulties due to the world depression. The advice of Van Raalte is more or less in accordance with the Doty (1964a) and Soemarwoto reports (1963). The decision has therefore been made that the field of operation of the NBI will be in so-called oriented fundamental research. Except for specific reasons, applied research will not be tackled at this institute.

PRESENT SITUATION

Scientific manpower is the most crucial factor for a research institute. For the NBI this has been the weakest point. Although biological research in Indonesia can be traced back for a few centuries, i.e., when Rumphius started his studies in the Moluccas in the seventeenth century, and although as of this date the Botanic Gardens are 150 years old, Indonesia started its independent life without a single Indonesian biologist. It is to be regretted that Indonesians did not have a share in the fame of the Botanic Gardens in prewar years, except as low-level technicians. Understandably, the emphasis of Professor Kusnoto, the first Indonesian director of the Botanic Gardens, was to recruit Indonesian biologists. This was by no means an easy task. Only a handful of students were enrolled at the Department of Biology of the University of Indonesia in Bandung. To enhance the recruitment program, a three-year college of biology was established in Tjiawi in 1955. Most of the present staff members of the NBI are graduates of this college.

Needless to say, with the shortage of personnel the scientific work was seriously jeopardized. Furthermore, the Japanese occupation left its mark. The war for independence was also still raging until 1949. When independence was finally gained, several Dutch scientists remained to work at the institute. Unfortunately, the dispute about West Irian was still unsettled, and in the mid-1950s the Dutch scientists departed. The Indonesians were not yet prepared to take over the scientific work, and research came to a grinding halt. What could be done consisted of curatorial work to preserve the existing invaluable collections of the Botanic Gardens, the Herbarium, and the Zoological Museum. It should be said that in spite of the great odds the collections were well taken care of and to this day are generally still in excellent condition. Indeed, the curators deserve to be praised for this job.

With the departure of the Dutch scientists and professors, the opportunity for higher education in biology in Indonesia was completely nullified. The only way was to send the students abroad. Most of them have now returned with higher degrees. The present scientific personnel of the NBI is shown in Table 4:1.

It is interesting to note that the students were not sent to a single country, but studied in many different ones—the U.S.A., England, Canada, Germany, Russia, Japan, and Australia. Thus their academic background is heterogeneous and they have different ideas and concepts about science and the development of science. Certainly this will have a positive effect on the progress of the NBI.

From this table one would expect the NBI to be able already to shift into high gear. Unfortunately this is not the case. There are still factors which prevent the NBI from coming into full capacity. These are at least as follows:

1. As mentioned by Van Raalte in his report (1965), the work of fundamental research is based on accumulated experience and tradition. If this fundamental research is interrupted, it takes many years to redevelop research of high quality. This fact has been felt strongly at the NBI.

TABLE 4:1   Scientific Personnel of the National Biological Institute

Field of Specialization	Number			
	Ph.D.	M.S.	B.S.	Other
Plant Taxonomy	3	–	2	1
Mycology	1	–	–	–
Plant Physiology	1	3	–	–
Plant Anatomy	2	1	–	–
Phytochemistry	–	1	2	–
Animal Taxonomy	1*	3	2	–
Insect Physiology	1	1	–	–
Microbiology	1	3	1	–
Biometry	–	2	–	–
Marine Sciences	1	3	11	1
Horticulture	–	–	4	1
TOTAL	11	17	22	3

* "Permanent visitor" from the Department of Biology, University of Indonesia.

The academic atmosphere and tradition are lost and have to be cultured anew. While abroad, the young staff members did enjoy good training, but they still lack the experience for independent research. Normally young Ph.D.'s would work for a few more years with senior scientists. Therefore, it will take some years before the desired conditions for high-quality research have been reestablished.

2. The economic situation of the country has been deteriorating from year to year and inflation has rocketed sky-high. Government officials are badly underpaid, with salaries too low to cover even the basic needs of food. Consequently, our scientists are forced to seek additional sources of income, a circumstance which naturally depresses their scientific productivity. Moreover, laboratory supplies are very hard to obtain. It may take months or even more than a year to get a certan chemical, herbarium paper, burette, and the like. Water, gas, and electricity are insufficient, and the supply is notoriously unreliable. All in all, it is almost impossible to do proper research.

3. Before the abortive coup of the Communists, the country was virtually in a continuous turmoil. The country lived on great slogans. Every work, we were told, should be devoted to the revolution, and science was no exception. Anybody practicing science for the furtherance of knowledge was labeled a textbook-thinker or even as counterrevolutionary. The scientists were faced with the hard choice of riding with

the tide or keeping quiet. Riding with the tide gave a means for securing funds to do so-called research. Keeping quiet left the scientists to work with their bare hands. Superficially, the government seemed to pay great interest to research, but in actuality the spirit and tradition of true scientific research were blacked out.

Freedom and democracy have now been restored in the country, though it will take time to bring the decisions which were made by our Congress into our daily life. But at least the dawn of hope has emerged from the dark night.

PLAN FOR THE FUTURE

Before we embark on the discussion of plans for the future, let us summarize the preceding discussion. With the foundation of the National Biological Institute, the fragmentation process of the departments should be reversed. For this purpose, a master plan of the NBI is being worked out and a broad guideline for an integrated operation is being formalized. The scientific collections of the NBI are still in good condition and are being well taken care of. A young generation of well-trained scientific staff is present and eager to move forward. These are all indications of a great potential residing at the NBI. With this in mind, efforts are to be directed toward eliminating the factors which inhibit the potentialities of the NBI to come into operation.

1. The creation of an academic atmosphere and tradition is of utmost importance. With the present staff, who for the greater part have had training at good institutions abroad, this can safely be expected. However, with the shortage of funds, the process will certainly proceed at a slow pace. In this age of rapid progress of science, this would mean a further lag behind the advanced countries.

At the turn of the nineteenth century, Treub wisely founded the Visitor's Laboratory. It proved to be a great success, and up to the time of World War II many great scientists worked for a shorter or longer period at the Botanic Gardens. The NBI is still frequently visited by scientists from many countries, but many of them stay for a few days only. Efforts are being made to attract scientists to work again at the NBI as visitors. The present change of the political situation is favorable to this purpose, and it is hoped that more success can be achieved. These visiting scientists would undoubtedly have a stimulating effect on our young staff members and would leave behind some of their experience, knowledge, and, above all, their scientific spirit.

2. Kistiakowsky mentions in his report that a research institute which does not have a close tie with a university will in the long run become sterile (Kistiakowsky 1962). Our staff members are therefore

encouraged to teach at the university. Opportunities are also given students to work on their theses in one of the departments of the NBI under the supervision of NBI staff members.

Recently the NBI submitted a proposal to MIPI for the establishment of a "Regional Center for Research, Training and Graduate Study in Biology" and offered its facilities for this center. Briefly, the program would consist of seminars for senior scientists, specialized courses of four to six weeks for junior research workers, and long-term courses leading toward higher degrees. This latter program would be conducted cooperatively with the universities in Bogor and Bandung. Such a center would not only benefit the NBI and the national needs of the country but also could become a great asset for the region of Southeast Asia. This proposal is in line with one of the recommendations of the Doty report. In this respect it is appropriate to mention that, before Indonesia withdrew from the United Nations, Bogor was mentioned as a potential site for a key zoological collection for Southeast Asia, which was one of the projects of the International Advisory Committee of the Humid Tropics Research of UNESCO. At that time discussions were also under way with UNESCO to make the scientific journal *Treubia* a regional one for Southeast Asia.

3. Indonesia has agreed to participate in the International Biological Program (IBP). A National Committee was formed, with the NBI serving as the nucleus. From the very beginning it was realized that due to the limiting factors previously mentioned, Indonesia will never be able to participate fully in the program. However, Indonesia is eager to learn from others and to share in their accumulated knowledge and experience. Furthermore, ties formerly broken by political problems are being reestablished. From being an isolated institution in the past few years, the NBI has again entered the international network of scientific cooperation. These efforts have already paid off. The Udjung Kulon Nature Reserve is now recognized as a field station of the IBP, and the International Union for the Conservation of Nature and the World Wildlife Fund have donated a power boat to patrol the reserve. From November 1966 to March 1967 a Belgian scientist worked at this reserve. His work will be continued by a Swiss scientist. It should be mentioned here that the Forestry Service plays an important role in this project.

The US-IBP National Committee has also indicated interest in helping to develop this site and others.

4. The Doty report stressed the importance of public service. This was also recognized by the Soemarwoto committee. Biology is a field of science which is little understood by the public and as such is not highly appreciated. Among high school students biology has the reputation of being dull and is regarded to be reserved for those with low I.Q.'s. This skepticism of the public has a depressing effect on the young biologists

who are at the beginning of their careers. Furthermore, the government tends to place biological research on a low level of priority. It could be assumed that if the Botanical Gardens and their departments did not exist in 1962, the chances are great that the foundation of the National Biological Institute would not have been included in the First Overall National Development Plan.

As a public service, therefore, the NBI has a duty to explain to the public the share biological research contributes to the economic development of the country and its potential role in and relationships to agriculture, fisheries, medicine, etc. This is being carried out by the publication of articles in daily newspapers and magazines, and by radio lectures. For a long time there has been a need of guides for visitors to the Botanic Gardens and the Zoological Museum, but due to several difficulties this has not yet been realized.

It is also important that the methods of teaching biology in high schools should be improved. The present method is very bookish and dull. This problem is of general nature in Southeast Asia, as was apparent during the discussions at the conference on the Conservation of Nature and Natural Resources in Tropical Southeast Asia, which was held in Bangkok in late 1965. In August 1965 the NBI held a two-week workshop for biology teachers of West Java. The workshop aroused the enthusiasm of the teachers and opened their eyes to a great challenge for improving high school instruction in biology.

Strictly speaking, research in methods of teaching biology is not a duty of the NBI. The purpose of the workshop was not to take over duties of the Teacher's College, but rather to stimulate thinking for improving teaching methods along modern lines. If the teaching methods could be substantially improved, biology would become interesting to the students and the recruitment program of the NBI would benefit from it. There would also be a general stimulating effect on the progress of biology in the country.

5. The most difficult problem in developing the NBI lies in its financing. This problem is inherently related to the economic situation of the country. There is little hope that within the near future the salaries of the scientific staff will be improved substantially. And yet, without this improvement all the efforts mentioned above would fail. Unless it can provide enough salary to cover the basic needs of a human being, the great potentialities of the NBI will remain idle, with a great waste of the money already invested for the education of the scientific staff and for the maintenance of the collections. Such a situation would be like that of a factory in which money has been invested for buildings and machinery, but without further investment to buy the fuel to run the plant. Faced with such a prospect, we should therefore look for possibilities to attract funds from outside the country. Several possibilities could be explored.

a. An arrangement could be made with a foreign university by which the NBI would offer its facilities to be used for the curricular activities of the university concerned. The students working at the NBI would be supervised by the senior scientists of the NBI. If necessary, professors of the university could take residence at the host institution. The university would be requested to make contributions for the general expenditures of the NBI and for honorarium for the staff members in return for the hospitality and services rendered to the students.

For a university that is keenly interested in tropical biology, this scheme would work better than the establishment of a department of tropical biology at the university itself, because at the NBI the students would be fully exposed to the tropical habitat. Presumably this scheme would also be cheaper than the building of a vast system of greenhouses to accommodate the tropical plants, which would be poor imitations of the lush tropical environment. A greenhouse system, no matter how extensive, would never surpass the opportunities for research and teaching to be found at such stations as Tjibodas and Udjung Kulon.

b. Cooperative research and joint expeditions could also be organized within this scheme. This mutual program would not necessarily be limited to a bi-institutional agreement, but could be expanded to a multiinstitutional or even multinational one. Thus, in effect, a regional or international center as outlined above would be of interest to UNESCO, which could act as one of the parties.

c. Technical aid such as that given by the U.S.A., the Netherlands, and other countries and by UN agencies should also be sought. However, the NBI prefers to have a two-way relationship, rather than to become a sole recipient.

d. If the Indonesian government allows, a long-term loan with low interest would be beneficial, too. This loan should be invested both in improving the working facilities and in supplementing the salaries of the scientific staff to enable the release of the potentials of the NBI for scientific production.

THE PLACE OF THE NBI IN THE WORLD SCIENTIFIC COMMUNITY

It is normal that in developing the NBI the needs of Indonesia are always kept in mind. While serving these national needs, the NBI may also be of value to the world scientific community.

The history of the Visitor's Laboratory demonstrated that scientists of many countries came to Bogor to work on certain aspects of biology. The work of these visitors was of great value to science. However, in recent years, under impact of modern chemistry and physics, the emphasis of biological research has shifted from the field into the laboratories.

With the availability of modern chemical techniques and sophisticated instruments, cellular, subcellular, and molecular studies flourish. Modern techniques have also enabled scientists to construct conditioned growth chambers, where almost any combination of climatic types can be simulated. When the great biologists came to Bogor they studied flowering, photosynthesis, etc., as it happened in nature. Now the modern biologists study the same phenomena in growth chambers, ranging from the level of whole organisms to the molecular level. From these latter studies emerge conceptions of long and short-day plants, of transformations of light energy into ATP, of regulations of enzyme synthesis by genes, etc. The modern scientists feel at home between the four walls of their laboratories and are confident that in time they will elucidate the secrets of the life processes with their electronic gadgets. Why should they wander to far countries like Bogor, as was done by their predecessors? For pleasure, yes, but not to do research!

Of course, the taxonomists still need the field work. But they could send well-trained collectors to the far corners of the world, and the scientists themselves could study the material at ease at their laboratories. This does not mean that there are no taxonomists who go into the jungles. Fortunately many still do. But with the increasing complexity of organizing and administering science, many of them cannot spend much time outside their home office. The tendency is that more and more assistants and collectors are the ones who go out on expeditions, while the scientists remain at home. There are examples of famed taxonomists who are at a loss to name living plants.

In this modern time of research, then, what could Bogor contribute to the advancement of biology? In my opinion the role of Bogor in biological research has not come to an end. In the temperate regions, with the relatively poor flora and fauna, field studies are perhaps less challenging than work in the laboratories. It is true that the biochemical and biophysical researches now going on in the advanced laboratories are of great value for the furtherance of our understanding of the life processes. But the danger exists that the scientists who are probing deeply into the secrets of life in these laboratories lose the great picture of what they are looking for. They are buried in the detailed but only small aspects of the intricate and complex life processes. Their mental picture of life is limited to the etiolated seedlings of oats, of *Drosophila* flies, etc. In their vacations they camp in the redwood forests and observe the wild animals. But their minds wander back to the growth chambers and the electronic equipment in their labs. Do they realize that the very processes they are studying in their labs are going on vigorously in the giant trees, the bear, the deer, etc.? In my opinion, if they could free themselves for even a brief period to spend some time in the natural surroundings of the great tropical forests together with field biologists, they would be intrigued to extrapolate their accumulated knowledge for the understanding of life as it exists in nature, which is, after all, the goal of the science of biology. This would refresh their minds, and, above all, their researches with the etiolated oat coleoptile, rat liver mitochondria, etc., would always be projected on the screen of the natural life.

For the education of biology students, I suggest that it is a must for them to work for a certain period in a field station as part of their curricular requirements, whether they would choose taxonomy or molecular biology as their future field of specialization.

The explorations of the rich tropical nature are not only useful for the progress of such fields as taxonomy and ecology but also have important bearing on the progress of other branches of "laboratory" biology. Van Raalte illustrated this nicely in his inaugural speech at his appointment as professor of plant physiology at the University of Groningen (Raalte 1959). He said that a botanical garden such as that existing in Bogor, with the associated nature reserves, would broaden the minds of the plant physiologists and at the same time would present endless problems for the inquiring mind and open roads for new techniques in modern research with more appropriate plant material.

In the tropics there are still many natural phenomena which are not yet understood scientifically. The whole of the Indonesian archipelago lies approximately 6 degrees north and 10 degrees south latitude and belongs to the tropical zone. To visitors from the temperate regions the tropical climate is monotonous, and seems to be uniform from day to day the year-round. To them this is a country of eternal summer. But for us there is no summer or winter. We know only the dry and the wet seasons. Nor are there pronounced differences in day-length. For Bogor the difference is only about forty minutes between the longest and shortest days. As an example the climate of Bogor is presented in Table 4:2. It is of course not representative of the whole country, since the climate varies from place to place and with the altitude. However, the table does give an idea of the general nature of the humid tropical climate, except that Bogor does not have a pronounced dry season.

The table shows that there are no large variations in temperature throughout the year. Differences in the mean monthly temperatures are even smaller than diurnal variations of the mean daily temperatures.

These data suggest many questions. I remember that while waiting for the plane at the airport in Bangkok, the late Dr. Graham said that the problem with educating biology students from the tropics in advanced institutions which are located in the temperate regions, is that upon their return home they would have to unlearn many concepts which presumably do not hold for the tropics. Several will be mentioned here as examples.

Does the concept of classifying plants respectively into long-day,

TABLE 4:2   The climatic nature of Bogor. Location 6°36′ south latitude; 106°48′ east longitude; 240 m. above sea level (from Braak 1921–1929)

	J	F	M	A	M	J	J	A	S	O	N	D	Annual Mean
Mean temperature in °C	24.1	24.2	24.5	25.0	25.1	25.0	25.0	25.1	25.3	25.3	24.7	24.4	24.8
Mean daily maximum temperature in °C	28.0	28.2	28.6	29.8	30.1	29.8	30.0	30.6	31.0	30.7	29.9	28.8	29.6
Mean daily minimum temperature in °C	21.5	21.6	21.6	21.9	21.9	21.4	21.0	21.1	21.5	21.8	21.5	21.6	21.5
Mean daily differences between maximum and minimum temperature in °C	6.5	6.6	7.0	7.9	8.2	8.4	9.0	9.5	9.5	8.9	8.4	7.2	8.1
Mean daily maximum relative humidity in percentage	88	89	87	85	83	82	79	77	78	79	83	83	83
Mean rainfall in mm.	434	394	393	400	360	269	248	246	327	428	406	346	4251+)
Mean number of rainy days	24	23	23	20	17	13	12	12	14	19	21	22	219+)
Mean sunshine in percentage of the day-length	43	42	53	64	67	71	78	78	78	72	62	48	63

+)Yearly total

short-day, and neutral-day hold for Indonesia, which lies at the equatorial belt? Under experimental conditions, several plants do react to differences in day-length. For example, Bolhuis has suggested that the flowering of *Hibiscus* sabdariffa is determined by day-length (Bolhuis 1940). But at least from the pedagogical point of view, it does not make sense to teach our students of long-day plants which flower under conditions of day-length of more than, for example, sixteen hours and of short-day plants which flower at day-length shorter than say eight hours, except for comparative purposes. It is difficult for our students to digest this concept. The result is that they learn it just to pass the examination.

And yet in Indonesia many plants flower more or less at fixed seasons. This is shown in Figure 4:1, which is compiled from the data of

FIGURE 4:1

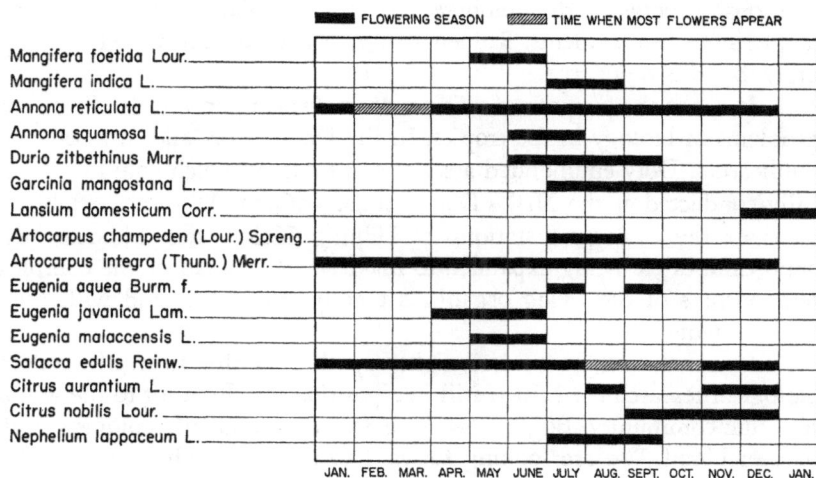

| | FLOWERING SEASON | TIME WHEN MOST FLOWERS APPEAR |

Mangifera foetida Lour.
Mangifera indica L.
Annona reticulata L.
Annona squamosa L.
Durio zitbethinus Murr.
Garcinia mangostana L.
Lansium domesticum Corr.
Artocarpus champeden (Lour.) Spreng.
Artocarpus integra (Thunb.) Merr.
Eugenia aquea Burm. f.
Eugenia javanica Lam.
Eugenia malaccensis L.
Salacca edulis Reinw.
Citrus aurantium L.
Citrus nobilis Lour.
Nephelium lappaceum L.

JAN. FEB. MAR. APR. MAY JUNE JULY AUG. SEPT. OCT. NOV. DEC. JAN.

Ochse (1931). The factor(s) affecting this fruiting season is still practically unknown. In many tropical plant species, periodicity in growth and leaf-fall occur also (Arens 1922; Coster 1923, 1925; Kerling 1941; Smith 1922). In several instances the periodicity could be attributed to temperature (Coster 1925; Vries 1950–1954), drought (Coster 1925), or rainfall (Kerling 1941). In others no correlation with external factors could be identified (Ochse 1931). In the case of flowering, both temperature and rainfall did not initiate the differentiation of the flower primordia, but merely broke the dormancy of the fully developed flower buds (Coster 1925; Kerling 1941). The questions which remain to be solved are to identify the factors that initiate the differentiation of the vegetative meristematic tissue into flower primordia and the mechanism of the breaking of dormancy of the flower buds. In temperate regions research of this type has developed to the level of biochemistry and enzymology.

In relation to the seasonal cycle, questions of the migration of birds were asked at an informal lecture given by Dr. McClure of the Migratory Animals and Pathological Survey. Their migration from the temperate or arctic regions to the tropics can be attributed to the lowering temperature or shortening of days with the approaching winter. But once they are in the tropics, how do they know the time to fly back to their place of "origin"? I have put the word origin within quotation marks to indicate that the tropical man has the same right to claim that the place of origin of the birds is the tropics.

Epiphytism is a phenomena which is very common in the humid tropics. In the Botanic Gardens in Bogor and Tjibodas virtually all trees bear epiphytes. For a long time epiphytism has been thought of as a loose relationship between the epiphyte and the host plant and is still being taught as such to students. Ruinen (1950–1954) demonstrated convincingly that this is not true.

It is not the purpose of this paper to dwell upon the details of the problems of biology in the tropics. In the Doty report and in a separate publication, Doty enumerated a series of problems which could be fruitfully conducted at the NBI (Doty 1964a, 1964b). With the establishment of the biological stations at Udjung Kulon and Tjibodas, the opportunities are being expanded to make *in situ* studies of the complex relationships of the living organisms among themselves and with their environments.

In conclusion, then, we might say that in this time of modern biological research the NBI is still in a position to offer a lot to the world scientific community. Bogor is waiting for the arrival of biologists with pioneer blood. We are looking forward to that time when imaginative research will again be carried out actively at the NBI and daring new concepts will emerge from this institution.

REFERENCES

Arens, P. 1922. Periodishe Blutenbildung bei einigen Orchidee n. *Ann. Jardin Bot. Buitenzorg* 32: 103–24.

Bolhuis, G. G. 1940. Bloeiwaarnemingen bij *Hibiscus* sabdariffa L. en *Hibiscus cannabinus* L. *Med. Alg. Proefst. Landb.* No. 44, 9 pp.

Braak, C. Het Klimaat van Nederlandsch-Indië. 1921–1929. *Verh. Kon. Magn. Met. Obs. Batavia* 8.

Coster, Ch. 1923. Lauberneuerung und andere periodishe Lebensprozesse in dem trockenen Monsun-Bebiet Ost-Java's. *Ann. Jardin Bot. Buitenzorg* 33: 117–89.

——. 1925. Periodische Blüteerscheinungen in den tropen. *Ann. Jardin Bot. Buitenzorg* 35 (1): 125–62.

Doty, M. S. 1964a. *The National Biological Institute of Indonesia, an opportunity for American research in the botany of the old world tropics and a series of recommendations for its future development*. Terminal report to the National Science Foundation, 55 pp.

——. 1964b. The American botanist and the Biological Institute of Indonesia. *Bioscience* 14 (12): 36–41.

Kerling, L. C. P. 1941. The gregarious flowering of *Zephyranthes rosea* Lindl. *Ann. Bot. Gardens, Buitenzorg* 51 (1): 1–42.

Kistiakowsky, G. B. 1962. Observations on technical higher education and scientific research in Indonesia, 3 pp.

Ochse, J. J. 1931. *Fruits and fruit culture in the Dutch East Indies*. Batavia: Kolfe Co., 180 pp.

Raalte, M. H. van. 1959. *Proefplanten, methodiek en problemen in de plantenfysiologie*. Groningen: J. B. Wolters, 20 pp.

——. 1965. Advies uitgebracht aan de Directeur van Lembag Biologi Nasional. Unpublished, 7 pp.

Ruinen, J. 1950–1954. Epiphytosis. A second view on epiphytism. *Ann. Bog.* 1 (2): 101–57.

Smith, J. J. 1922. Periodischer Laubfall bei *Breynia cernua* Muell. *Arg. Ann. Jardin Bot. Buitenzorg* 32: 97–102.

Soemarwoto, O. 1963. Report of the Advisory Committee on the Future Development of the National Biological Institute to the President of the Council for Sciences of Indonesia. Unpublished.

de Vries, Jeane T. 1950–1954. On the flowering of *Phalaenopsis schillariana* Rchb. f. *Ann. Bog.* 1 (2): 61–76.

CHAPTER 5

Maxwell S. Doty and Aprilany Soegiarto   **The Development of Marine Resources in Indonesia**

The major problems of rapidly developing nations include communication, food, foreign exchange, and, not least, fulfilling their roles as members of the international community of nations.[1] The problem before us at the moment is how such needs are being met by Indonesia through development of its marine resources. It is pleasing to report that steps have been taken and that more are planned toward utilizing the opportunities provided by Indonesia's geography (Figure 5:1) via the pathway of scientific development. This paper will first review some of Indonesia's problems in apposition to the physical nature of the country; then present a historical résumé of major scientific developments; and last, will relate some details of recent and planned activities.

Communication involves not only messages but the transport of people and material between different places within a nation and back and forth between it and other nations. For Indonesia, this is no small problem, for the country includes more than 3,000 islands, surrounded by marine areas totaling some 3 million square kilometers.

Food must be adequate both in quantity and quality, and for Indonesia this too is a problem, for there are over 116 million people to be fed, plus an increase of about 3 million per year. Much of the 2 million square kilometers of land is unproductive, and area for area the surrounding sea is about as productive as the land.

Any rapidly developing nation nowadays imports a disproportionately large amount of material and technology, and the availability of foreign exchange and credit determines the rate such a nation can change by means of such imports. Indonesia has unusually ready access to the ocean and its vast resources as a useful asset.

Each nation has obligations to play a role in activities of the community of nations, much as any people have obligations to the society in which they live. Indonesia's objective and nonpolitical contribution to the world's fund of scientific information, theory, and methodology is one of the ways in which this duty can be fulfilled.

Indonesia and the Philippines are unique among nations in their insular dispersion. Japan and the United Kingdom have had the similar fate of being insular but have developed mightily. However, their problems were far less severe, with respect both to time and the number of their islands. Their solutions to these same problems have involved turning to the sea for much of their strength in communication, food provision, foreign exchange, and the role they play among nations. The maritime and air transport systems of Japan and England, their fishing fleets, their export of marine products, machinery, and technology, and their roles among nations in marine legal and scientific affairs are almost national peculiarities.

Indonesia's very marine nature sets it aside from most other similarly developing nations. The Indonesian part of the ocean is large; it is in major international sealanes and in the heart of the Old World Tropics. Thus it would be natural for Indonesia's role in marine matters to become large. Actually, the archipelago covers much of the Old World Tropics between 97° and 141° east longitude and 4° north to 11° south latitude. This is a most complex system of waterways, of shallows and deeps. Basically it consists (Figure 5:1) of the broad shallow Sunda and the Sahul shelves and the intervening and bordering deep seas.

To realize return from its maritime opportunities, Indonesia is devoting considerable attention to scientific survey of its marine self. The major restrictions to more rapid investment, advancement, and return, aside from almost excruciating growing pains, are in a shortage of properly trained, properly oriented, and properly rewarded personnel. Five moderate to splendid research ships carry the Indonesian flag and have been well equipped.

THE MARINE ENVIRONMENT OF INDONESIA

Indonesia has long been considered a paradise to both oceanographers and marine biologists. The roots of marine research in Indonesia extend from the times when Amboina was a headquarters for the Dutch East Indies Company. However, modern marine research stems from the Siboga Expedition of 1899–1900 (Tydeman 1903) which focused its attention on the marine flora and fauna and its biogeography, besides the making of hydro- and bathymetric observations. The "Visscherij Station" at Pasar Ikan, in the oldest part of Djakarta, was established in 1904 and is still in operation there as a semiautonomous department of the National Biological Institute, the Institute of Marine Research. Physical oceanography was brought to the fore by two expeditions in 1929–1930, that of the *Snellius* (Van Riehl 1932) and the *Dana,* though the latter essentially passed through, as did the more recent world-renowned *Albatross* and the *Galathea* expeditions in 1948 and 1951, respectively.

From these and other sources (Wyrtki 1961) it has been learned that largely the marine waters of Indonesia are part of the Pacific Ocean water mass. Considerable amounts of surface water from the Pacific flow continuously through the several passages and channels into Indonesia. Part of this water mass eventually returns to the Pacific. A certain amount flows on to the Indian Ocean, in some cases somewhat altered. Thus,

Rochford (1961) was able to detect Banda Sea intermediate waters far out in the Indian Ocean.

Monsoonal winds affect the marine waters strongly, since Indonesia is located near the equator between the Asian and the Australian continents. Indonesia is thus ideal for studying the effect of the monsoons on both water circulation and the seasonal distribution of its physical, chemical, and biological properties.

Generally the northwest monsoon lasts from about December to February and the east monsoon from June to August. The rest of the year represents the transition periods from the west to the east monsoons (March–May) and back from the east to the west monsoons (September–November). While the effect of the monsoons on the surface circulation has not been studied in detail all over Indonesia, the effects in the Java Sea can be summarized as follows: During the northwest monsoon the wind blows eastward and causes heavy rainfall throughout most of the Indonesian archipelago. This, with the heavy runoff of many rivers from Sumatra, Java, and Borneo, results in a general lowering of the salinity near shore. Sometimes the isohaline (thirty parts per thousand) is pushed far toward the open sea. At the same time the surface current from the South China Sea brings this low-salinity water into the West Java Sea pushing the waters of higher salinity eastward. With the onset of the southeast monsoon, these low-salinity waters are transported back westward and into the West Java and South China seas, i.e., the low-salinity water north of Java is replaced by waters of higher salinity from the Makassar Strait and Flores Sea. In September the water masses of high salinity reach their maximal westward penetration.

Basic to an understanding of geographic, seasonal, and other types of biological variation is an understanding of the related variations in primary productivity, the conversion rates of inorganic matter to organic form. In Indonesia this has only been done (Figure 5:2) in respect to phytoplankton primary productivity. Allen and Cupp (1935) described the commonly found diatoms in the Java Sea. A first step toward understanding their variation there was the work of Delsman (1939), who studied the seasonal distribution of phosphate and phytoplankton. He found that there was no marked difference in phosphate content between April and October. He observed a slight increase toward the coasts of Java and Kalimantan. He also noted similar phenomena in respect to plankton settling volume, although the average volume in October was somewhat higher ($0.9 \text{ ml}^3/\text{m}^3$) than that found in April ($0.7 \text{ ml}^3/\text{m}^3$).

Tjia and Nontji (in preparation) have tried to interpret the phytoplankton data of the First Baruna Operation in the Java Sea and relate them to hydrographic conditions. Praseno and Tjee (1966) made a quantitative study of the zooplankton of the waters around Java during

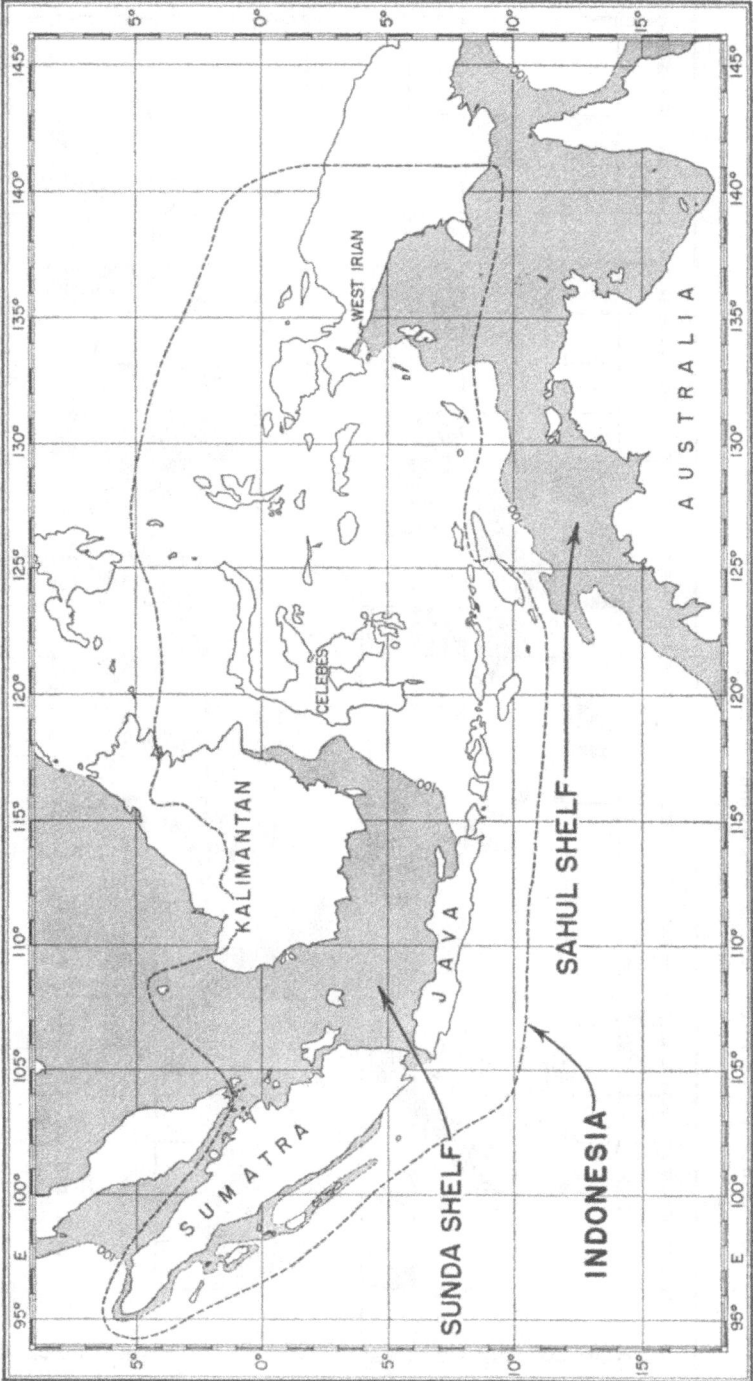

FIGURE 5:1 Map of Indonesia, showing major areas of nearby sea less than 100 fathoms deep.

FIGURE 5:2   Food productivity in the sea near and within Indonesia.

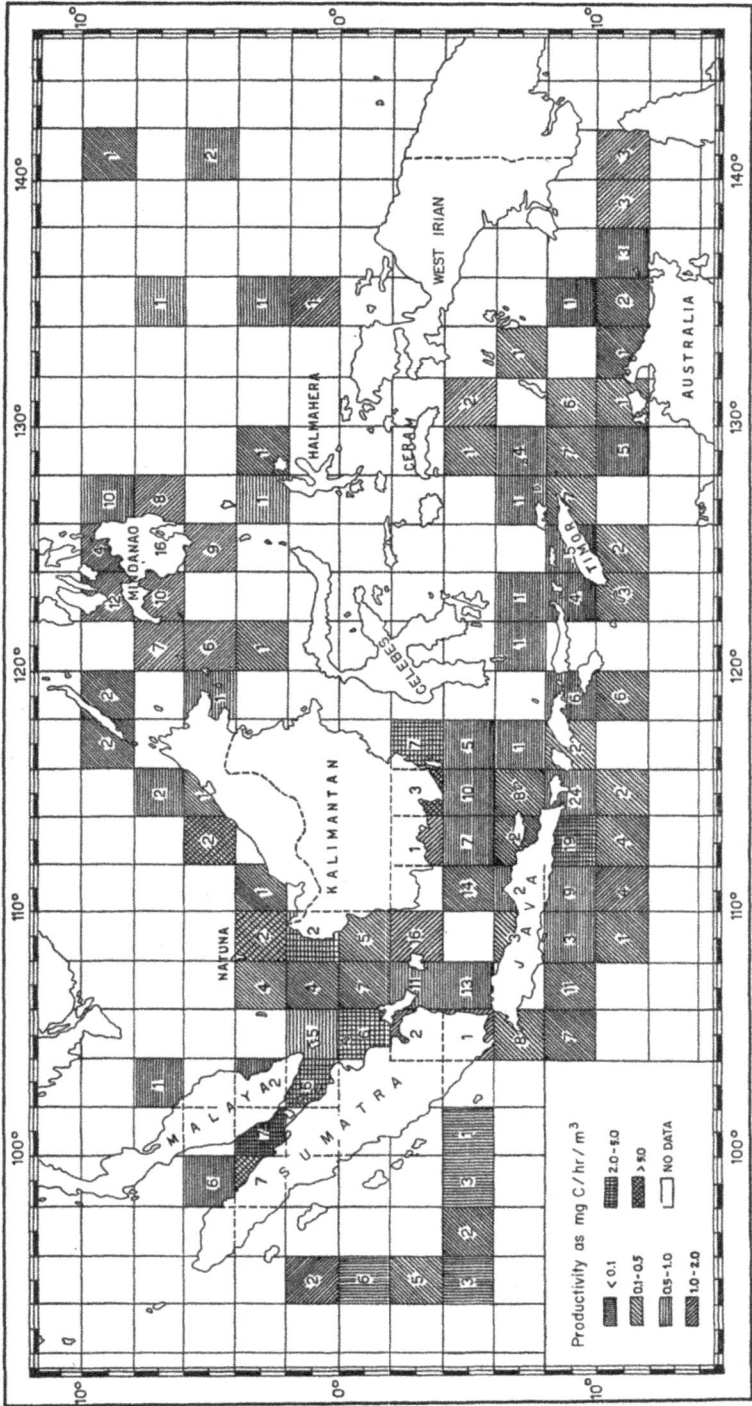

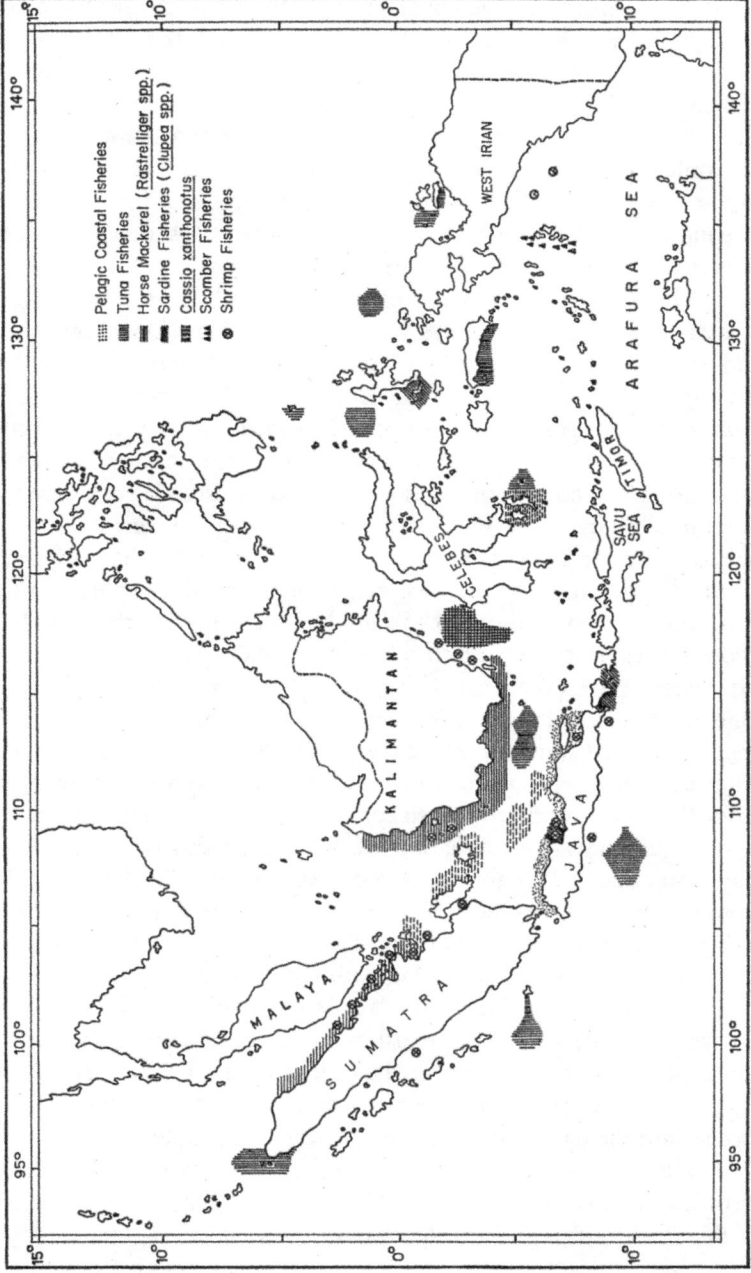

FIGURE 5:3   Locations of known fishing grounds in Indonesia.

the 1964 (September–October) cruise. The plankton displacement volumes of samples from the Java Sea are higher than those from the Indian Ocean. Foraminifera are found in abundance in Bali Strait, but are absent in samples collected from the Java Sea and the Indian Ocean.

Bogorov and Vinogradov (1961) report a very dense population of phytoplankton in the waters south of Java ($>$ 150ml/1000m^3). According to them, the main factor creating conditions favorable for this phenomenon is the upwelling of water near the shore and conditions related to divergences or eddies in the open ocean.

The primary productivity of these waters had been investigated by Steemann-Nielsen and Aabye-Jensen (1957), by Doty, Suriaatmadja, and Soegiarto (1963), and by Soegiarto and Nontji (1966a and b). Among these, only Soegiarto and Nontji attempted to study the effect of monsoonal changes on primary productivity. It was a pity that only two out of the four cruises, planned in accordance with the four seasons, were carried out. Anyhow, a comparison of the two seasons reveals that the surface productivity in the Java Sea recorded during the west monsoon (December–February) is somewhat lower than that of the east monsoon (June–August). During the west monsoon (December–February) there is also a rather strong indication of a gradual increase in surface productivity as one passes from the western part of the Java Sea (0.04 mg C/hr/m^3) to the eastern part (6.92 mg C/hr/m^3). There are also some unusually high rates recorded from three stations in the Bali Strait (28.54, 31.97, and 44.71 mg C/hr/m^3, respectively) during the east monsoon (June–August). This probably can be related to the upwelling phenomenon (Wyrtki 1962) along the south coast of Java in the same season.

Figure 2 is a compilation of surface productivity in Indonesian waters summarized by areas 2 $\times$ 2 degrees square. The data were derived from many cruises, including those of non-Indonesian vessels. It is interesting to compare the regions of high rates in this figure with those (Figure 5:3) of the known pelagic fishing grounds.

One of the most important factors influencing productivity in tropical waters is the rate of replenishment of the inorganic fertilizer salts. The replenishment process over the deeper waters is governed by upwelling or by divergent movements causing more fertile water below to ascend into the euphotic zone. This process occurs only locally.

The presence of such upwelling in Indonesian waters had been recorded notably in two regions. Wyrtki (1961) reported its occurrence in the Arafura Sea and in northwestern Australian waters. In 1962 he gave a detailed account of the upwelling in the water along the south coast of Java (Figure 5:3) up to the entrances of the Savu Sea. The upwelling there reaches its full height in about September (east monsoon), adding about 2.4 million m^3/sec to the flow of the South Equatorial current. The region of upwelling is characterized by high plankton biomasses (see also Bogorov and Vinogradov 1961), high rates of production (Soegiarto and Nontji 1966), low water transparency and a high concentration of inorganic phosphorus, especially at the bottom of the euphotic layer. This account is supported by the findings of Rochford (1962), who also described the upwelling in the Arafura Sea. The process probably takes place earlier here (August) than upwelling along the south coast of Java. However, both occur during the east monsoon period.

Indonesians are noted as courageous seafarers. For instance, during the Sriwidjaja (between seventh and ninth centuries A.D.) and Modjopahit (between sixteenth and eighteenth centuries) kingdoms, they made voyages with their small vessels to Indo-China and even to China and Madagascar. However, there is no record to indicate the existence of scientific exploration before the arrival of the Dutch (seventeenth century), when during the establishment of the Dutch colonies various remarks and notes were recorded by the officials, who for the most part merely marveled at the beauty and variety of the tropical marine life they saw.

As in most parts of the world, exploration in marine sciences began with biological investigations. For marine research in Indonesia, 1904 was an important year, for it was then that the director of the Bogor Botanical Gardens established the "Visscherij Station" in Pasar Ikan. Since that time research in marine biology has continued, although in most cases it was still classified as fisheries research. In 1919 this station was renamed as the Institute of Marine Research (in Dutch, *Laboratorium voor het Onderzoek der Zee;* in Indonesian, *Lembaga Penelitian Laut*). By then one public aquarium and several laboratories had been added to the original building.

THE ORGANIZATION OF MARINE RESEARCH IN INDONESIA

In 1962 almost all the scientific institutions belonging to the Botanical Gardens, including the Institute of Marine Research, were transferred from the Ministry of Agriculture to the Council for Sciences of Indonesia. Part of the reason was that these institutions were, and still are, doing basic research. The Council for Sciences realized the importance of marine research and the urgent need of combining and coordinating the efforts of the scientists and institutions to "exploit the wealth of the sea" for the Indonesian people, not an entirely academic objective. In addition to the buildings, laboratories, and staff, two ships were available, the *Samudera* of 150 tons and the *Aries* of 50 tons. These were gifts from the

U.S.A. and the U.S.S.R., respectively. Doty (1964) describes these and other related facilities briefly.

In the same year, a National Committee on Oceanic Research (NCOR) was established to coordinate research activities and to advise the Council for Sciences of Indonesia on the scientific aspects of these activities. The committee consists of several member institutions: the Institute of Marine Research, the Naval Hydrographic Directorate, the Institute of Marine Fisheries Research, the Directorate of Meterology and Geophysics, the Directorate of Geology and Mining, and the universities, which have marine science programs.

At present there is strong feeling toward reorganizing this committee and expanding its membership so as to include all the agencies, both government and private, connected with marine activities.

INDONESIAN MARINE RESEARCH ACTIVITIES,
1960–1966

Since the Indian Ocean is so little known in comparison to relatively detailed knowledge of the Atlantic and the Pacific, UNESCO in 1959 initiated the International Indian Ocean Expeditions (IIOE), an international study of this ocean. Many countries took part in the work, which officially lasted five years, starting in 1960. Indonesia, which has thousands of kilometers of coast bounded by the Indian Ocean, used this opportunity by sending out cruises (Figure 5:4) to gather information in order to facilitate expansion of marine fisheries and to gain a general picture of what effects this ocean may have on the Indonesian archipelago. Unfortunately, however, due to lack of available facilities, and especially to a lack of oceangoing ships with up-to-date equipment, only after 1963 was Indonesia able to take part actively in the IIOE. In that year Indonesia obtained the 748-ton oceangoing oceanographic research vessel, *Jalanidhi* (Figure 5:5). In the same year four cruises were conducted into the Indian Ocean, southwest of Sumatra, to study hydrography, meteorology, and bottom topography.

Between 1964 and 1965 four further cruises were planned to study seasonal changes in primary productivity and related oceanographic and ecological factors in cooperation with the University of Hawaii in the waters around Java. Unfortunately, however, due to the very limited budget only two of the four cruises were carried out. These two cruises were conducted during the west and the east monsoons, respectively.

Three papers were presented in the Eleventh Pacific Science Congress; one master's thesis and several more papers are still in preparation as a result of this seasonal study. The first of the papers presented

FIGURE 5:4 Indonesian work at sea in association with the International Indian Ocean Expeditions, 1960–66.

I. *Jalanidhi* Cruise I (IIOE): June 4–12, 1963
II. *Jalanidhi* Cruise II (IIOE): June 15–24, 1963
III. *Jalanidhi* Cruise III (IIOE): Aug. 10–27, 1963
IV. *Jalanidhi* Cruise IV (IIOE): Sept. 24–31, 1963
V. BARUNA I/Jln. V (IIOE): May 9–July 27, 1964
VI. *Jalanidhi* Cruise VI (IIOE): Sept. 20–Oct. 17, 1964

VII. *Jalanidhi* Cruise VII (IIOE): March 10–April 5, 1965
VIII. *Jalanidhi* Cruise VIII (IIOE): Feb. 10–March 10, 1966
IX. BARUNA II: Nov. 21, 1966–Feb. 18, 1967

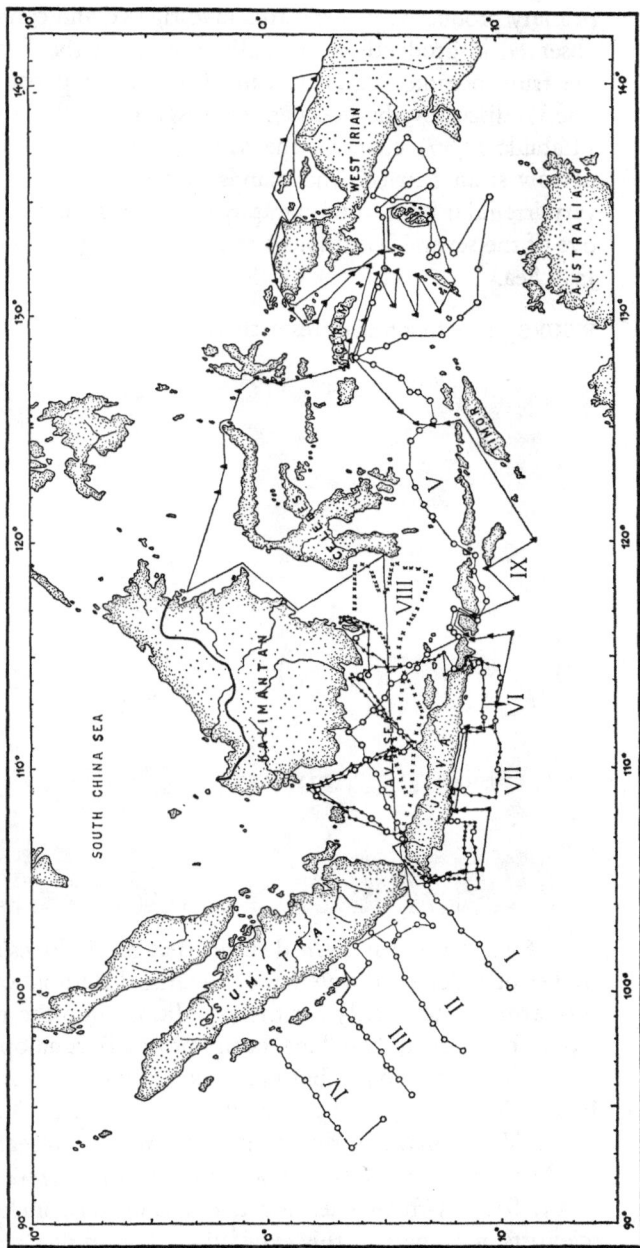

(Soegiarto and Nontji 1966) deals with the seasonal changes in the primary productivity of the area investigated and compares the differences observed in productivity in shallow water of the Java Sea with those of the truly oceanic Indian Ocean. The second paper (Praseno and Tjia 1966) discusses the zooplankton aspects of the study. A third paper (Ilahude 1966) concerns the hydrographical conditions in Bali Strait, a narrow strait between the islands of Bali and Java. This strait, with its very irregular bottom topography and very strong currents, is representative of the several hazardous straits connecting the Indian Ocean with the Java Sea.

FIGURE 5:5   Indonesian research vessel *Jalanidhi.*

Recently it has been decided that all Indonesian Marine Institute studies of Indonesian waters will be termed Baruna[2] operations. Formerly, this term was used only for the expeditions into the more eastern waters. Up to the present, there have been but two Baruna operations.

The three-month Baruna I expedition was carried out in eastern Indonesian waters, May 9 through July 29, 1964. Three ships were used: the R. V. *Jalanidhi* of the Institute of Marine Research, the *Djadajat* of the Ministry of Sea Communication, and the *Tamrau* of the Indonesian Navy. Seventy-three scientists and technicians, including five Japanese scientists, took part in this expedition. The studies were of many aspects of marine science, including oceanography, marine biology, geology, meteorology, and fisheries. The main objective was to make an inventory of the as-yet-untapped marine resources of eastern Indonesia.

Two research vessels were assigned to the Baruna II expeditions (Figure 5:4): the R. V. *Burudjulasad* (2,000 tons) of the Naval Hydrographic Directorate, newly arrived from Germany in June 1966, and the R. V. *Jalanidhi*. This second expedition was to last about three months (November 27, 1966–February 18, 1967). However, due to engine trouble the second vessel began its work in April 1967. Besides routine oceanographic and hydrographic surveys, the program of Baruna II included a survey of radioactive fallout in the Easter Islands, research on diseases common to pearl oyster divers at Dobo Island, and meteorological observations. The data are still in an early stage of processing.

The current Seribu[3] Islands project is a special research project carried out by the Institute of Marine Research to study the biology and ecology of this group of mostly very small islands. These islands are situated in front of Djakarta Bay, where they form a north–south "barrier." During the east monsoon, they tend to force the westward-moving water to turn into Djakarta Bay. This water usually is rich in schools of fish. The area is the main source of supply for fresh and dried fish for metropolitan Djakarta, a population of about 4.5 million people. These islands also represent a biotopic "prototype" of the Java Sea. Therefore, they are areas of great interest, both biologically and ecologically.

Special attention has been given to one of the Seribu Islands, Pari Island, because of the richness of its shores in seaweed, e.g., *Eucheuma* spp., and the pearl oyster, *Pinctada margaretifera,* as well as other useful species. At this stage an intensive study is being carried out in order to promote establishment of pearl oyster culture and experimentally cultivate *Eucheuma.*

Research on commercial seaweeds has been carried on since April 1966, when the Institute of Marine Research launched explorations for them. This project was implemented to determine the potential commercial seaweed productivity of several islands of the Lesser Sunda group, but chiefly Sumbawa. The data, eventually, will support the Indonesian government in its export-effort on soft products, including resources from the sea. The surveys include geographical and seasonal distribution, measuring the potential productivity for each season, ecological study, chemical analyses, and measuring the nutritional value of edible seaweeds.

Unfortunately, Indonesia's ability to supply seaweed is being neglected at present. The reason seems to be the unreliable content of the different shipments made. The colloid material most sought, kappa-carrageenin from *Eucheuma spinosum,* is very different from the colloid material in the irregularly intermixed seaweeds of other kinds that often dominate the different lots. The largest buyer refused (in 1967) to purchase Indonesian seaweed until some reliable quality standards are effected. Steps are being explored that may remedy this trouble.

Even now it should be possible to produce at least 50 tons of *Eucheuma spinosa* per month in good merchantable form. It is now about 80 percent of the seaweed exported. One problem is the provision of supervisory manpower for the twelve days per month when the tides favor a half-day of harvesting the beds, which are, themselves, remote from population centers. Supervision and training are essential to quality control. Transportation is a major problem, requiring capital investments. Thus far, the slow financial turnover and return of profits is hindering development, especially since further investment of capital would seem necessary before the industry will stabilize and grow to its potential of at least 100 to 200 tons per month.

It has been determined that in a free enterprise area such as the Philippines the seaweed industry, which is the object of the present effort, is exceptionally rewarding in that it is a new product for most areas, is of no value locally at present, and over 50 percent of the foreign exchange value goes to the individual fishermen who deliver the seaweed from the water. This would mean at current prices 10 to 20 thousand dollars a month, with an additional few thousand per month going to the middle-men and exporters. It should be remembered that this return goes into the hands of maritime communities which have little opportunity otherwise. The ultimate size of the industry is limited, it would seem, by the highest sustained yield; thus, further research in this direction is planned.

INDONESIAN MARINE RESEARCH ACTIVITIES, 1967

The use of only one research vessel was planned for the research activities of 1967, i.e., the R. V. *Burudjulasad*. The R. V. *Jalanidhi* was continuing the work for Baruna II.

The operation *Tjenderawasih*[4] is a name given for the exploration and other activities in West Irian. In 1967 several teams were establishing the borderline between Indonesian West Irian and the Australian half of the island. The R. V. *Burudjulasad* was assigned to function as a logistics and supply ship for all teams. At least three trips were planned to West Irian for this year. While going back and forth between Djakarta and West Irian, the vessel was scheduled to carry out oceanographic observations in some of the waters. Figure 5:6 is the cruise track for the three trips as presently planned.

Indonesia is participating in the Cooperative Study of the Kuroshio (CSK) current. Formerly this CSK program was confined to the Kuroshio current proper, but during an organizational meeting in Tokyo there was a strong suggestion that the activities should be expanded to the adjacent waters. This suggestion was accepted favorably by representatives of the Southeast Asian countries. An extension program of the CSK

FIGURE 5:6 Planned cruise tracks for research vessel *Burundjulasad* in 1967.

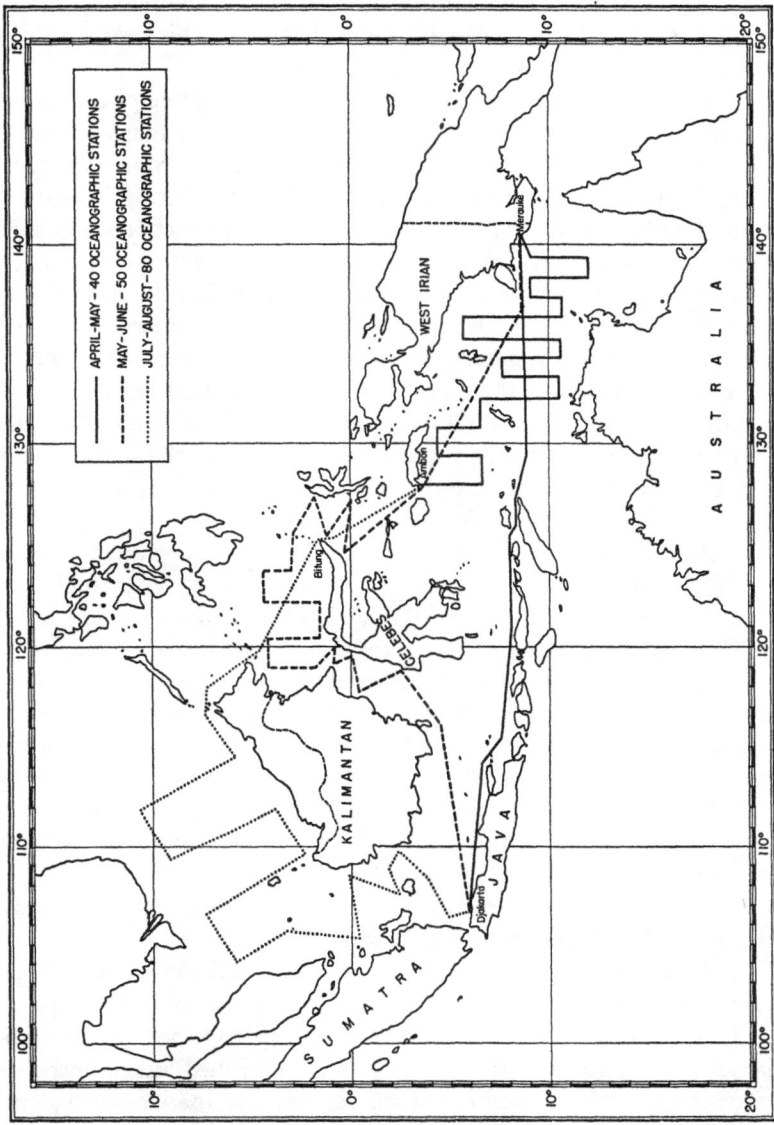

APRIL–MAY – 40 OCEANOGRAPHIC STATIONS
MAY–JUNE – 50 OCEANOGRAPHIC STATIONS
JULY–AUGUST–80 OCEANOGRAPHIC STATIONS

SUMATRA

KALIMANTAN

CELEBES

JAVA

WEST IRIAN

AUSTRALIA

Djakarta

Bitung

Ambon

Merauke

into the South China Sea officially was scheduled to start on July 1, 1967. In May 1967, UNESCO sponsored a meeting among representatives of the Southeast Asian countries to plan together, according to their abilities, the kinds of work to be carried out.

Since Indonesia already had a research program in the South China Sea (see the long-term program, below), it was only a matter of shifting the designated year. The third cruise for the operation *Tjenderawasih* (Figure 5:6), scheduled for July and August of this year, could serve Indonesia as a kind of trial cruise for the program.

A *long-term research program* for Indonesia is one of the important functions of the NCOR in coordinating activities in marine sciences. It will require the coordinated efforts of many governmental agencies, especially those which are members of the NCOR. During its early years, it will involve substantial investments for the construction and operation of ship and shore facilities for research and surveys, the development of new instruments to chart the seas, gathering data, and the training of new scientific manpower. For this purpose the NCOR submitted a "Ten Year Program on Marine Research" to the Indonesian government, and began the implementation of this in 1965. This program outlines not only the research activities, but includes also all aspects of activities in the marine environment, such as the construction of tide gauges and harbors, surveys, and the exploitation of natural resources, as well as enhancing the education and recruitment for the scientific staffs.

As for the research program itself, Indonesian waters are divided into five different zones (Figure 5:7). Each zone will be studied intensively for two years. It is hoped that after the initial ten-year period there will be a clearer picture of what is there and what is really going on.

The research activities in each zone are planned in such a way that all their aspects will be in accord with the development of marine science in Indonesia, such as the number of research vessels, manpower, budget, etc. It must be kept in mind that this zoning is not rigid, but is rather flexible. If it is necessary, the predetermined period can be shifted accordingly. For example, in order to participate in the extension program of the Cooperative Study of the Kuroshio current in the South China Sea, instead of carrying out the research program in 1968–1969, the activities in this area were expected to begin in 1967.

A foundation has been laid to standardize all techniques and procedures for field and laboratory operations related to hydrographic and oceanographic surveys. The data will be kept together in the National Oceanographic Data Center that has been established just recently. Reference stations will be established throughout the Indonesian waters and will be visited regularly, so that a continuous and consistent flow of data

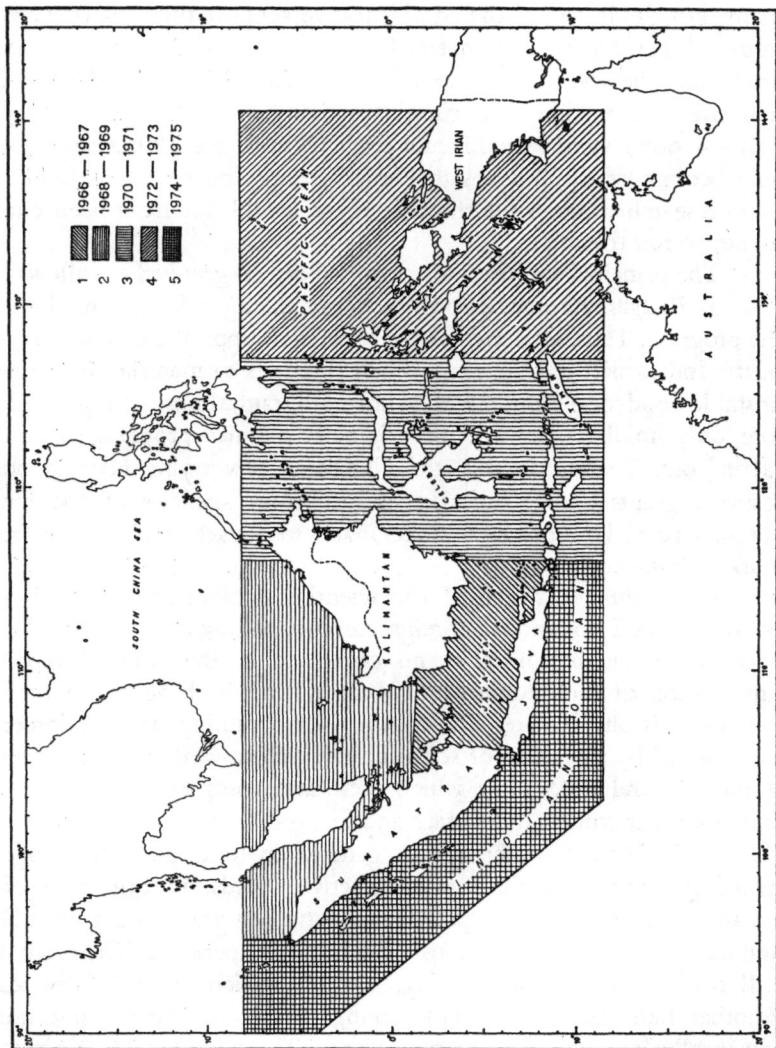

FIGURE 5:7 Areas designated for 10-year program of initial studies of the sea near and within Indonesia.

will be accumulated from these prefixed positions. Particularly, this will facilitate interpretation of the data on a seasonal basis.

CURRENT PROBLEMS OF SIGNIFICANCE

The problems faced in developing Indonesia's marine resources are many, but the largest is the administrative support that can be given in terms of manpower and material. Although sound programs can be drawn and the several activities can be carried out successfully, this does not mean everything is running smoothly. The last two years (1965–1967) were very difficult years. Most of the cruises were fielded only because of the Indonesian Navy's strong and persistent interest in these research programs. Otherwise there would not have been enough money to run the ships.

The principal problems encountered can be grouped as follows:

a. *Budget.* At present only government agencies are working for the program. Thus, all activities are dependent upon the financial support of the Indonesian government. When this fails to materialize due to an unstable or adverse economy, the entire program almost collapses. Therefore, only small fractions of the originally planned programs have been carried out. To remedy this, the NCOR is now trying both to obtain research grants and technical assistance from agencies of the United Nations (e.g., UNESCO and FAO) and to attract foreign scientists to work in Indonesian waters.

b. *Equipment.* Much of the scientific equipment is out of order because there is not enough foreign currency to buy accessories and spare parts. Indonesia has little or no capability in the field of repair or improvision of such equipment. Much of it will have to be replaced because it is out of date. The urgency for obtaining new equipment is accentuated by the trend of scientific research toward standardization of techniques and procedures which facilitates comparison of the results from different cruises, Indonesian and foreign.

c. *Manpower.* Although in general there is enough manpower quantitatively to meet the increasing activity needs, most of the researchers and assistants are young people who have just graduated from colleges and universities, and with almost no working experience. Therefore, they still need guidance and training, both of which are woefully scarce. Another handicap is that these young people mostly are not trained specifically for research in marine science. There are but few universities in Indonesia which have any oceanographic training programs.

It is now realized that sending young people abroad for training only solves the problem partially; eventually they have to reorientate themselves to working on problems of a tropical nature under conditions very different from those of their classrooms in the temperate regions. Manpower able to improvise and interested in maintaining equipment is essentially lacking, be it for ships or pencils. Rewarding jobs must be provided that will result in the encouragement of technical staff development in such areas, as well as in the scientific area itself. Toward this end, use of the adequate vessels and buildings for training programs sponsored by such agencies as UNESCO is to be encouraged.

IN CONCLUSION

The rate at which Indonesia is able to develop marine sciences could be greatly speeded by improving the personal rewards for jobs well done, not only in science itself but in the supporting roles so necessary for science's moving ahead smoothly. Recognizing work that can be done with the present technical know-how and facilities and encouraging such work while, at the same time, developing for the more esoteric scientific work of tomorrow is one way of advancing steadily and at the same time enhancing the reputation and productivity of Indonesia in science. Perhaps one way of augmenting this process would be through bringing instructors from overseas—not just as instructors per se but as scientists who would work with their Indonesian colleagues at operational levels compatible to the current conditions for work and the current status of the particular discipline in Indonesia.

Perhaps the kind of assistance most needed to hurry development is that which will get the results from the actually executed parts of the present plans *analyzed, reduced, interpreted,* and *published.* Most other aspects and *the production of results* as raw data tables are now within the power and grasp of Indonesia itself. It would seem pointless to continue planting crops in an arid area until such a time as water can be provided to bring the crop to bear.

As is, Indonesia is moving as rapidly as can be expected toward developing marine science further and gaining information so that the sea can be better understood and utilized for the nation's good in *communication,* in *food production,* and as a source of exports that will bring in *foreign exchange.* Finally, in contributing to the world's scientific knowledge and participating in international scientific affairs, Indonesia is moving toward playing a conspicuous role in the community of nations.

PERTINENT PUBLICATIONS

Those professional papers which largely concern the results of recent Indonesian efforts are preceded with an asterisk (*).

Allen, W. E., and Cupp, E. E. 1935. Plankton diatoms of the Java Sea. *Ann. Jard. Bot. Buitenzorg* 44 (2), 174 pp.

*Anonymous. 1964. Laporan Ekspedisi Ilmiah Laut Operasi Baruna. (Report on the scientific marine expedition "BARUNA OPERATION"), *Sie-Pen. KOTI,* 161 pp.

Bogorov, V. G., and Vinogradov, M. E. 1961. Some features of plankton biomass distribution in the surface water of the Indian Ocean during the winter of 1959–1960. *Okeanol. Issled* No. 4: 66–71. (In Russian.)

Delsman, H. C. 1939. Preliminary plankton investigation in the Java Sea. *Treubia* 17: 139–81.

*Doty, M. S., Soeriaatmadja, R. E., and Soegiarto, A. 1963. Observations on the primary marine productivity of Northwestern Indonesian waters. *Mar. Res. Ind.* 5: 1–25.

*Doty, M. S. 1964. The American botanist and the Biological Institute of Indonesia. *BioScience* 14 (12): 36–41.

*Fukai, R., Soegiarto, A., and Ruamragsa, S. 1961. An attempt to use radiophosphorus (P^{32}) for productivity determination of the sea. *Proc. IPFC,* Sections 2 and 3: 7–8.

*Hardjasasmita, H. S. (In press). Primary notes on the amphibians and reptiles collected during the Baruna expeditions. *Proc. Baruna Exp.* 1 A.

*Hartono, H. M. S. (In press). Age and correlation of the geological formations found in Kangean. *Proc. Baruna Exp.* 1 B.

*Ilahude, A. G. 1966. Oceanographic observations in Bali Strait. (Paper submitted to the Eleventh Pacific Science Congress.)

*McConnoughey, B. H. 1964. The determination and analysis of plankton communities. *Mar. Res. Ind.* Special Number: 1–40.

*Nontji, A., and Houw, T. O. (In preparation). Plankton diatoms of the Java Sea of the Baruna expedition.

*Praseno, D., and Tjee, O. H. 1966. A quantitative study on the zooplankton of the waters around Java. (Paper submitted to the Eleventh Pacific Science Congress.)

*Rahardjo, G., and Ilahude, A. G. (In press). Temperature and salinity observations in the Java Sea. *Proc. Baruna Exp.* 1 C.

van Riehl, P. M. 1932. The Snellius Expedition. *J. Cons. Inst. Explor. Mer* 7: 212–17.

Rochford, D. J. 1961. Hydrology of the Indian Ocean. I. The water masses in the intermediate depths of the Southeast Indian Ocean. *Austr. J. Mar. Freshw. Res.* 12 (2): 129–49. (Also in Coll. Repr. of the IIOE Vol. 1. UNESCO.)

————. 1962. Hydrology of the Indian Ocean. II. The surface waters of the Southeast Indian Ocean and Arafura Sea in the spring and summer. *Austr. J. Mar. Freshw. Res.* 12 (2): 226–51. (Also in Coll. Repr. of the IIOE Vol. 1. UNESCO.)

*Romimohtarto, K. 1967. The oxystomatous crabs of the Baruna expedition. *Mar. Res. Ind.* 8, 15 pp.

*Serene, R., and Romimohtarto, K. 1963. On some species of *Eumedoninae* of the Indo-Malayan region. *Mar. Res. Ind.* 6: 1–14.

*Soegiarto, A. 1965. The development of oceanology in Indonesia. *Research in Indonesia, 1945–1965* 3: 213–30. (In Indonesian.)

*———. 1966. Oceanic research in Indonesian Waters, 1960–1965. (Paper presented in the Eleventh Pacific Science Congress.)

*Soegiarto, A., and Nontji, A. 1966a. Notes on the usages of isotopic carbon for measuring primary marine productivity in Indonesian waters. (Paper presented in the first symposium on the application of radioisotopes in Indonesia.)

*———. 1966b. A seasonal study on primary marine productivity in Indonesian waters. (Paper presented in the Eleventh Pacific Science Congress.)

*Soerjodinoto, Soegiarto, A., and Pardaningsih, N. 1966. Edible marine algae of Southern Seribu Islands, with special reference to the coral islands in which they grow. (Paper submitted to the Eleventh Pacific Science Congress.)

*Somadihardjo, S. 1965. Notes on the radula of some species of Cypraeidae. *Mar. Res. Ind.* 7: 1–25.

Steemann-Nielsen, E., and Aabye-Jensen, E. 1957. Primary oceanic production. *Galathea Report* 1: 49–125.

*Tisna-Amidjaja, D. A. (In press). On the growth rate of coral reefs in the Kei Island. *Proc. Baruna Exp.* 1 A.

*Tjia, H. D. (In press). Preliminary geological report of the Baruna expedition. *Proc. Baruna Exp.* 1 B.

*———. (In press). Orientation on two modern beaches. *Proc. Baruna Exp.* 1 B.

Tydeman, G. F. 1903. Hydrographic results of the Siboga Expedition. *Siboga Exped.* 3, 93 pp.

*Usna, Ismail. (In press). The occurrence and formation of autogenic pyrite in Manumbai Strait—Aru Island. *Proc. Baruna Exp.* 1 B.

Wyrtki, K. 1961. Physical oceanography of the Southeast Asian waters. *Naga Report of Scripps Inst. of Ocean.* Vol. 2, 163 pp.

———. 1962. The upwelling in the region between Java and Australia during the Southeast monsoon. *Austr. J. Mar. Freshw. Res.* 13 (3): 217–25.

[1] Financial assistance from the Office of Naval Research and the United States Atomic Energy Commission via contracts with the University of Hawaii, and vessel time provided aboard the United States Coast and Geodetic Survey vessel *Pioneer* and aboard the National Biological Institute of Indonesia's vessels *Jalanidhi* and *Samudera* are gratefully acknowledged, especially in reference to the activities that made Figure 5:2 possible.

[2] Baruna or Varuna is the name of the god of the sea in Sanskrit.

[3] Seribu = one thousand.

[4] Tjenderawasih = Bird of Paradise.

Karl J. Pelzer   **Geographical Literature on Indonesia**

The purpose of this essay is to survey the geographical literature dealing with Indonesia, going back to the end of the eighteenth century. Not that we do not have writings of a geographical nature dating back to the sixteenth and seventeenth centuries and earlier, but for economy of space this survey starts with the literature of the last quarter of the eighteenth century. No attempt will be made to include every author who has written on some aspect of the natural-physical or cultural ecology of Indonesia.[1] Instead, a selection will be made of the more important publications of the late eighteenth or the nineteenth centuries. The writings of geographers of the first half of the twentieth century, especially of American geographers, will be examined in greater detail. The final part of this essay will look forward and outline some of the more important problems of the natural and cultural environment which deserve special attention of geographers, in particular those concerned with planning.

GEOGRAPHICAL LITERATURE OF THE LAST
QUARTER OF THE EIGHTEENTH AND THE NINE-
TEENTH CENTURIES (ca. 1775 to 1900)

Because geography emerged as a formal academic discipline only during the second half of the nineteenth century, it is readily understood that the earlier writings of a geographical nature are credited to scholars who were not geographers as such but rather administrators, students of "political economy and history," naturalists, and the like. Some of the best writings of a geographical nature, of real importance to the student of cultural and physical ecology of Indonesia, come from the pens of nongeographers.

WILLIAM MARSDEN

The early writings do not deal with what constitutes Indonesia today, but with those sections of the country that were of special interest to European powers. That Great Britain's share of Indonesia—except for the period 1811–1816—was limited to parts of Sumatra is reflected in the writings of William Marsden (1754–1836), who served the British East Company at Fort Marlborough on the west coast of Sumatra from 1771 to 1779. Marsden, one of the best orientalists of the eighteenth century, had great influence on the development of a number of disciplines and made major contributions to our knowledge in such fields as natural and agricultural history, customary law,[2] public administration, and history in the modern sense of the term. In other words, Marsden's remarkable book far exceeds what today we regard as boundaries of historical writing. This is brought out very clearly in the long subtitle of his *History of Sumatra.* As far as I know, the first and one of the best descriptions of the *ladang* system, or shifting cultivation, comes from the pen of Marsden (*History of Sumatra,* 3d ed. 1811, pp. 68–73). Just as important is his description of pepper cultivation (3d ed. 1811, pp. 129–46). Even today careful study of Marsden's writings proves most rewarding.

ADOLPH ESCHELS-KROON

When Marsden was preparing the first edition of his *History of Sumatra* he was not aware of Adolph Eschels-Kroon's account of Dutch commercial establishments and trade along the west coast of Sumatra, first published in Germany in 1781. Of considerable historical interest, Eschels-Kroon's new map of Sumatra identified major political units, such as Het Ryk van Pasi, van Dilli (Deli), Bangkalo (Bengkalis), Andragiri (Indragiri), Palimbang (Palembang), Maningcabo (Minangkabau), and Sinkil (Singkil). A study of this valuable historical map shows that the west coast of Sumatra was much better known than the opposite coast facing the Strait of Malacca, with its broad belt of mangrove swamps and multitude of islands providing an abundance of hideouts for pirates. The west coast was studded with innumerable small ports and trading establishments of the British and Dutch East Indies Companies, most of which have lost all importance and are by now forgotten. The knowledge of Sumatra's interior was extremely limited. Eschels-Kroon and his contemporaries knew nothing about either the location or even the existence of Lake Toba and other great lakes in the interior of the island.[3]

THOMAS STAMFORD RAFFLES

One of the great names in geographical writings on Indonesia is that of Thomas Stamford Raffles (1781–1826). Born in the year that Eschels-Kroon's volume on Sumatra was published and that Marsden was writing his monumental account of that island, Raffles died at the age of forty-five. How much more would he have written had he reached the same age as his friend Marsden or had he not lost the bulk of his collections in the fire of the S. S. *Fame* in 1824?[4]

Raffles was one of the early great English orientalists and probably the first Southeast Asia area specialist with a catholic interest in the natural sciences, humanities, and social sciences. He started with the study of Malay, later shifting to the study of Malay-Indonesian history, maritime law, social institutions, and physical geography, with special emphasis on the faunistic and floristic riches of Southeast Asia. He never neglected the study of local economy, including internal and external trade. There were always a number of copyists and translators on his staff, engaged in adding to his manuscript collection. In his dealing with Malays and Indonesians he revealed a high measure of empathy for Southeast Asians and even seems to have preferred their company to that of Europeans. His mind was highly imaginative, and he possessed an acute and superb feeling for geographic location, most effectively demonstrated in his recognition of the great strategic value of Singapore's location, which in turn led to his raising the British flag on Singapore island in 1819.

His writings on Indonesia, especially on Java and Sumatra, are still worth reading, not only by historians but also by social scientists. Raffles made important contributions to our knowledge of the physical and cultural ecology of Sumatra by undertaking long and difficult trips into the interior of that island. To the best of my knowledge, he was the first European to undertake an exploratory expedition into the hinterland of Padang, the Minangkabau Highlands, where he reached Lake Singkarak. One of his personal ambitions was to be the first European to reach the shores of Lake Toba, thereby proving the existence of that lake, about which he had collected hearsay stories,[5] but the authorities in London issued binding instructions that kept Raffles from penetrating the hinterland of the Bay of Sibolga in his effort to locate the mysterious lake and the place of residence of the priest-king of the Taba Bataks, the feared Singa Mangaradja, whose *huta* was Bakara.[6]

Raffles was a lifelong student of Southeast Asia. His language studies paid off handsomely in his first post as Secretary to the Governor of Penang and his far more important assignment as Agent of the Governor-General to the Malay States, Lord Minto, with headquarters in Malacca. Throughout his years of service, first in Penang and Malacca and, subsequently, in Batavia and Fort Marlborough, Sumatra, he employed Malay, Indonesian, and European assistants and scientists who collected, transcribed, and translated documents for him and who collected geologic, botanical, zoological, and archaeological specimens for him. He was an untiring collector of historic, economic, sociological, anthropological, and political data. While serving as Lieutenant Governor of Java, Raffles revived the Royal Batavian Society, which showed more life and activity during the five years of his chairmanship (1811–1816) than during any other five-year period of the nineteenth or twentieth centuries. In South Sumatra Raffles founded an Agricultural Society, and established the first printing press in Sumatra, which printed the first books in Sumatra, among them the *Proceedings* of the Agricultural Society of Sumatra and *Malayan Miscellanies*. The two volumes of the latter contain papers on Nias Island, cannibalism among the Toba

Bataks, the laws of Moko-Moko, and on the annals of Acheh, while the *Proceedings* contain the results of a series of investigations into Indonesian society of the British possessions in Bencoolen which had been undertaken by members of Raffles's staff.

THOMAS HORSFIELD

Among the scientists whose work was directed by Sir Stamford was the American Thomas Horsfield (born in Bethlehem, Pa., 1773, died in London 1850). Horsfield first reached Batavia as a ship's doctor in 1800. He became so enamored with the fauna and flora of tropical Java that he returned in 1802 and entered the service of the Royal Batavian Society as a naturalist. After the British conquest of Java he befriended Raffles, who in 1814 commissioned him to survey the island of Banka and its tin industry, which he did to Raffles's full satisfaction. In 1818 Horsfield accompanied Sir Stamford and Lady Raffles on their expedition to Lake Singkarak. Shortly after their return to Fort Marlborough, Horsfield sailed with his herbarium of some 2,200 Javanese plant species to London, where he was given a position at the Indian Museum in Leadenhall Street.

JOHN CRAWFURD

John Crawfurd (born 1783 on the isle of Islay, West Scotland, died in South Kensington 1868) was the third great orientalist who contributed significantly to our knowledge of Southeast Asia in general and Indonesia in particular. He served from 1811 to 1816 as a high official in Java and was therefore on the staff of Raffles's administration of that island. In 1808, he had followed Raffles to Penang, where he studied Malay and joined Lord Minto's expedition to Java in 1811. Crawfurd was a harsh competitor of Raffles, of whose work he was critical. Raffles published his *History of Java* in 1817, Crawfurd his *History of the Indian Archipelago*[7] in 1820. As Bastin[8] has pointed out, although Crawfurd planned to go beyond Marsden's work on Sumatra and Raffles's work on Java by covering the whole of the Indonesian archipelago, the Philippines, and Malaya, actually he concentrated so much on Java that P. de Haan's translation into Dutch carries the more limiting title *De Indische Archipel: In het bijzonder het eiland Java.* Crawfurd followed the design which had been developed by Marsden and further refined by Raffles by dealing not only with history in the traditional sense but also with natural history, fauna, flora, agricultural techniques and production, internal and external trade, character of the people, languages, customs, customary laws, art achievements, and the like. For other writers of the nineteenth century, "history" of the Indian archipelago was in the main the story of the development of European conquest and trade.[9] Crawfurd's most important work is his *Dictionary of the Indian Islands,* the first encyclopedia of Indonesia, Malacca, Mainland Southeast Asia, and the Philippines. A testament to Crawfurd's great knowledge, his range of interest, and his power of observation, his dictionary is still worthy of use.

JOHN ANDERSON

In the years 1819 to 1824, the Governor of Prince of Wales Island (i.e., Penang) and Raffles became rivals in trying to strengthen the trade between their particular territorial bases and Sumatra. To gain more knowledge about Sumatra and to link the Sumatran states along the east coast of Sumatra with Penang, the government of Penang dispatched John Anderson, Deputy Secretary to the Governor of Prince of Wales Island and Malay Translator, to the east coast of Sumatra. He sailed from Penang on January 9, 1823, spent the next three months visiting all Sumatran states between Langkat and Siak, and returned to Penang on April 9, 1823.

His account, *Mission to the East Coast of Sumatra,* is a most valuable landmark in the geographical literature of this area. It is the first detailed survey of the natural and cultural environment of that part of Sumatra which was to overshadow all other parts of the Outer Islands as a result of the later development of plantation agriculture and oil mining. The book enables us to draw a detailed picture of the level of economic development and of the political organization of East Sumatra during the first quarter of the nineteenth century. Since there is no evidence of striking changes in East Sumatra between 1823 and 1863, the year of the arrival of Nienhuys, the first planter, we are justified in relying on Anderson for the historic benchmark at the outset of the revolutionary changes to come during the last four decades of the nineteenth century.

FRANZ WILHELM JUNGHUHN

Franz Wilhelm Junghuhn (1809–1864) entered the Dutch colonial service in January 1835 as a health officer and in October of that year arrived in Java, where he devoted most of his energy to botanical and geological studies. In 1839 he was transferred to Padang, where he received orders to survey the Batak lands. This assignment was completed by 1842, and the results of his field research were published in German in 1847. His fame is based on his researches in Java, which he published in a number of volumes, and in a large map, in four sheets. While on furlough in Europe he established contact with Alexander von Humboldt. In the 1850's Junghuhn devoted his energies mostly to the development of cinchona plantations in West Java. In 1860 the famous German geographer Ferdinand von Richthofen visited Java and traveled with Junghuhn for over one month through the Preanger Highlands.

Junghuhn, who was given the honor to be called "the Humboldt of Java," was buried in a grove of cinchona trees near Lembang, north of Bandung, on the slope of the volcano Tangkubanperahu.

PIETER JOHANNES VETH

Another great name among the orientalists of the nineteenth century is that of Pieter Johannes Veth (born in Dordrecht 1814, died in Arnhem 1895). He began his academic career as a linguist and subsequently became professor of geography and anthropology at the University of Leiden. Although he never visited Indonesia, he made a great name for himself with his geographical writings on Borneo, Java, and Sumatra. His book *Atchin* was written in the record time of four weeks, after the Dutch declaration of war on that country. Veth received several honors for his monumental work on Java, among them medals by the International Geographical Congresses in Paris (1872) and Venice (1881). In 1894 his colleagues honored him by issuing a *Feestbundel* to which linguists, historians, geographers, and ethnologists contributed.

GEOGRAPHICAL WRITINGS OF THE TWENTIETH CENTURY

Toward the end of the nineteenth and during the first fifteen years of the current century, a large number of expeditions were undertaken by individual scholars and by groups of scholars. Several of these expeditions were financed by geographical societies or by government agencies. All contributed to our knowledge of Indonesia and helped fill in the white patches of *terra incognita* on the official maps of Indonesia. This applies especially to Sumatra, Kalimantan (Borneo), and Sulawesi (Celebes), but also to the smaller islands and island groups of eastern Indonesia.

P. AND FR. SARASIN

In Sulawesi the cousins P. and Fr. Sarasin traveled in the 1890's and in 1902–1903, publishing their observations in a handsomely illustrated set of two volumes. The first presents an account of travels in the Minahassa area in the north—a first crossing of the peninsula to the Gulf of Tomini and a second crossing starting from Buol. The second volume reports crossings from the west coast to the Gulf of Bone and travels in the southwestern peninsula of Sulawesi.

K. MARTIN, W. H. NIEUWENHUIS, WILHELM VOLZ, J. W. IJZERMAN, M. MOSZKOWSKI

The Moluccas attracted K. Martin, while W. H. Nieuwenhuis conducted ethnological surveys in Kalimantan during the 1890's and published his findings in two volumes in 1904 and 1907 respectively. In Sumatra, the German geographer Wilhelm Volz conducted years of field research in the Gajo lands of Atjeh and in the adjacent Karo and Pakpak Highlands. This work was financed by the Humboldt Foundation of the Royal Prussian Academy of Sciences in Berlin. In Central Sumatra, engineers of the Indonesian State Railroad Service, under the leadership of J. W. Ijzerman, investigated possible routes between the Ombilin coalfield and the east coast as well as the west coast of Sumatra. M. Moszkowski traveled in the Sultanate Siak and the adjacent Rokan States in 1907 and made very interesting studies in the field of cultural geography.

HERBERT LEHMAN, KARL HELBIG

World War I interrupted the series of large-scale expeditions for a brief period, but they were resumed in the 1920's and 1930's: there followed—not necessarily in this sequence—the Snellius Expedition, Middle East Borneo Expedition, Leo Frobenius Expedition, Deutsche Sunda Expedition, Insulinde Expedition des Frankfurter Völkermuseums, and others. These expeditions were usually interdisciplinary in their orientation and covered oceanography, limnology, geology, vulcanology, climatology, botany, zoology, ethnology, geography, and other fields. Among geographers who traveled extensively without the cumbersome apparatus of a full-fledged expedition and wrote prodigiously on Indonesia are the Germans Herbert Lehman and Karl Helbig. The latter used his membership in the German Seaman's Union repeatedly to work his way to Indonesia, where on several occasions he conducted extensive field research in Java, Sumatra, and Kalimantan especially. No other geographer of the period between 1925 and 1940 has published as much that is based on original field work as has Dr. Helbig. After World War II, Helbig continued to publish the data which he had gathered on his earlier trips, especially his 3,000-kilometer trek across Kalimantan from Pontianak on the west coast to Samarinda and Balikpapan on the east coast, a trip which he made accompanied only by one Indonesian, who helped him in carrying the scanty equipment and supplies.

WALTER BEHRMAN, JULES SION, E. H. G. DOBBY, CHARLES A. FISHER, NORTON GINSBURG, CHARLES ROBEQUAIN, JOSEPH E. SPENCER

No Dutch geographer or, as a matter of fact, no geographer of any nationality, has attempted a full-length and comprehensive regional geography of Indonesia. Several have written rather short regional treatments as their contribution to large compendia or handbooks, as did Walter Behrman for the *Handbuch der Geographischen Wissenschaft* and Jules Sion for *Géographie Universelle*. Others treated Indonesia in textbooks dealing with Southeast Asia as a whole: E. H. G. Dobby in his *Southeast Asia*, Charles A. Fisher in his *Southeast Asia*, Norton Ginsburg in *Pattern of Asia*, Charles Robequain in *Le Monde Malais*, and Joseph E. Spencer in *Asia East by South*. None of these does or was intended to do full justice to Indonesia.

The Geographical Section of the Naval Intelligence Division of the British Admiralty compiled a very useful handbook on the Netherlands East Indies during World War II.

SAMUEL van VALKENBURG

Samuel van Valkenburg began his professional career as a geographer, serving in the Topographical Service of the Netherlands East Indies for a number of years before joining Clark University. From his years of service in the Dutch colonial service came a number of scientific papers on Indonesian topics, although in later years van Valkenburg turned to other subjects.

JAN O. M. BROEK

Jan O. M. Broek, who wrote on aspects of Indonesian economy during World War II, contributed material on Indonesia to geographical handbooks prepared by the Office of Strategic Services, and served as visiting professor and geographical adviser at the University of Indonesia at Batavia in 1947 during a leave of absence from the University of Utrecht. Since then he has undertaken port studies on Kalimantan while holding a Fulbright visiting professorship at the University of Malaya.

KARL J. PELZER

Karl J. Pelzer, whose doctoral dissertation at the University of Bonn dealt with plantation labor migrations in Southeast Asia, including Indonesia, in 1940–1941 undertook field research in the Philippines and Indonesia under the auspices of the Johns Hopkins University and the former Institute of Pacific Relations. He studied problems of land use, the impact of different systems of land utilization on the landscape, and lastly, internal migrations of pioneer settlers in the Philippines and in Indonesia, especially of Javanese to the Outer Islands. During World War II and the years immediately following, Pelzer found an opportunity to make use of his firsthand knowledge of Southeast Asia as a Philippine and Indonesia area specialist in the Far East Division of the Office of War Information and of the Office of Foreign Agricultural Relations in the United States Department of Agriculture.

During the postwar period Pelzer investigated the changes in the economic, sociological, and political structure of East Sumatra. These manifest themselves above all in the Social Revolution of 1946, the squatter problem, the shrinkage of the plantation lands, and, finally, the nationalization of all Dutch plantations in 1958–1959.

WILLIAM A. WITHINGTON

William A. Withington served two years as visiting professor of Nommensen University, Medan, Sumatra. This exposure to Sumatra and a later field trip lead to a series of articles dealing above all with the urban geography and rural-urban migration in Sumatra.

JAN F. ORMELING, H. T. VERSTAPPEN

To the small number of Dutch geographers who did field work in Indonesia and who wrote extensively on the subject belong above all Jan F. Ormeling, a cultural geographer and onetime head of the Geographical Institute in Djakarta, and H. T. Verstappen, a geomorphologist and former member of the same institute.

PRESENT STATUS OF GEOGRAPHIC RESEARCH IN INDONESIA

Both before and after World War II, a number of doctoral dissertations accepted by Dutch, German, and, less frequently, American universities have dealt with either physical or cultural aspects of the geography of Indonesia. However, in most instances the authors have since then for one reason or another—mainly because of their inability to undertake field research in Indonesia—turned their research interests to other countries.

With Indonesian political independence came the development of universities which included departments of geography. Especially important is the department at Gadjah Mada University of Jogjakarta, which publishes *Madjalah Ilmu Bumi Indonesia* (Indonesian Journal of Geography). Gadjah Mada as well as other Indonesian universities had to appoint "expatriate" geographers because of the great shortage of scholars with advanced training. The same applies to all other disciplines and reflects the prewar Dutch educational policy.

The prewar Topographical Service of the Indonesian Army has continued and expanded its Geographical Institute, or *Balai Geografi,* since 1950. It too had initially to depend on scientific personnel from the Netherlands (Messrs. Ormeling and Verstappen, and later, from India, Mr. Bhatta). Gradually Indonesia begins to staff such technical services as its Geological, Volcanological, Meteorological, Topographical, and Soil Survey Services with Indonesians who have received scientific training both at home and abroad. All these services have need for geographers to a varying degree.

The need for geographers is most pressing in the institutions of higher learning, i.e., the teachers colleges, institutes of technology, and universities. It may take concentrated efforts extended over a period of fifteen to twenty years before the needs for geographers can be met by the training centers, which at present are themselves badly understaffed.

FUTURE DIRECTION OF GEOGRAPHIC RESEARCH

In the past, geographical writing has been in the main of a descriptive nature and has often emphasized the relationship between man and his environment. In the 1920's and 1930's, geographers were concerned with regional descriptions. No doubt both types of studies will continue to appear, but the new trend, especially in American geographical thought, points in the direction of topical and systematic research rather than regional and descriptive. This trend began during World War II and gained momentum in the postwar period.[10]

Recently Ullman[11] recognized, besides the topical-systematic emphasis, the following five approaches: (1) a genetic or historical one applied especially by Carl O. Sauer;[12] (2) a quantitative approach stressing measurement, the use of statistics, and the development of mathematical models;[13] (3) a functional or interaction approach concerned with circulation, interaction, transportation, and communications;[14] (4) a theoretical approach which combines the interaction and quantitive approaches and is concerned with systems; and (5) the predictive approach of those geographers who see as the ultimate goal of geography the codification of spatial relations, their rigorous analysis for the purpose of making predictions, of participating in planning—be it regional or local —activities.[15]

Turning now to Indonesia, one can identify a number of research frontiers for students of physical and cultural ecology, all of direct practical bearing on the solution of the often staggering problems which confront the leaders of this country. Groups of scholars with special interests and special training in physiography, river hydraulics, soil science, and related subjects are needed to provide technical analysis of such problems as alarming changes in river basins, coastal lowlands, and coastlines which adversely affect the natural vegetation, the transport system—both land and water—and the output of such economic sectors as forestry, smallholder and plantation agriculture, and fishing and fish farming. The East Sumatran landscape, for example, is studded with the ruins of once flourishing plantations, of once prosperous peasant villages which have been either totally abandoned or at least depopulated because of serious ecological changes or because of the complete breakdown of the transport system, and of harbors which can no longer be reached by coastal steamers because of extensive silting. The current ineffectiveness of the Public Works Department, the stoppage of river and harbor dredging, the inability of the Forestry Service to prevent the invasion of forest reservations and the destruction of forests protecting critical watersheds, the ineffectiveness of the Agricultural Extension Service in the fight against manmade, accelerated soil erosion, and other administrative shortcomings—all have contributed to the mounting of problems in the affected areas and to the development of economically "dying lands" and "graveyards." One finds them everywhere—in the highlands of the interior and in the lowlands of the coastal regions. The research undertaken at the Coastal Studies Institute of the Louisiana State University at Baton Rouge could provide stimulating models for research badly needed throughout Indonesia, especially on Java, Kalimantan, and Sumatra.

There is no lack of research topics for the student of cultural ecology. The spatial arrangement of Indonesia's 116 million people, the rapid increase in population, the demographic structure, the striking cultural variations within Indonesia's population, the widespread hidden and overt unemployment—these contribute to a large cluster of research topics concerned with man, his numerical size, his spatial distribution, his economic activities, and his technical ability to manipulate the environment and its resource potential. The striking regional differences in production and consumption demand an efficient network of trade channels and communications lines. The student of location theory and regional planning can only feel overwhelmed by the abundance and complexity of research problems. Planning has to cover a wide range of topics such as natural increase, migration of people, creation of new settlements, development of new and expansion of existing systems of transportation, expansion of agricultural areas, conversion of land from the swidden to the permanent-field system of agriculture, rationalization and intensification of forest use, development of fishing and mining industries, conversion of coastal swamp lands either into belts of fish ponds—capable of producing large quantities of animal protein—or into fields for the raising of wet rice.

The traditional subdivisions of geography—economic, urban, and transportation—are bound to play an important role because of their practical applicability to the problems of Indonesia. These subfields have recently made significant advances by the application of mathematical concepts and have advanced beyond mere description to a high level of generalizations. The methods and concepts developed in these subfields have enabled the practitioners to offer their services to agencies concerned with urban and regional planning or corporations confronted by the problem of selecting locations for plants, warehouses, and stores. Their working procedure is analytic and usually highly quantitative.[16]

Certain other problems would lend themselves to study by geographers who have an analytical orientation. These include the rapid urbanization of Indonesia as a result of rural-urban migration; the decline of land values in some areas as a result of serious deterioration of the road network; the increase in land values in other areas through rehabilitation of roads and the expansion of the existing network beyond the pioneer fringe into heretofore completely undeveloped and isolated parts. In these fields geographers share the work with economists, sociologists, and highway engineers and planners. In the United States the common interests of geographers, regional economists, sociologists, city planners, regional planners, and engineers has led to the formation of the Regional Science Association.

Indonesia offers great research opportunities for the type of practitioners who have a professional interest in the new subfield of regional science.

LITERATURE

A. ATLASES

Atlas Nasional Seluruh Dunia untuk Sekolah Landjutan (Djakarta, Bandung, 1960).
Atlas van Tropisch Nederland (Batavia, 1938).
"Maps and Charts of the Netherlands East Indies." Appendix III of *Netherlands East Indies,* Geographical Handbook Series, Naval Intelligence Division (London, 1944), Vol. 1, pp. 439–88.
Indonesia, Department of Agriculture, Industry and Commerce. *Landbouwatlas van Java en Madoera.* Bulletin of the Central Bureau of Statistics, No. 33 (Batavia, 1926).

B. BIBLIOGRAPHIES

Anderson, Benedict R. *Bibliography of Indonesian Publications. Newspapers, Non-Government Periodicals, and Bulletins, 1945–1948, at Cornell University.* Data Paper No. 33 (Ithaca, N.Y., 1959).
Bouterwek, Konrad. "Hinterindien und Indonesien 1913–25," *Geographisches Jahrbuch,* Vol. 42, 1927 (Gotha, 1928), pp. 40–82.
Cense, A. A., and Uhlenbeck, E. M. *Critical Survey of Studies on the Languages of Borneo.* Bibliographical Series No. 2 ('s-Gravenhage, 1958).
Helbig, Karl. "Länderkunde der Aussereuropäischen Erdteile: Hinterund Insel-Indien. Teil C. Insel-Indien," in *Geographisches Jahrbuch 1942,* Vol. 57, II, pp. 547–769. The most valuable geographical bibliography on Indonesia, which covers the period from 1926 to 1940. The same author has also surveyed the literature from 1940 to 1946 in *Naturforschung und Medizin in Deutschland 1939–1946,* Part II, pp. 53–61.

Hicks, George L., and McNicoll, Geoffrey. *The Indonesian Economy, 1950–1965* (New Haven, Conn., 1967).

Hoykaas, J. C., Hartman, A. et al. *Repertorium op de literatuur betreffende de Nederlandsche kolonien, 1595–1932.* 11 vols. (Amsterdam, Den Haag, 1877–1934).

Kennedy, Raymond. *Bibliography of Indonesian Peoples and Cultures.* Revised edition by Thomas W. Maretzki and H. Th. Fischer (New Haven, Conn., 1955).

Quelle, Otto. "Indonesien 1904–07." *Geographisches Jahrbuch,* Vol. 32, 1909 (Gotha, 1909), pp. 301–309.

———. "Indonesien 1908–1912." *Geographisches Jahrbuch,* Vol. 37, 1914 (Gotha, 1915), pp. 246–56.

Research Catalogue of the American Geographical Society, Vol. 13 (Boston, 1962) pp. 9602–78.

Schleifer, Hedwig. *Bibliography on the Economic and Political Development of Indonesia.* Edited by Douglas Paauw (Cambridge, Mass., 1953).

Teeuw, A., with the assistance of H. W. Emanuels. *A Critical Survey of Studies on Malay and Bahasa Indonesia.* Bibliographical Series No. 5 ('s-Gravenhage, 1961).

Wallace, J. Allen, Jr. "An annotated bibliography of climatic maps of Indonesia." U.S. Weather Bureau, mimeographed (Washington, 1962).

C. ENCYCLOPEDIA AND HANDBOOKS

Aardrijkskundig en Statistisch Woordenboek van Nederlandsch Indie. 3 vols. (Amsterdam, 1861–1869).

American University, Special Operations Research Office, Foreign Area Studies Division. *U.S. Army Area Handbook for Indonesia* (Washington, 1964).

van Bemmelen, R. W. *The Geology of Indonesia.* 2 vols. in 3 pts. (The Hague, 1949).

Bezemer, T. J. *Beknopte Encyclopaedie van Nederlandsch-Indie* (Leiden, 's-Gravenhage, Batavia, 1921).

Braak, C. *Het klimaat van Nederlandsch-Indie. Verhandelingen* No. 8, Koninklijk magnetisch en meteorologisch observatorium te Batavia, vol. 1 (Batavia, 1921), vol. 2 (Weltevreden, 1929).

British Admiralty, Geographical Section, Naval Intelligence Division. *Netherlands East Indies.* 2 vols. (London, 1944). Each chapter concludes with a brief bibliographical note.

Dutch East Indies. Department van Binnenlandsch Bestuur. Afdeeling Bestuurszaken der Buitengewesten. *Mededeelingen.* 35 vols. (Batavia, 1911–1928). *Mededeelingen.* Series A, 13 vols. (Batavia, 1927–1931).

Encyclopaedie van Nederlandsch-Indie. Edited by J. Paulus, S. de Graaff, D. S. Stibbe, and others. 8 vols. ('s-Gravenhage, 1917–1936). This valuable encyclopedia is a goldmine for the geographer.

Hadikusumo, Djajadi. *Report on the volcanological research and volcanic activity in Indonesia for the period 1950–1957.* Bandung, Departemen Perindustrian Dasar/Pertambangan. Djawatan Geologi. (Bandung, 1961).

van Hall, C. J. J., and van de Koppel, C. *De Landbouw in den Indischen Archipel.* 3 vols. in 4 pts. ('s-Gravenhage, 1946–1950).

Heyne, K. *De nuttige Planten van Nederlandsch-Indie* (Batavia, 1927).

———. *De nuttige Planten van Indonesie.* 2 vols. ('s-Gravenhage, Bandung, 1950).

Honig, Pieter, and Verdoorn, Frans, eds. *Science and Scientists in the Netherlands Indies* (New York, 1945).

Koninklijke Akademie van Wetenschappen, Amsterdam. *Science in the Netherlands East Indies.* Edited by L. M. R. Rutten, secretary of the "I.C.O." Committee (Amsterdam, 1929).

McVey, Ruth T., ed. *Indonesia* (New Haven, Conn., 1963).

Scientific Results of the Snellius-Expedition in the Eastern Part of the Netherlands East Indies, 1929–1930 (Utrecht and Leiden, 1934–1941).

Sion, Jules. *Asie des Moussons,* in *Géographie Universelle,* vol. 9 (Paris, 1928). Part 2, pp. 479–504.

Sutter, John O. *Scientific Facilities and Information Services of the Republic of Indonesia* (Honolulu, 1961).

D. BOOKS, MONOGRAPHS, AND ARTICLES

Allen, G. C., and Donnithorne, Audrey G. *Western Enterprise in Indonesia and Malaya: a study in economic development* (New York, 1957).

Anderson, John. *Mission to the East Coast of Sumatra, in MDCCCXXIII under the Direction of the Government of Prince of Wales Island: including historical and descriptive sketches of the country, an account of the commerce, population, and the manners and customs of the inhabitants and a visit to the Batta Cannibal States in the interior* (Edinburgh, 1826).

Anderson, John. *Acheen, and the Ports of North and East Coasts of Sumatra* (London, 1840).

Behrman, Walter. "Die Malaiische Inselwelt," in *Handbuch der Geographischen Wissenschaft: Vorder- und Südasien in Natur, Kultur und Wirtschaft* (Potsdam, 1937), pp. 453–523.

van Bemmelen, R. W. "The influence of geologic events on human history (an example from Central Java)," *Verhandelingen van het K. Nederl. Geologisch-Mijnbouwkundig Genootschap.* Geologische Serie 16 (1956): 20–36.

Bennett, Don C. "Population Pressure in East Java." Ph.D. dissertation, Syracuse University, 1957.

———. "The basic food crops of Java and Madura," *Economic Geography* 37 (1961): 75–87.

Bhatta, J. N. *Soal-soal transmigrasi di Indonesia, istimewa Sumatra Selatan (Regarding internal migration in Indonesia with special reference to*

South Sumatra). Republic of Indonesia. Kementerian Pertahanan. Direktorat Topografi Angkatan Darat. Balai Geografi, Publikasi No. 7 (Djakarta, 1957).

————. *The future Census (October 1961) of Indonesia.* Djakarta, Departemen Angkatan Darat. Direktorat Topografi. Dinas Geografi. Publikasi No. 10 (Djakarta, 1961).

————. *Source and reliability of demographic data in Indonesia.* Djakarta, Departemen Angkatan Darat. Direktorat Topografi. Dinas Geografi. Publikasi No. 11 (Djakarta, 1962).

Bintarto, R. "Geography and population in the area of Jogjakarta," *Indonesian Journal of Geography* 1, 2–3 (1961): 29–31.

————. "Man, rice and problems in Jogjakarta," *Indonesian Journal of Geography* 3 (1961/63): 34–39.

Blink, H. *Nederlandsch Oost- en West-Indie geographisch, ethnographisch en economisch beschreven.* 2 vols. (Leiden, 1905, 1907.)

————. "Nederlandsch Oost-Indie als productie- en handelsgebied," *Tijdschrift voor Economische Geographie* 5 (1914): 193–320.

————. "Sumatra's Oostkust in hare opkomst en ontwikkeling als economisch gewest," *Tijschrift voor Economische Geographie 1918,* pp. 57–156.

————. "De Inlandsche landbouw in Nederlandsch Indie," *Tijdschrift voor economische geographie* 17 (1926): 349–98.

————. *Opkomst en ontwikkeling van Sumatra als economisch-geographisch Gebied* (Den Haag, 1926).

Brenner, Joachim Freiherr von. *Besuch bei den Kannibalen Sumatras. Erste Durchquerung der unabhängigen Batak-Lande* (Würtzburg, 1894).

Boeke, J. H. *The Interests of the Voiceless Far East: Introduction to Oriental Economics* (Leiden, 1948).

————. *Ontwikkelingsgang en Toekomst van Bevolkings- en Ondernemings-Landbouw* (Leiden, 1948).

Breman, J. C. "Java: bevolkingsgroei en demografische structuur," *Tijdschrift K. Nederl. Aardrijkskundig Genootschap,* 2nd ser. 80 (1963): 252–308.

Broek, Jan O. M. "The economic development of the Outer Provinces of the Netherlands Indies," *Geographical Review* 30 (1940): 187–200.

————. *Economic Development of the Netherlands Indies* (New York, 1942).

————. "War and postwar problems of the Netherlands Indies." *Global Politics,* edited by Russell H. Fitzgibbon (Berkeley, Calif., 1944), pp. 119–34.

————. "Man and resources in the Netherlands Indies," *Far Eastern Quarterly* 5 (1946): 121–31.

————. "Indonesia," *Focus* 7, 4 (1956).

————. *Indonesia* (Garden City, N.Y., 1957).

Broersma, R. *Oostkust van Sumatra.* Part I, *De Ontluiking van Deli* (Batavia, 1919). Part II, *De Ontwikkeling van het Gewest* (Deventer, 1922).

Burton and Ward, "Report of a journey into the Batak country in the interior of Sumatra," *Transactions of the Royal Asiatic Society* 1 (1827): 485–513.

Castles, Lance. "The ethnic profile of Djakarta," *Indonesia* 3 (1967): 153–204.

Crawfurd, John. *History of the Indian Archipelago.* 3 vols. (Edinburgh, 1820).

———. *De Indische Archipel, in het bijzonder het eiland Java beschouwd in de zeden, wetenschapen, talen, godsdienst, beschaving, koloniale belangen en koophandel van derzelver inwoners.* 3 vols. (Haarlem, 1823–1825).

———. *A Descriptive Dictionary of the Indian Islands and Adjacent Countries* (London, 1856).

Cunningham, Clark E. *The Postwar Migration of the Toba-Bataks to East Sumatra* (New Haven, Conn., 1958).

Dobby, E. H. G. *Southeast Asia* (London, 1950).

Eichelberger, R. "Regenverteilung, Pflanzendecke und Kulturentwicklung in der ostindischen Inselwelt," *Geographische Zeitschrift* 1924, pp. 108–16.

Eidman, Franz Erich. "Die Aufgaben der Forstwirtschaft bei der Lösung bevölkerungspolitischer Probleme in tropischen Ländern unter besonderer Berücksichtigung der Verhältnisse in Niederländisch-Indien," *Zeitschrift für Weltforstwirstschaft* 5 (1938): 527–37.

Eschels-Kroon, Adolph. *Beschreibung der Insel Sumatra, besonders in Ansehung des Handels, und der dahingehörigen Merkwürdigkeiten. Nebst einer neuen Original- Charte, von Adolph Eschels-Kroon, vormaligen Residenten der Holländischen, Ostindischen Compagnie, zu Ayerbangis, auf Sumatra.* Herausgegeben mit einer Vorrede von Gottlob Benedict von Schirach (Hamburg, 1781).

———. Dutch edition: *Beschrijving van het eiland Sumatra* (Haarlem, 1783).

Fiedler, H. *Die Insel Timor* (Friedrichsegen, 1929).

Fisher, Charles A. "Southeast Asia," in East, W. Gordon, and Spate, O. H. K., *The Changing Map of Asia. A Political Geography* (London, 1950), pp. 179–246.

———. *South-East Asia. A Social, Economic and Political Geography* (London, 1964). Part II. "The Equatorial Archipelago: Indonesia," pp. 205–403.

———. "Economic Myth and Geographical Reality in Indonesia," *Modern Asian Studies* 1, 2, (1967): 155–89.

Fryer, Donald W. "Indonesia's Economic Prospects," *Far Eastern Survey* 23 (1954): 177–82.

———. "Economic Aspects of Indonesian Disunity," *Pacific Affairs* 30 (1957): 195–208.

———. *Indonesia* (Melbourne, 1957).

———. "Recovery of the sugar industry in Indonesia," *Economic Geography* 33 (1957): 171–81.

————. "Indonesia, the Economic Geography of an Underdeveloped Country." Ph.D. dissertation, University of London, 1958.

————. "Jogjakarta—economic development in an Indonesian city state," *Economic Development and Cultural Change* 7 (1959): 452–64.

Fuchs, F. W. "Moderne Kolonisation in Niederländisch-Indien," *Koloniale Rundschau* 29 (1938): 316–42.

Fumneaux, Rupert. *Krakatoa* (Englewood Cliffs, N.J., 1964).

Geertz, Clifford. *Agricultural Involution: The Processes of Ecological Change in Indonesia* (Berkeley, Calif., 1963).

————. *Peddlers and Princes: Social Change and Economic Modernization in Two Indonesian Towns* (Chicago, 1963).

————. *The Social History of an Indonesian Town* (Cambridge, Mass., 1965).

Geldern, J. van. "Western enterprises and the density of population in the Netherlands Indies," in Koninklijk Bataviaasch Genootschap van Kunsten en Wetenschappen. *The Effect of Western Influence on Native Civilizations in the Malay Archipelago.* (Batavia, 1929).

Ginsburg, Norton, ed. *The Pattern of Asia* (Englewood Cliffs, N.J., 1958), chap. 17, pp. 344–69.

Gould, James W. *Americans in Sumatra* (The Hague, 1961).

Gretzer, W. K. G. *Grundlagen und Entwicklungsrichtung der landwirtschaftlichen Erzeugung in Niederländisch-Indien* (Berlin, 1939).

Hamerster, M. *Bijdrage tot de kennis van de afdeeling Asahan*, Mededeelingen, Oostkust van Sumatra Instituut No. XIII (Amsterdam, 1926).

Hanrath, Joh. J. "Transmigratie in Indonesie in het algemeen en in Celebes in het bijzonder," *Tijdschrift voor economische en sociale geografie* 45 (1954): 133–38.

Helbig, Karl. *Batavia, eine tropische Stadtlandschaftskunde im Rahmen der Insel Java.* Ph.D. Thesis, University of Hamburg (Bad Segeberg, 1931).

————. "Bevölkerungsprobleme von Niederländisch-Indien," *Zeitschrift für Geopolitik* X (1933): 76–89.

————. "Die ländlichen Siedlungen auf Sumatra," in Fritz Klute, ed., *Die ländlichen Siedlungen in verschiedenen Klimazonen* (Breslau, 1933), pp. 122–30.

————. "Die Insel Sumatra," *Geographische Zeitschrift* 1934, pp. 89–101.

————. "Studien auf Sumatra und Nias," *Zeitschrift der Gesellschaft für Erdkunde zu Berlin* 1934, pp. 102–23.

————. "Bau und Bild der Insel Java," *Zeitschrift der Gesellschaft für Erdkunde zu Berlin,* 1935, pp. 102–25.

————. "Landschafts- und Wirtschaftsstufung in südlichen Batakland auf Sumatra," *Zeitschrift für Erdkunde* 4 (1936): 961–66, 1018–26, 1057–71.

————. "Bali. Eine tropische Insel landschaftlicher Gegensätze," *Zeitschrift für Ethnologie* 1939, pp. 357–79.

————. "Beiträge zur Landeskunde von Sumatra. Beobachtungen zwischen Asahan und Barumun, Toba-see und Malakkastrasse," *Wissenschaftliche*

Veröffentlichungen des Deutschen Museums für Länderkunde, N.S. 8 (1940): 133–251.

―――. "Die Insel Bangka. Beispiel des Landschafts- und Bedeutungswandel auf Grund einer geographischen 'Zufallsform'," *Schriften der Bremer Wissenschaftlichen Gesellschaft,* Reihe C: *Deutsche geographische Blätter* 43 (1940): 133–207.　　　　　・

―――. "Nusa Penida, eine tropische Karstinsel," *Mitteilungen der Geographischen Gesellschaft Hamburg* 1940, pp. 391–410.

―――. *Urwaldwildnis Borneo. 3000 Kilometer Zickzack-Marsch durch Asiens grösste Insel* (Braunschweig, 1940).

―――. *Indonesiens Tropenwelt* (Stuttgart, 1947).

―――. *Indonesien. Eine auslandskundliche Übersicht der malaiischen Inselwelt* (Stuttgart, 1949).

―――. *Paradies in Licht und Schatten* (Braunschweig, 1949).

―――. *Am Rande des Pazifik: Studien zur Landes- und Kulturkunde Südostasiens* (Stuttgart, 1949).

―――. "Glaube, Kult und Kulturstätten der Indonesier in kulturgeographischer Betrachtung," *Zeitschrift für Ethnologie* 76 (1951): 246–87.

Helfferich, E. "Kapital und Arbeit in Niederländisch-Indien," *Mitteilungen der Geographischen Gesellschaft in Hamburg* 36 (1924): 137–58.

―――. "Wirtschaft und Ethik in Niederländisch-Indien," *Mitteilungen der Geographischen Gesellschaft in Hamburg* 40 (1929): 148–65.

Hoeven, Anny van der. "Die wirtschafts-geographischen und rechtlichen Grundlagen des Ladangbaus im Malaiischen Archipel, unter besonderer Berücksichtigung der Insel Sumatra." Dissertation, Universität Hamburg (Typescript. Hamburg, 1944).

Hollerwöger, F. "The Progress of the River Deltas in Java," in UNESCO, *Scientific Problems of the Humid Tropical Zone Deltas and their Implications; Proceedings of the Dacca Symposium,* 1964 (Paris, 1966).

Horsfield, Thomas. *The natural history of Java, including besides the Flora Javana, a detailed account of the zoology and mineralogy of that interesting island* (London, 1817).

―――. *Zoological Researches in Java and the Neighbouring Islands* (London, 1824).

―――. "Report on the Island of Banka (1814)," *Journal of the Indian Archipelago and Eastern Asia* 2 (1848): 299–336, 373–427, 705–25, 779–824.

Horstman, Kurt. "Die Industrialisierung Indonesiens," *Verhandlungen des Deutschen Geographentages* [Würzburg, 1957] 31 (1958): 304–307.

―――. "Indonesien: Bevölkerungsproblem und Wirtschaftsentwicklung," *Geographisches Taschenbuch.* Jahrweiser zur deutschen Landeskunde 1958/9, pp. 410–23.

―――. "Die Bevölkerungsverteilung in Indonesien: geographische Betrachtungen zu einem Grundproblem der Entwicklungsplanung," *Die Erde* 95 (1964): 167–80.

Ijzerman, J. W., van Bemmelen, J. F., Koorders, S. H., and Bakhuis, L. A., *Dwars door Sumatra. Tocht van Padang naar Siak* (Haarlem, 1895).

Junghuhn, Franz Wilhelm. *Die Battaländer auf Sumatra.* 2 vols. (Berlin, 1847).

———. *Topographische und naturwissenschaftliche Reisen durch Java. Topographischer und naturwissenschaftlicher Atlas* (Magdeburg, 1849).

———. *Java, deszelfs gedaante, bekleding en inwendige structuur.* 4 vols. (Amsterdam, 1852).

———. *Java, seine Gestalt, Pflanzendecke, und innere Bauart.* 3 vols. (Leipzig, 1852–1854).

———. *Java, zijn gedaante, zijn plantentooi en inwendige bouw.* 4 vols. (Amsterdam, 1853–1854).

———. *Licht en schaduwbeelden uit de Binnenlanden van Java* (Leiden, 1854).

Kennedy, Raymond. *The Ageless Indies* (New York, 1942).

———. *Islands and Peoples of the Indies.* Smithsonian Institution, War Background Studies, No. 14 (Washington, 1943).

Keyfitz, Nathan. "The ecology of Indonesian cities," *American Journal of Sociology* 66 (1961): 348–54.

———. "Indonesian population and the European industrial revolution," *Asian Survey* 5 (1965): 503–14.

Khan, M. Halim. "The rise and decline of cash crops in Java," *Indonesian Journal of Geography* 1, 2–3 (1961): 47–55.

———. "An introductory study of water in mid-Java," *Indonesian Journal of Geography* 4, 8 (1964): 48–58.

———. "Water in Gunung Kidul [Java]," *Indonesian Journal of Geography* 4 (1964): 50–60.

Klaveren, Jan Jacob van. "Das niederländisch-koloniale Bodenrecht in seinem Zusammenhang mit der Struktur der Niederländisch-Ostindischen Landwirtschaft." Dissertation, Technische Hochschule München (Typescript. München, 1945).

Kornrumpf, M. *Mensch und Landschaft auf Celebes.* Dissertation, University of Breslau. Beiheft No. 8, *Geographische Wochenschrift,* 1934.

Kuperus, G. *Het cultuurlandschap van West-Soembawa.* Dissertation, University of Utrecht (Groningen and Batavia, 1937).

———. "The Relation between Density of Population and Utilization of Soil in Java," in *Comptes Rendus du Congrès International de Géographie Amsterdam 1938* (Leiden, 1939), II, Sec. IIIc, pp. 465–77.

Lehmann, H. "Kulturgeographische Wandlungen in Südost-Sumatra," *Zeitschrift der Gesellschaft für Erdkunde zu Berlin,* 1933, pp. 161–75.

———. "Die Landschaft Ngada auf Flores: Eine länderkundliche Skizze aus den Sundainseln," *Geographische Zeitschrift* 1935, pp. 339–52.

———. "Zur Vegetationsgliederung in Niederländisch-Ostindien," *Koloniale Rundschau* 1935, pp. 319 ff.

———. "Das Antlitz der Stadt in Niederländisch-Indien," in *Länderkund-*

liche Forschung. Festschrift für Norbert Krebs, edited by H. Louis and W. Panzer (Stuttgart, 1936) pp. 109–39.

————. *Morphologische Studien auf Java,* Geographische Abhandlungen, III Reihe, No. 9 (Stuttgart, 1936).

————. "Die Bevölkerung der Insel Sumatra," *Petermann's Mitteilungen,* 1938, pp. 3–15.

————. "Die koloniele Oberschicht der Bevölkerung von Niederländisch Indien," *Koloniale Rundschau* 1938, pp. 97–114.

Lekkerkerker, C. *Land en volk van Java.* Vol 1: *Inleiding en algemeene beschrijving* (Groningen, 1938).

Marsden, William. *History of Sumatra, Containing an Account of the Government, Laws, Customs, and Manners of the Native Inhabitants, with a Description of the Natural Productions and a Relation of the Ancient Political State of that Island.* 1st ed. 1783, 2d ed. 1784, 3d ed. 1811. Also available are a French and German translation of the 1783–1784 editions. Marsden's widow published his autobiography under the title *A Brief Memoir of William Marsden* (London, 1838).

Martin, K. *Reisen in den Molukken, in Ambon, den Uliassenn, Seran und Buru* (Leiden, 1894, 1903).

Matoušek, Vladimir. "Overpopulation in agricultural areas of Java," *Journal of the Czechoslovak Geographical Society,* Supplement for the 20th International Geographical Congress, 1964 (Prague, 1964), pp. 157–61.

Milone, Pauline D. "Contemporary Urbanization in Indonesia," *Asian Survey* 4 (1964): 1000–1012.

————. *Urban Areas in Indonesia: Administrative and Census Concepts* (Berkeley, Calif., 1966).

Moszkowski, M. *Auf Neuen Wegen durch Sumatra* (Berlin, 1909).

Nieuwenhuis, A. W. *In Centraal Borneo.* 2 vols. (Leiden, 1900).

Nitisastro, Widjojo. "Migration, Population Growth and Economic Development in Indonesia: A Study of the Economic Consequences of Alternative Patterns of Interisland Migration." Ph.D. Thesis (Berkeley, Calif., 1961).

Notohadiprawiro, R. M. Tedjojuwono. "A comparative study of two adjacent soil profiles under different vegetation and use (Teak forest and extensive dry farming)," *Indonesian Journal of Geography* 4 (1964): 36–49.

————. "A Soil survey in the Bena Plain on the island of Timor," *Indonesian Journal of Geography* 4, 8 (1964): 1–29.

Ormeling, Jan Ferdinand. "Agrarische planologie in Indonesie," *Geografisch Tijdschrift* 3 (1950): 199–208.

————. "Enige opmerkingen over verkeer en bodemgebruik in West-Java," *Geografisch tijdschrift* 6 (1953): 49–62, 97–105, 153–62, 199–212, 216–66.

————. *The Timor Problem: A Geographical Interpretation of an Underdeveloped Island* (Djakarta, 1955).

————. "Het visvijver landschap langs Java's Noordkust," *Tijdschrift K.*

Nederlandsch Aardrijkskundig Genootschap, 2d series, 67 (1950): 469–86.

Paauw, Douglas S., ed. *Prospects for East Sumatran Plantation Industries. A Symposium* (New Haven, Conn., 1962).

Palmier, Leslie. *Indonesia* (New York, 1965).

Pannekoek, A. J. "Geomorfologische waarnemingen op het Djampang-Plateau in West-Java," *Tijdschrift K. Nederl. Aardrijkskundig Genootschap,* 2d ser., 63 (1946): 340–67.

———. "Outline of the geomorphology of Java," *Tijdschrift K. Nederl. Aardrijkskundig Genootschap,* 2d ser., 66 (1949): 270–326.

Paravincini, E. "Die ländlichen Siedlungen Javas," *Geogr. Zeitschrift* 33 (1927): 392–404.

Pédelaborde, Pierre. *The Monsoon* (London, 1963), pp. 111–32.

Peekema, Wibo. "Colonization of Javanese in the Outer Provinces of the Netherlands East-Indies," *Geographical Journal* 101 (1943): 145–51.

Pelzer, Karl J. *Arbeiterwanderungen in Südost-asien: Eine bevölkerungs-undwirtschafts-geographische Untersuchung* (Hamburg, 1935).

———. *Pioneer Settlement in the Asiatic Tropics: Studies in Land Utilization and Agricultural Colonization in Southeastern Asia* (New York, 1945).

———. "Tanah Sabrang and Java's population problem," *Far Eastern Quarterly* 5 (1946): 133–42.

———. "Agrarian Conflict in East Sumatra," *Pacific Affairs* 30 (1957): 151–59.

———. "Physical and Human Resource Pattern" and "The Agricultural Foundation," chapters 1 and 4 in Ruth T. McVey, ed., *Indonesia* (New Haven, Conn., 1963), pp. 1–23, 118–54, 475–79, 498–504.

Peper, Bram. "Groote en groei van Java's Inheemse bevolking in de negentiende eeuw," Publicatie No. 11, Afdeeling Zuid en Zuidoost-Azie, Anthropologisch-Sociologisch Centrum, Universiteit van Amsterdam (Mimeographed. Amsterdam, 1967).

Pitkanen, Allan M., and Riis, Jacob A. "The geopolitical pattern of Indonesia," *The Social Studies* 48 (1957): 198–205, 237–42, 279–85.

Purcell, Victor. *The Chinese in Southeast Asia* (London, 1951). "The Chinese in Indonesia," pp. 441–568.

Raffles, Thomas Stamford. *Substance of a Minute Recorded by the Honourable Thomas Stamford Raffles, Lieutenant-Governor of Java and its Dependencies, on the 11th February 1814: on the Introduction of an Improved System of Internal Management and the Establishment of a Land Rental on the Island of Java* (London, 1814.)

———. *History of Java* 2 vols. (London, 1817).

———. "On the Malayan Nation with a translation of its maritime institutions," *Asiatic Researches* 7 (1818): 102–58.

Raffles, Lady Thomas Stamford. *Memoir of the Life and Public Services of Sir Thomas Stamford Raffles, F.R.S. Particularly in the Government of Java, 1811–1816, and of Bencoolen and its Dependencies, 1817–1824, with Details of the Commerce and Resources of the Eastern Archipel-ago, and Selections from his Correspondence* (London, 830).

Regelink, Z. *Bijdrage tot de kennis van het bevolkingsvraagstuk op Java en Madoera.* Dissertation, University of Utrecht (Enschede, 1931).

Reiner, Ernst. *Die Molukken. Petermanns Geographische Mitteilungen,* Ergänzungsheft 260 (Gotha, 1956).

Reinhard, R. "Das Bevölkerungsproblem in Java," *Berichte der Mathi-Phys. Königlich Sächsischen Akademie der Wissenschaften Leipzig* 93 (1941): 69–92.

Reksodihardjo, Iso, and Mukkadas. Arifin. "Population density and swamp paddy cultivation with irrigation facilities in the Asian monsoon-tropics, with special reference to Java (Indonesia)," *Indonesian Journal of Geography* 1, 2–3 (1961): 5–11.

Reksodihardjo, Iso, and Reksodihardjo, Soedarsono. "Double cropping in wet-rice cultivation in relation to soil and climate," *Indonesian Journal of Geography* 3 (1961/63): 10–14.

Robequain, Charles A. "Problèmes de colonisation dans les Indes Néerlandaises," *Annales de Géographie* 50 (1941): 37–57, 114–36.

——. *Malaya, Indonesia, Borneo and the Philippines: A Geographical, Economic and Political Description of Malaya, the East Indies and the Philippines.* Translated by E. D. Laborde (London, 1954).

Roch, G. *Die politisch-geographische Entwicklung von Sumatra.* Dissertation, University of Leipzig (Dresden, 1936).

Sarasin, P., and Sarasin, Fr. *Reisen in Celebes, ausgeführt in den Jahren 1893–96 und 1902/3.* 2 vols. (Wiesbaden, 1905).

——. *Versuch einer Anthropologie der Insel Celebes* (Wiesbaden, 1906).

Schmitthenner, Heinrich. "Die Insel Java," *Geogr. Zeitschrift* 1922, pp. 148–65.

Spencer, J. E. *Asia East by South. A Cultural Geography* (New York, 1954).

Staub, W. "Die wirtschaftliche Bedeutung der grossen Sunda-Inseln," *Der Schweizer Geograph* 19 (1942): 66–76.

van Steenis, C. G. G. J. "Maleische vegetatieschetsen. Toelichting bij de plantengeografische kaart van Nederlandsch Oost Indie," *Tijdschrift K. Nederl. Aardrijkskundig Genootschop,* 2d ser., 52 (1935): 25–67, 171–203, 363–98.

——. "Hoofdlijnen van de plantengeografie van de Indische Archipel op grond van de verspreiding der phanerogamen-geslachten," *Tijdschrift K. Nederl. Aardrijkskundig Genootschap,* 2d ser., 65 (1948): 193–208.

Tan, Goantiang. "Growth of cities in Indonesia, 1930–1961," *Tijdschrift voor Econ. en Sociale Geografie* 56 (1965): 103–108.

Tennekes, J. "De bevolkingsspreiding der residentie Besoeki in 1930," *Tijdschrift K. Nederl. Aardrijkskundig Genootschap,* 2d ser., 80 (1963): 309–423.

Terra, G. J. A. "Mixed-garden horticulture in Java," *The Malayan Journal of Tropical Geography* 3 (1954): 33–43.

——. "Some sociological aspects of agriculture in Southeast Asia," *Indonesie* 6 (1963): 297–316, 439–63.

Tieman, Ilse. *Das Plantagengebiet der Ostküste von Sumatra.* Dissertation, University of Leipzig (Dresden, 1936).

United States Economic Survey Team to Indonesia. *Indonesia: Perspective and Proposals for United States Economic Aid* (New Haven, Conn., 1963).

van Valkenburg, Samuel. "Economisch-geografische beschouwingen over de productie van het groot-landbouwbedrijf op Java en Madoera," *Tijdschrift voor economische geographie* 16 (1925): 269–84.

———. "Java, the Economic Geography of a Tropical Island," *Geographical Review* 15 (1925): 563–83.

———. "Java. A study in population," *Papers Michigan Academy of Science, Arts and Letters, XIV,* 1930, pp. 399–415.

———. "Agricultural Regions of Asia," *Economic Geography* 12 (1936): 27–44.

Van der Kroef, Justus M. "Population pressure and economic development in Indonesia," *American Journal of Sociology* 12 (1953): 355–71.

———. "Indonesia's human resource pattern," *Journal of Geography* 58 (1959): 186–94.

Verstappen, H. T. *Djakarta bay: a geomorphological study on shoreline development* ('s-Gravenhage, 1953).

———. "Het kustgebied van Noordelijk West-Java op de luchtfoto," *Tijdschrift K. Nederl. Aardrijkskundig Genootschap,* 2d ser., 71 (1954): 146–52.

———. "Geomorphological observations on Indonesian volcanoes," *Tijdschrift K. Nederl. Aardrijkskundig Genootschap,* 2d ser., 80 (1963): 237–51.

———. "The geomorphology of Sumatra," *Journal of Tropical Geography* 18 (1964): 184–91.

———. "Some volcanoes of Halmahera (Moluccas) and their geomorphological setting," *Tijdschrift K. Nederl. Aardrijkskundig Geonotschap,* 2d ser., 81 (1964): 297–316.

Veth, Pieter Johannes. *Borneo's Westerafdeeling geographisch, statistisch, historisch, voorafgegaan door eene algemeene schets des ganschen eilands.* 2 vols. (Zalt-Bommel, 1854–1856).

———. "Sumatra," in *Aardijkskundig en statistisch Woordenboek van Nederlandsch Indie.* Vol. 3, (Amsterdam, 1869), pp. 661–797. (An excellent article with a long bibliography of twenty pages.)

———. *Java, geographisch, ethnologisch, historisch.* 3 vols. (Haarlem, 1875–1882).

———. *Atchin en zijne Betrekkingen tot Nederland, topographisch-historische Beschrijving, met eene schetskaart van het rijk Atchin,* enz. door W. F. Versteeg (Leiden, 1873).

Volz, Wilhelm. *Nord-Sumatra. Bericht über eine im Auftrage der Humboldt-Stiftung der Königlich Preussischen Akademie der Wissenschaften zu Berlin in den Jahren 1904–06 ausgeführten Forschungsreise.*
Band 1: *Die Batakländer* (Berlin. 1909).
Band 2: *Die Gajoländer* (Berlin, 1912).

————. *Im Dämmer des Rimba, Sumatra's Urwald und Urmensch* (Breslau, 1921).

————. "Die südostasiatische Inselwelt," in Andree-Heiderich-Sieger, *Geographie des Welthandels. Eine wirtschaftsgeographische Erdbeschreibung.* 4th ed. (Wien, 1927). Vol. 2, pp. 397–440.

van Vuren, L. "Zur Anthropogeographie van Zentral-Celebes." *Zeitschrift der Gesellschaft für Erdkunde zu Berlin,* 1929, pp. 108–13.

————. "Westlicher Einfluss auf die einheimische Kultur im Malaiischen Archipel," *Zeitschrift der Gesellschaft für Erdkunde zu Berlin,* 1930, pp. 178–85.

————. *De Merapi. Bijdrage tot de Sociaal-Geographische Kennis van dit Vulkanisch Gebied.* Mededeelingen von het Geographisch-Geologisch Instituut, Rijksuniversität Utrecht. Anthropogeogr. Reeks No. 2 (Utrecht, 1932).

de Waard, J. "De Oostkust van Sumatra," *Tijdschrift voor economische geographie* 25 (1934): 213–21, 255–74, 282–301.

Watts, Kenneth. "How to make an urban planning survey based on Djakarta, Indonesia," *Ekistics; reviews on the problems and science of human settlements* 13, No. 79 (1962): 300–312.

————. "Tanggerang: A case study in planning policy for a small town within a tropical metropolitan region [Java]," *Planning Outlook* 5 (1962): 5–21.

Wellan, J. W. J., ed. *Zuid-Sumatra. Economisch overzicht van de gewesten Djambi, Palembang, de Lampongsche Districten en Benkoelen* (Wageningen, 1932).

Wertheim, W. F. "Sociological aspects of inter-island migration in Indonesia," *Population Studies* 12 (1959): 184–201.

Withington, William A. "Medan, regional metropolis of northern Sumatra, Indonesia." Association of American Geographers, Southeastern Division. *Memorandum Folio* 11 (1959): 115–24.

————. "Amount and variability of tropical rainfall in North Sumatra." Association of American Geographers, Southeastern Division. *Memorandum Folio* 12 (1960): 98–104.

————. "Upland resorts and tourism in Indonesia: some recent trends," *Geographical Review* 51 (1961): 418–23.

————. "Medan: primary regional metropolis of Sumatra," *Journal of Geography* 61 (1962): 59–67.

————. "The cities of Sumatra," *Tijdschrift voor Econ. en Sociale Geografie* 53 (1962): 242–46.

————. "The Kotapradja or 'king cities' of Indonesia," *Pacific Viewpoint* 4 (1963): 75–86.

————. "The distribution of population in Sumatra, Indonesia, 1961," *Journal of Tropical Geography* 17 (1963): 203–12.

————. "Changes and Trends in Patterns of North Sumatra's Estate Agriculture, 1938–1959," *Tijdschrift voor Econ. en Sociale Geografie* 5 (1964): 8–13.

————. "The Major Geographic Regions of Sumatra, Indonesia," *Annals of the Association of American Geographers* 57 (1967): 534–49.

————. "Migration and Economic Development: Some Spatial Changes in the Population of Rural Sumatra," *Tijdschrift voor Econ. en Sociale Geografie* 58 (1967): 153–63.

Zoetmulder, P. J. "The mutual relationship between geography and history of Indonesian culture and literature," *Indonesian Journal of Geography* 1, 1 (1960): 21–25.

NOTES

[1] For a listing of the more important bibliographies, see the titles in the bibliographical appendix.

[2] C. van Vollenhoven regarded Marsden as one of the pioneers in the study of customary law. See his *De ontdekking van het adatrecht* (Leiden, 1928), pp. 14–19.

[3] As late as 1845 Junghuhn doubted the existence of Lake Toba, though Raffles had indicated its approximate location on his map of Sumatra, published in 1830 (Carte de l'île de Sumatra d'après Sir Th. St. Raffles. Etablissement Géographie de Bruxelles, fondé par Ph. Vandermaelen en 1830.) F. W. Junghuhn, *Die Battaländer auf Sumatra.* (Berlin, 1947).

[4] The greatest loss ever suffered in the field of Southeast Asia Studies was caused by the fire which completely destroyed the S. S. *Fame.* The S. S. *Fame* left Benkoolen on February 2, 1824, having aboard the retiring Lieutenant Governor Thomas Stamford Raffles and his family and staff. Aboard the ship were also the fruits of Raffles's lifework as a student of Southeast Asian affairs. In his report to the directors of the East India Company, Raffles stated that in some 120 large boxes were packed

"endless volumes and papers of information on the civil and natural history of nearly every island within the Malay Archipelago, collected at great expense and labor, under the most favorable circumstances, during a life of constant and active research, and in a special manner calculated to throw light not only on the commercial and other resources of these islands, but to advance the state of natural knowledge and science, and finally to extend the civilization of mankind.

"These, with all my books, manuscripts, drawings, correspondence, records, and other documents, including tokens of regard from the absent, and memories from the dead, have been all lost forever in this dreadful conflagration. . . ."

"*Of Sumatra*—A map on a large scale, constructed during a residence of six years, from observations made by myself and persons under my authority, European and native, calculated to exhibit, at one view, the real nature and general resources of the country, on a very different scale to what was formerly supposed; together with statistical reports, tables, memoirs, notices, histories of the Battas, and other original races, native and European vocabularies, dictionaries and manuscripts in the different languages, contained in several cases.

"*Of Borneo*—A detailed account of the former history, present state, population, and resources, of that long-neglected island, already drawn out to the extent of upwards of one thousand pages of writing with numerous notes, sketches, details of the Dayak population, their government, customs, history, usages, etc. with notices of the different ports, their produce, and commercial resources.

"And of Java and the Moluccas—the whole of the voluminous history, as carefully abstracted from the Dutch archives while I was in Java, with careful translations of the most valuable native books, vocabularies, memoirs, and various papers intended principally to assist in a new edition of my History of Java." (C. E. Wurtzburg, *Raffles,* pp. 684–85).

As the account goes on, covering several more pages, the weight of the losses becomes almost unbearable. It was truly an irreplacable loss that the world of scholars suffered on the evening of February 2, 1824. The next morning Raffles and his family and friends landed at Fort Marlborough with nothing but the scanty clothing they were wearing the evening before.

[5] The first European to reach Lake Toba from the west coast of Sumatra was the linguist Dr. A. Neubronner van der Tuuk, who in February 1853 was the guest of Ompu Sohahuron, also known as Singa Mangaradja, in Bakara on the southern shores of the lake. The first European coming from the Strait of Malacca was the Dutch district officer Cats Baron de Raet, who in 1868 saw the lake from the heights on the north side. The first European to cross the length of Lake Toba by boat was the Austrian Joachim Freiherr von Brenner, who crossed the lake from north to south, coming from Negori on the northern shores via Ambarita on the island of Samosir and finally landing at Laguboti on the southeastern shores. In Laguboti resided a member of the Rhenish Mission, Ludwig I. Nommensen, who happened to be on a trip to the Silindung Valley at the time of von Brenner's visit to Laguboti.

[6] Shortly after Raffles's final departure from Sumatra, two English missionaries, Burton and Ward, carried out the instructions of their patron and undertook a carefully prepared trip to the Silindung Valley where they reached what is now Tarutung. They were not able to proceed beyond Tarutung for two reasons. First and above all, the Toba chiefs of the Silindung Valley told them they had to carry out strict orders of the Singa Mangaradja not to allow any European to reach the shores of the sacred lake. Second, Burton became seriously ill, and the two missionaries thought it wiser to return to the coast.

[7] Crawford coined the term "Indian Archipelago," a term which became very popular in nineteenth-century writing on Southeast Asia.

[8] John Bastin, "English Sources for the Modern Period of Indonesian History," in Soedjatmoko and Mohammad Ali, G. J. Resink. and G. McT. Kahin, eds., *An Introduction to Indonesian Historiography* (Ithaca, N.Y., 1965), p. 266.

[9] Horace St. John, *The Indian Archipelago: Its History and Present State* (London, 1852). See also Bastin, pp. 266–67.

[10] Ackerman, Edward A., "Geographic Training, War Time Research and Immediate Professional Objectives," *Annals of the Association of American Geographers* 35 (1945): 121–43.

[11] Ullman, Edward L., "Geographical Prediction and Theory: The Measure of Recreation Benefits in the Meramec Region," mimeographed.

[12] Sauer, Carl O., *Land and Life* (Berkeley, Calif., 1963).

[13] Haggett, Peter. *Locational Analysis in Human Geography* (London, 1965). See also the writings of Wm. L. Garrison, Brian J. Berry, Wm. Warntz, and others.

[14] Ullman, Edward L., "The Role of Transportation and the Bases for Interaction," in William L. Thomas, ed., *Man's Role in Changing the Face of the Earth* (Chicago, 1956), pp. 862–80.

[15] See Ullman, "Geographical Prediction."

[16] *The Science of Geography.* Report of the Ad Hoc Committee on Geography, Earth Science Division, National Academy of Sciences–National Research Council (Washington, D.C., 1965), pp. 44–45.

CHAPTER 7

R. P. Koesoemadinata and V. E. Nelson **Mineral Resources in Indonesian Development**

One of the basic prerequisites for successful economic development of a nation mentioned by Ambassador Suwito Kusumowidagdo is mineral wealth. He included this wealth as an area of hope for the future economic development of Indonesia. Since no second crop may be expected, rich diverse mineral deposits are one of a nation's most valuable but ephemeral possessions. They might be termed its quick assets. It is the purpose of this paper to attempt an assessment of these assets in only the most general terms. Special emphasis is given to petroleum resources because they are somewhat better known and more fully developed than most others, and because they are the largest generator of foreign exchange for Indonesia at the present time.

Information regarding a nation's mineral position is a necessity if decisions are to be made wisely regarding industrial development, expansion, foreign affairs, international trade, defense, and many other areas of concern. For this reason it is imperative that in a developing nation an early part of the program must be an appraisal, as accurate as possible, of its mineral resources. If their extent and quality are unknown, high priority should be given to arrangements which will supply this basic information.

Full development of the potential mineral resources of Indonesia will require extensive effort by geologists, geophysicists, geochemists, mining engineers, and related earth scientists. Ideally, they should be primarily Indonesian nationals with perspective on full development and conservation of the nation's mineral wealth. To attain this ideal, the small number of Indonesians currently trained for mineral exploration and exploitation will have to be increased manyfold. Currently there are approximately 120 professionally trained Indonesian geologists. Though this number is small, it is evidence of encouraging growth when compared with the three such persons available at the time of independence to undertake geological studies, assume teaching positions in the institutions of higher learning, and provide administrative personnel for various agencies such as *Direktorat Geologi* and *Directorat Pertambangan* (Mining).

The problem of developing the corps of Indonesian geologists so useful in national economic development is somewhat different from that of many other professional groups. There is difficulty in attracting students within the universities to choose geology or related earth sciences as their profession. A very large segment of the group will have to be directly engaged in mineral exploration and exploitation or engaged in the early phases of major developmental projects. Such duties require, for the most part, the discomforts and inconveniences associated with a nomadic type of existence in mostly undeveloped areas. Thus, when students have an opportunity to obtain a university education, they tend to choose a profession in which they feel they will be rewarded with creature comforts as well as intellectual satisfaction and prestige. The problem is not unique to Indonesia. Its solution in most instances has been accomplished by increased monetary compensation for persons required to perform their duties under adverse living conditions. What Indonesia's methods should be in dealing with the problem is an internal matter. However, some means of creating prestige commensurate with that of the other professionals will be necessary if the persons needed are to be recruited from the student population.

Indonesia, with a land area of approximately 575,000 square miles, is geologically an extremely complex area. The entire nation lies within the tropical zone, and geological investigations are particularly difficult to carry out because of deep rock-weathering and the wide extent of dense vegetation. These conditions require that conventional methods of surface geological mapping be augmented by sophisticated geophysical and geochemical techniques, many of which have to be developed and modified for a particular area if its existing mineral wealth is to be located.

Tales of the mineral wealth of the islands go far back into history. These resources in tropical countries under Spanish influence, for example, were quite well known by the beginning of the nineteenth century. Very little had been recorded regarding the mineral wealth of Indonesia, however, before 1850. Since that time a number of resources have been found and developed, but not enough to place the country in a leading position among others in known ore reserves of most metallic or nonmetallic ore substances. In attempting to evaluate the potential resources, one must make speculative estimates on the basis of the area involved and the general geological setting or conditions. The geological processes responsible for mineral concentration in deposits of economic value are numerous and varied. They are not the same for all mineral commodities, nor even for all deposits of a single metallic or nonmetallic material source. In the Indonesian archipelago, it is the area itself and the great variety of geological phenomena exhibited which indicate that, with intensive exploration, there should be uncovered extensive resources of a number of the materials necessary for industrial development and growth. Much of the basic and early phase of exploration for new deposits will possibly have to be carried on by government agencies in order to encourage private enterprise to invest risk capital into new mining ventures. Even in countries such as the United States, governmental agencies have found it necessary to initiate interest in regions of potential mineral production through generalized geological mapping programs and the employment of new exploration techniques.

Indonesian mining law is such that mineral wealth to be found within the boundaries of the individual landowner is the property of the government and thus belongs to the entire community. This common ownership allows full development of resources which might otherwise be hampered by detrimental actions of individual property owners. It also makes possible the orderly exploitation of any resource, avoiding expensive duplication, wasteful operating methods, etc. Consequently, it is possible for the nation to utilize its mineral wealth to the best advantage in the total development program. This, of course, means that the government must maintain adequate controls of concessions assigned to private corporations for exploration and exploitation.

Table 7:1 shows production data for various mineral resources currently being exploited, and the location is identified of known occurrences of various economically valuable substances exclusive of petroleum and natural gas (Figure 7:1). Many of these localities may not contain materials in amounts sufficient for economic development. Nevertheless, their large number and widespread occurrence attest to the many and varied ore-concentrating mechanisms which have been operative in the region. It seems only reasonable to predict that in a number of locations there should have developed deposits of commercial grade which await discovery.

PETROLEUM

Indonesian petroleum production, 1960–1968, is shown in Table 7:2. In evaluating potential future production, however, comparison with other producing regions of the world is instructive. Estimated proved probable reserves of crude oil for the entire world at the end of 1968 were 509.9 billion barrels (42 U.S. gallons per barrel). This represents a thirty-six year supply at current production rates. Indonesian proved reserves are estimated at 10 billion barrels, or approximately 2 percent of the world total (World Petroleum Report 1967). Fifty-six percent of the world total is in the Middle East and 12 percent is in North America. In petroleum-bearing regions where exploration has not been carried out intensely and steadily, proved reserves will decline, but with an intensive exploration program they are quite likely to rise for a number of years until all the available area has been subjected to careful exploration. Indonesia produced in 1968 a total of 219,365 thousand barrels, or approximately 1.5 percent of the world total. With vigorous exploitation and available markets Indonesian production could be raised considerably

TABLE 7:1 Indonesian Production of Selected Metals and Minerals: 1960–1966
(metric tons unless otherwise specified)

Commodity	1960	1961	1962	1963	1964	1965	1966
Bauxite	395,678	419,865	491,298	493,111	647,805	688,259	701,255
Gold (troy ounces)	5,660	5,337	4,469	4,437	6,400	6,720	4,115
Lead					650	N.D.*	N.D.*
Manganese ore	10,910	12,707	4,953	2,841	500	415	N.D.*
Nickel ore (3.5 percent nickel)	13,758	18,000	12,722	45,705	47,950	102,002	117,402
Silver (thousands of troy ounces)	311	324	248	280	290	299	221
Tin ore (metal content)	23,048	18,946	17,310	12,927	16,345	14,699	12,526
Sulphur	500	817	932	1,050	1,000	1,288	1,200
Coal	657,164	563,530	470,703	591,356	446,213	390,548	319,831

Data from U.S. Bureau of Mines, Minerals Yearbook 1964 and Office of Directorate General of Mines, Republic of Indonesia.
* No Data.

FIGURE 7:1

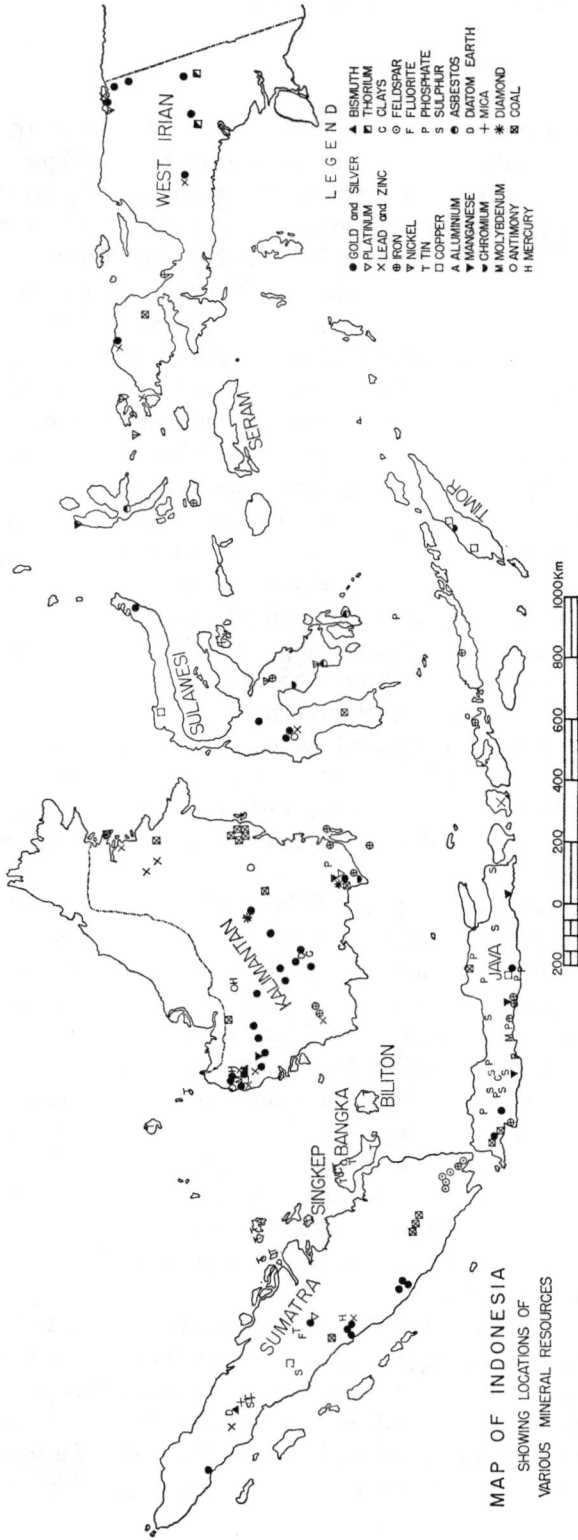

MAP OF INDONESIA

SHOWING LOCATIONS OF
VARIOUS MINERAL RESOURCES

LEGEND

● GOLD and SILVER   ▲ BISMUTH
▽ PLATINUM   ◪ THORIUM
✕ LEAD and ZINC   C CLAYS
⊕ IRON   ⊙ FELDSPAR
▼ NICKEL   F FLUORITE
T TIN   P PHOSPHATE
□ COPPER   S SULPHUR
▲ ALUMINIUM   ◆ ASBESTOS
▼ MANGANESE   D DIATOM EARTH
M CHROMIUM   + MICA
M MOLYBDENUM   ✳ DIAMOND
H ANTIMONY   ◙ COAL
H MERCURY

WEST IRIAN

SERAM

TIMOR

SULAWESI

KALIMANTAN

JAVA

BILITON

BANGKA

SINGKEP

SUMATRA

200 0 200 400 600 800 1000Km

in a comparatively short period of time. The year 1968 showed an increase of 18.3 percent over the previous year. Figure 7:2 is a map showing the location of sedimentary deposits possibly favorable for petroleum prospects as well as the known oil fields. The important producing areas to date are restricted to Tertiary basins of West Indonesia, and the discussion which follows deals essentially with those areas.

Several papers concerning the regional geology of petroleum in Indonesia have appeared during the last several decades, but opinions regarding oil possibilities are mostly based on age of sedimentary strata and geologic structure. Less attention has been paid to analyses of facies relationships and basin configuration. (Sedimentary facies are areally segregated parts of differing nature belonging to any genetically related body of sedimentary deposits.) The most obvious anticlinal accumulations have been discovered and developed, and knowledge of the geological occurrence of oil is accumulating; these facts have resulted in geological reasoning concerning oil possibilities based on basin studies of sedimentation, facies relationships, and basin development in general (Habitat of Oil 1958; Ismet 1962, p. 24).

Papers concerning oil occurrence in Indonesia and using this new approach have also appeared, notably for South Sumatra (Dufour 1957, pp. 172–81; Wennekers 1958, pp. 1347–58) and also for East Kalimantan (Borneo) and East Java (Weeda 1958, pp. 1337–46 and pp. 1359–64), but no discussions have appeared concerning the whole of Indonesia.

This analysis of oil possibilities is based partially on sources in the literature, but published data or available analyses are unfortunately limited. This makes it necessary to resort to deductive geological reasoning and speculation based on analogies among several basins with which the authors are most familiar. This method is also proposed by Mallory (1963, pp. 757–76): "Evaluation for petroleum is effected by the deduction of significant analogies developed in the comparison of an explored or partially explored region with similar regions that have mature production history." In this case South Sumatra is considered to be a region with a mature production history and for which opinions concerning the controls of oil occurrence have been published. For each basin only a general outline is presented, and geological details are not given in the following discussion.

The general regional tectonic framework of the Indonesian Tertiary basins is shown in Figure 7:2, which was compiled from several sources, including Umbgrove (1933), Beltz (1944), Schuppli (1946), Van Bemmelen (1949), and Weeda (1958). It can be seen that in the western part of Indonesia the Sunda shelf consists of a continental core of crystalline rocks (igneous and metamorphic), which tectonically has

TABLE 7:2 Indonesian Petroleum Production: 1960–1968 (in thousand barrels; 42 U.S. gallon barrels)

1960	1961	1962	1963	1964	1965	1966	1967	1968
152,988[1]	155,369[1]	167,777[1]	165,002[1]	169,250[1]	178,190[2]	169,118[2]	185,785[4]	219,365[4]

Total cumulative production through December 1968: 3,479,150[3]

[1] Source: *Bulletin* American Association Petroleum Geologists, Vol. 50, no. 8, Tulsa, Okla., 1966.
[2] Source: *World Oil*, Vol. 164, no. 3, Gulf Publishing Company, Houston, Texas, 1967.
[3] Source: Office of Directorate General of Oil and Natural Gas, Republic of Indonesia.
[4] Source: *World Petroleum Report*, Vols. 14 and 15, Mona Palmer Publishing Company, New York, 1968, 1969.

TABLE 7:3 Summary of Cumulative Production through December 1966 of West Indonesian Oil Fields in both Transgressive and Regressive Phases (in thousand barrels; 42 U.S. gallon barrels)

Stratigraphic Position	Oil Basin				
	N. Sumatra	C. Sumatra	S. Sumatra	E. Java	E. Kalimantan
Transgressive Phase	None	1,015,000	861,000	None	60,000
Regressive Phase	180,000	None	292,000	136,000	524,000

Source of information: Directorate General of Oil and Gas, Republic of Indonesia

FIGURE 7:2

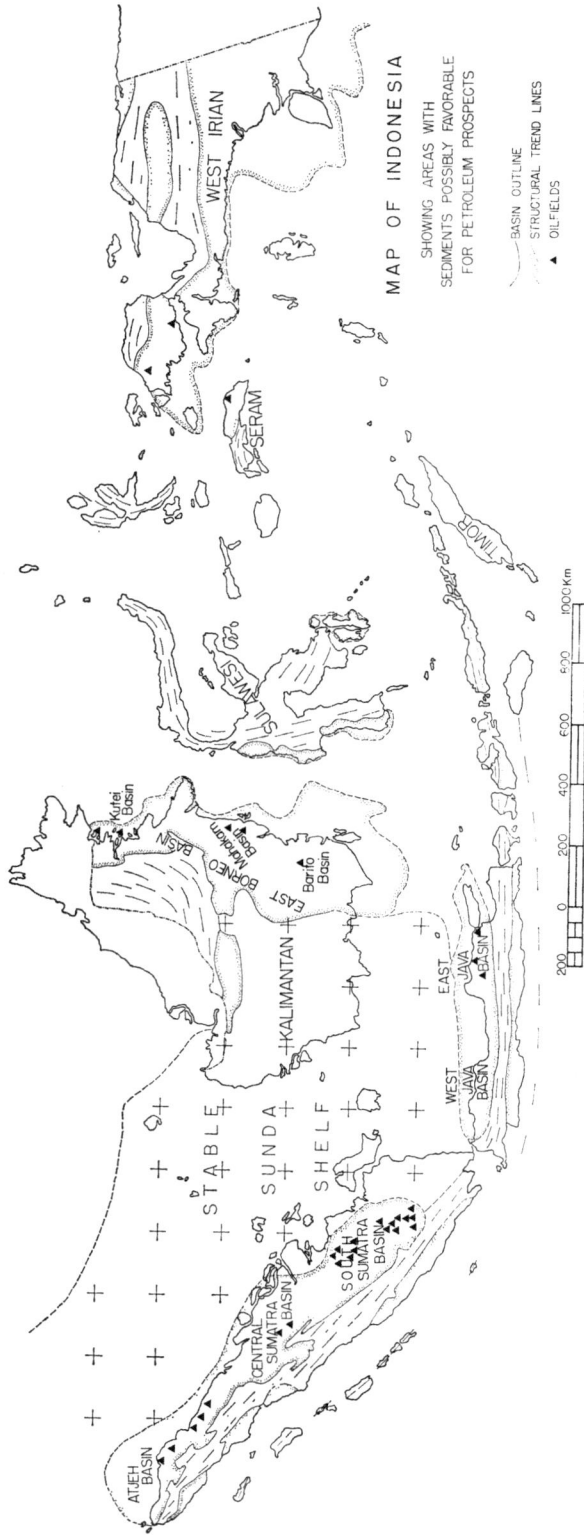

MAP OF INDONESIA

SHOWING AREAS WITH
SEDIMENTS POSSIBLY FAVORABLE
FOR PETROLEUM PROSPECTS

------ BASIN OUTLINE
········· STRUCTURAL TREND LINES
▲ OILFIELDS

WEST IRIAN

SERAM

TIMOR

SUNDA WEST

Kutei Basin
BORNEO BASIN
EAST
Mahakan Basin
Barito Basin

KALIMANTAN

STABLE SUNDA SHELF

EAST JAVA BASIN
WEST JAVA BASIN

SOUTH SUMATRA BASIN
SUMATRA BASIN
CENTRAL SUMATRA BASIN

ATJEH BASIN

200 0 200 400 600 800 1000 Km

been stable from the Tertiary to the present. This stable shelf is surrounded by mobile geanticlinal belts, consisting of a volcanic inner arc and a nonvolcanic outer arc, which during the Tertiary have been the loci of strong uplift and folding. The volcanic inner arc is represented in Sumatra by the Pegungan Barisan Range and in Java by the Central Volcanic Range. It is composed of folded pre-Tertiary and Tertiary formations, and in most places the older rocks are crowned by recent active volcanoes. The outer nonvolcanic arc is represented by the offshore islands west of Sumatra and, farther south, by the submarine ridge south of Java. It is mostly composed of Tertiary formations. Volcanic activity is entirely absent.

The area between these belts and the stable Sunda shelf is occupied by Tertiary sedimentary basins. Smaller sedimentary basins are also present between the inner and outer arcs, but these have not been extensively studied. Oil seeps and other indications of petroleum have been found in the basins between the arcs, but no oil has been produced. This discussion is only directed to the sedimentary basins directly adjoining the Sunda shelf. These basins are situated in a metastable area and are termed "ideogeosynclines" by Umbgrove (1933). In these areas, rapid sedimentation occurred during the Tertiary, in partially closed marine environments, followed by moderate to strong folding at the close of the Tertiary. The result was a gently folded thick prism of sediments, highly favorable for the occurrence of petroleum. Development of the individual basins may differ in the time of tectonic events, but a similar evolution and sedimentation cycle may be observed in each basin.

During the early Tertiary these areas formed elongated basins parallel to the geanticlinal belts. During a period of intra-Miocene orogenesis, the basinal areas were broken into smaller basins by the rise of median ridges composed of pre-Tertiary basement rocks. The resulting basins are, from west to east, the Atjeh Basin (North Sumatra Basin), the Central Sumatra Basin, the South Sumatra Basin, the West Java Basin, the East Java Basin, the Barito Basin, the Mahakam Basin, and the Kutei Basin. (The last three are in the East Kalimantan basinal area, as shown in Figure 7:2).

The East Kalimantan basinal area is more complicated than the other areas because it was influenced by geanticlinal belts of different ages on the northern and eastern sides.

The regional tectonic framework of the basins and the sedimentation history give some basis for comparison of the stratigraphy among the basins. Local conditions within the basins may vary considerably, but the general outline of basin history is much the same for all. The development of these basins differs in the age of stratigraphic sequences; some started earlier than others, but there were similar sedimentation cycles.

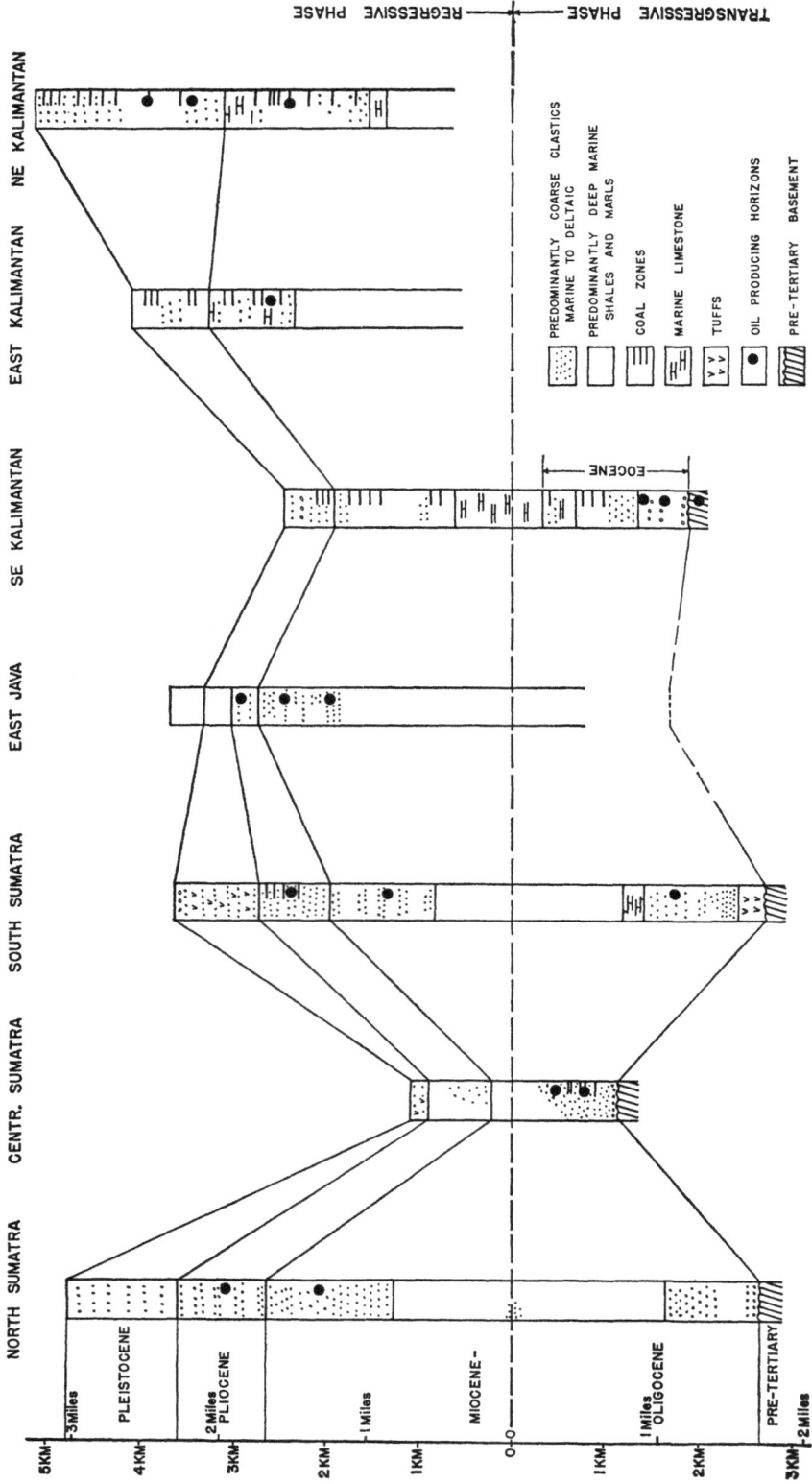

FIGURE 7:3

TERTIARY STRATIGRAPHY OF THE OIL BASINS IN WEST INDONESIA

FIGURE 7:4

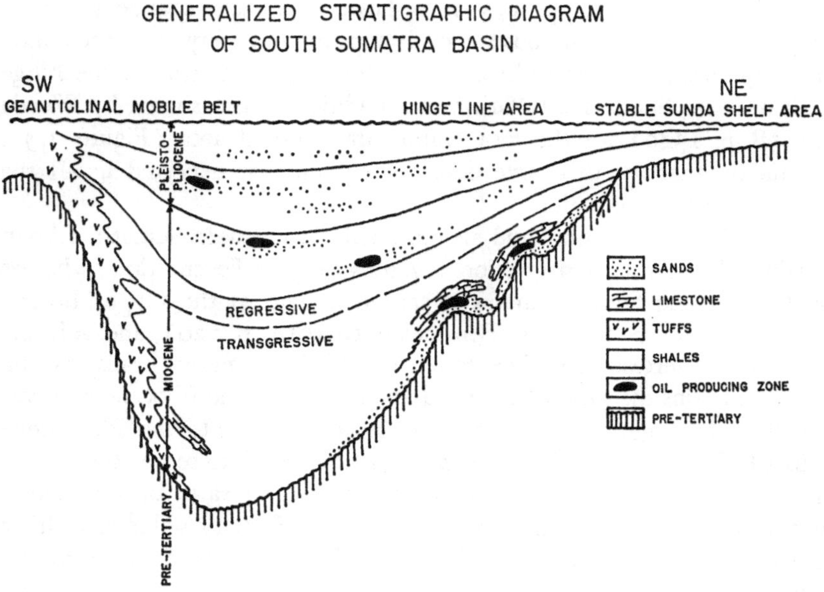

GENERALIZED STRATIGRAPHIC DIAGRAM
OF SOUTH SUMATRA BASIN

Figure 7:3 is a highly generalized outline of the stratigraphy of individual basins, compiled from various sources. Similarity in the stratigraphic succession is apparent. Each basin started with a transgressive facies, preceded in some basins with volcanic activity or terrestrial sedimentation, and littoral to neritic deposition was followed by bathyal shale deposition. At the close of the Tertiary this series of deposits was followed by sedimentation in the regressive environments resulting from basin filling. A final nonmarine sequence is indicated by numerous coal seams, with the exception of the East Java Basin, where such seams are rare (Weeda 1958, p. 1361).

For the South Sumatra Basin, de Sitter (1941, p. 231), Dufour (1957, p. 173), and Wennekers (1958, p. 1349) came to the conclusion that the whole sedimentary sequence can be regarded as a megacycle consisting of a lower transgressive facies which is mirrored in an upper regressive facies, with the plane of symmetry extending through the bathyal shale series (Figure 7:4). This is also the case in the East Kalimantan basinal areas (Figure 7:5), which are compared by Weeda (1968, p. 1340) with the South Sumatra Basin. Taking into consideration the regional tectonic framework and the similar stratigraphic successions in the different basins, it can be concluded that a similar sedimentation cycle may have existed in all West Indonesian basins lying between the Sunda shelf and the surrounding geanticlinal mobile belt.

Dufour (1957, pp. 173–74) shows that facies-change plays an important role in the various stages. It appears that away from the Sunda shelf the basin reached bathyal depths, but this is not true of the hinge belt near the Sunda shelf. This same condition is also shown by Weeda (1958, p. 1340) for the East Kalimantan basinal area (Figure 7:5). Again by analogy, this same development may be expected in all the basins under consideration.

In East Kalimantan and also probably in northern Sumatra (Atjeh Basin), the marine transgression began as early as Eocene time, whereas in Central and South Sumatra it started as late as the Oligo-Miocene (Dufour 1957, p. 172; Van Bemmelen 1949 IA, p. 120), and volcanic activity and terrestrial sedimentation preceded the marine transgression. In some basins the megacycle ended at the close of the Pliocene and was followed by orogeny; in other basins it continued into the Pleistocene (East Kalimantan, Weeda 1958, p. 1341) or even into recent time (East Java, Van Bemmelen 1949, Volla p. 553). The rates of subsidence, indicated by the maximum thicknesses of the Tertiary sediments, differ greatly from basin to basin (Atjeh Basin, 8,000 meters; South Sumatra, 4,600 meters, East Java, 6,000+ meters, East Kalimantan, 12,000 meters).

The formations in the transgressive and regressive sequences are composed mostly of coarse clastics which constitute favorable reservoir rocks. In line with the above reasoning, and as can be seen immediately in the stratigraphic diagram in Figure 7:3, oil and natural gas occur both in the formations of the regressive and transgressive facies, and practically none occurs in formations of the bathyal facies.

All the earlier-developed oil fields are located in the upper regressive facies (northeast Sumatra, South Sumatra, East Java, and Kalimantan). This is quite understandable because formations in the upper regressive facies are at shallow depths.

In the early days of exploration the lower-lying formations in the transgressive facies were not considered to be productive because oil seeps are absent, the strata were rarely penetrated in deeper areas, and at places where these formations are exposed, or are close to the surface, they are situated close to the mobile belt where they have been found to be nonproductive. Since the 1918 discovery of the Pendopo field (South Sumatra), with production from the lower transgressive facies, there has been a growing awareness of the potential of these formations. The discovery led to extensive exploration for oil in the lower transgressive facies, not only in South Sumatra but also in Central Sumatra and in southeastern Kalimantan. This exploration resulted in the discovery of

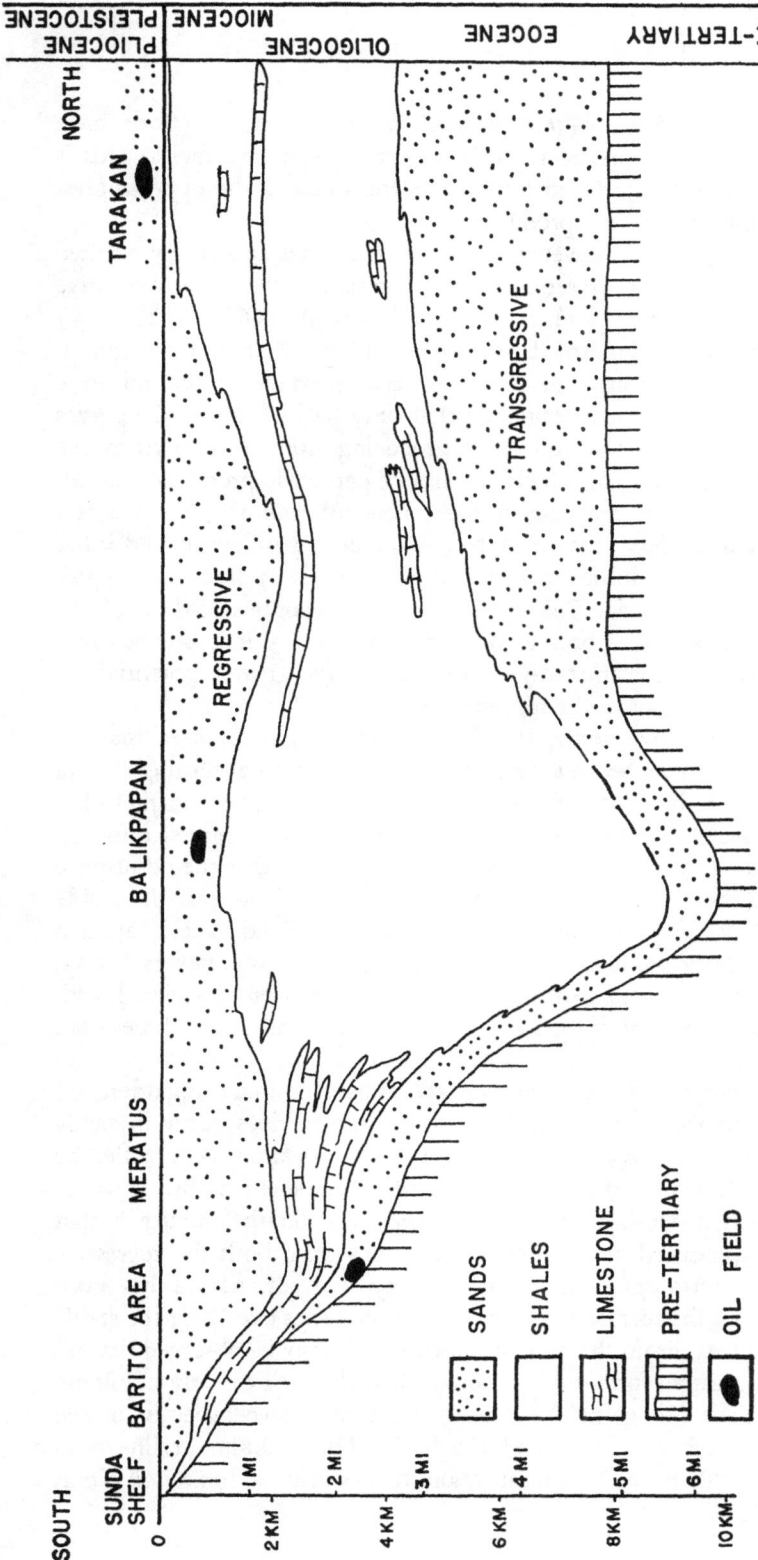

FIGURE 7:5

HYPOTHETICAL STRATIGRAPHIC SECTION OF EAST KALIMANTAN BASINAL AREA
(AFTER WEEDA, 1958)

large oil reserves. Since World War II, most exploration efforts have been directed toward prospects in the lower transgressive facies. This is especially true in Central Sumatra, where the strata in the upper regressive facies appear to be nonproductive.

Exploration of the lower transgressive facies has apparently resulted in discovery of larger oil reserves than are present in the upper regressive facies. The cumulative production figures through 1966 (Table 7:3) show that in South Sumatra the oil fields with production from formations in the lower transgressive facies have produced more oil in a relatively short time (it is estimated that only half of the total reserves have been produced) than oil fields producing from formations in the regressive facies (most of which are almost depleted; production began for most of them at the end of the nineteenth century). In Central Sumatra the transgressive facies is the sole producing sequence, and it has yielded more than 1 billion barrels within a relatively short time (production began in 1950). This is considered to be only one-third of the estimated ultimate total production. From Table 7:3 it is obvious that formations in the lower transgressive facies offer greater potential reserves than formations of the regressive facies.

For comparative study, the South Sumatra basinal area may be taken as a prototype, because more data and opinions concerning the oil occurrence there have been published than for other areas and there has been extensive exploration in both the transgressive and regressive formations. Dufour (1957, p. 175) came to the conclusion that the occurrence of reservoir rock in the transgressive facies in areas close to the stable Sunda shelf is controlled by the hinge belt. The Sunda shelf supplied most of the clastic sediments during the transgression. Wennekers (1958, p. 1348) observed also that some reservoir rocks were associated with basement highs where fringes of reservoir sands and reefal limestones were developed.

It appears that certain generalizations may be made regarding oil occurrences of the basins as follows: (1) that oil does occur in sandy formations of the transgressive facies; (2) its localization is controlled by the hinge belt against the Sunda shelf and by basement highs.

Another generalization broadly accepted in South Sumatra is that oil is never produced in commercial quantities from both the regressive facies and the transgressive at one locality. Further, no oil has been produced from the formations in the regressive facies overlying the stable Sunda shelf area. From the previous discussion it may be observed that oil in the transgressive formations is confined to the area directly adjoining the Sunda shelf (hinge belt), and oil in the regressive facies is located more toward the deeper part of the basin. This is quite in line with Weeks's (1958, p. 21) generalization that within a basin, oil fields show an arrangement related to basin configuration: oil in older formations is closer to the stable shield and oil in younger formations is in the deeper part of the basin. For our comparative study there is only one other truly basinal area in West Indonesia where both transgressive and regressive formations are known to be productive, namely East Kalimantan. Figure 7:5 (after Weeda 1958, pp. 1342–43) clearly shows this arrangement; there is a vertical shift in the reservoir rock facies and subsequent oil accumulation northward toward the deeper part of the basin. In Central Sumatra, oil in the regressive facies is thus far not known to occur, but the position of existing oil fields suggests that here also oil in the transgressive facies occurs at the margin of the Sunda shelf.

Lack of data for other basins prevents further comparative study. Since, however, these basins have similar stratigraphic successions and similar tectonic positions, with some reservation and taking into consideration oil occurrences so far known, we may expect that the generalization made for South Sumatra may have validity for all the basins in West Indonesia.

The observations and conclusions which have been made are of importance in the evaluation of potential oil reserves in West Indonesia.

There are possibilities for additional reserves in the regressive formations because there are many mappable surface and subsurface structures which remain untested. This is especially true for the East Kalimantan basinal areas, and perhaps also for Central Sumatra, where, up to now, the presence of oil in formations in the regressive phase has not been reported.

The authors believe that the great oil potential in western Indonesia Tertiary basins lies in reservoir formations of the transgressive phase, especially in basinal areas where no extensive exploration has been carried out (northwest Sumatra, East Kalimantan, North Java). Currently (1967), there is an exploration program underway in northwestern Java.

In exploring for oil, more consideration should be given to stratigraphic trapping conditions, such as updip pinch-outs toward the stable shelf, buried topographic highs, etc. This will entail more thorough subsurface studies and geophysical investigations.

In the North Sumatra (Atjeh) Basin the transgressive facies has thus far been devoid of oil and only the regressive facies is productive. In order to find oil in the lower transgressive facies one should look more toward the hinge belt at the edge of the Sunda shelf, in this case offshore to the east. The absence of oil in the lower transgressive facies in the Atjeh Basin is concluded from drilling to date only in areas close to the mobile belt (Bukit Barisan Range) in which the oil-producing horizons should indeed be in the upper formations of the regressive facies.

In the East Java Basin the base of the Tertiary has not been reached by the drill, but from comparison of the stratigraphy with other basins it can be inferred that transgressive coarse clastics should have preceded the "base marls." Future oil possibilities are, then, also present in the transgressive phase toward the north in the direction of the Sunda shelf. The updip rise of the formations in this direction should bring them within the reach of the drill. Weeks (1958, p. 28) is of the opinion also that the "base marls" would change facies into clastic formations toward the Sunda shelf.

The same line of argument would apply for the East Kalimantan basinal area, where production has already been established in the lower transgressive formations. This opinion is offered with reservation, however, because the tectonic framework of the area is not yet clearly understood.

It thus appears reasonable to conclude that great potential reserves of petroleum are still available in the Tertiary basins of western Indonesia, especially in the transgressive facies which has not been explored in much of the basinal area.

Figure 7:2 indicates a number of other areas of considerable extent, notably in Sulawesi and West Irian, where sediments occur which are possibly favorable for petroleum prospects. In fact oil has been found in two localities of West Irian, as indicated on the map. Some exploration has been done, but it cannot be said to be sufficiently extensive to evaluate the potential. Much of this possible area lies in the shallow water (less than 50 meters deep) off the coastal margins. Stratigraphic information known to the authors for this area is sufficient to warrant comparison with the basinal analysis attempted for the western portion of the archipelago.

NATURAL GAS

The occurrences of natural gas with petroleum, or in some instances alone but in traps in essentially identical geological circumstances, makes a detailed geologic discussion of this commodity unnecessary. Lack of demand has resulted in little or no effort to date to locate gas reserves. Primary use of that which has been produced in oil operations has been for extraction of gasoline and as a source of power within the oil fields. Reserve figures known for Indonesia unquestionably do not reflect potential production and will not until a market exists. *World Oil* reported proved reserves of 2,000 billion cubic feet, or about .002+ percent of the world total at the end of 1965. These reserve estimates will unquestionably show a sharp increase as the natural gas market expands and produces an incentive for gas discoveries.

COAL

Coal is present in a number of the islands of Indonesia, with major production in the past having come from the island of Sumatra and lesser amounts from mines on the island of Kalimantan. In 1941 total production exceeded 2 million metric tons. Production for recent years has shown a rather steady decline, as evidenced by production figures given in Table 7:1.

The workable coals are all of Tertiary age and are not limited to a single epoch but range from Eocene to Pliocene. They are bituminous to subbituminous in rank and have heating values from 9,000 to 15,000 B.T.U. They are for the most part friable and, due to water content, slake badly when stored for any length of time. Coking tests on Indonesian coals have been unsuccessful. This has contributed to the failure of numerous plans to establish an iron and steel industry in the country.

Currently work is being carried out to increase the coal production from the Bukit Asam coal mine in South Sumatra (*Minerals Yearbook* 1964). The Polish government has provided assistance to modernize and expand this operation. However, 1966 production figures showed a drop over 1965.

Though the proved reserves of coal in Indonesia are small by comparison to many of the producing areas of the world, tonnages are available in currently producing areas which, at production rates many times in excess of current ones, would be sufficient to last for several decades. Though careful estimates have not been made, it appears certain that if lignites and brown coals were included in coal reserves of the country, the total would certainly amount to several billion tons. The future of the coal industry in Indonesia will be governed largely by the uses to which the coal may be put, rather than availability of reserves.

It seems reasonable to expect that, with the increased need for electrical energy if development is to move forward, coal will be in increased demand for steam-generating electric power plants. One can also expect that new uses for coal will be found in the hydrogenation, gasification, gas synthesis, and carbonization processes.

TIN

Indonesia has long been a major producer of tin. This metal ranks as the second most important mineral commodity of the archipelago, following oil. In 1966, production accounted for 6 percent of the total world output. The nation ranked sixth among tin-producing countries of the world. As may be seen from the mineral resources map (Figure 7:1), the production comes from what are commonly referred to as the "tin islands," with Bangka, Billiton, and Singkep as the chief producing areas. Tin has been produced from both primary vein deposits and alluvial concentrations, the latter by far the more important source.

The tin occurrences of the "tin islands" are similar to the deposits of Malaysia, Thailand, and Burma. The primary ore occurs in veins and veinlets within post-Triassic granites, with cassiterite as the tin mineral. These primary occurrences in turn have been concentrated in many instances in residual hill-slope deposits remaining after intense tropical weathering and also as placer deposits in valley bottoms. Quaternary submergence drowned the lower reaches of the river valleys with their tinstone to depths of as much as thirty meters. Many such valleys can be traced out to sea and the tin recovered by sea dredges.

A rough estimate of total production from the inception of mining through 1966 is 1,887,000 metric tons. The writers do not have available reliable figures regarding current total reserve estimates, but at the close of World War II there was an estimated reserve of alluvial tin, obtained from the three main producing islands, of roughly 630,000 metric tons. Production from 1951 through 1964 averaged 25,529 tons per year. Annual production has shown nearly a continuous drop in the period from 1956 through 1966. This does not reflect a decrease of workable ore, but rather the continued deterioration of tin-mining equipment. The year 1964 showed a rather sharp increase in production, resulting from renovation of equipment and technical assistance provided by the Netherlands.

There should be an extensive exploration program carried out on the "tin islands" and their immediate offshore areas. Outside of these three islands there are further possibilities of significant deposits on many of the islands of the Kepulauan Riau. Small reserves are also indicated on Sumatra. There seems little reason to doubt that Indonesia can rank high among the tin-producing areas of the world for a number of decades, and there is no question that immediate production can be greatly increased by improvement in exploitation methods and equipment.

BAUXITE (ALUMINUM)

Bauxite (the only commercial source of aluminum) has been produced in Indonesia since 1935, when 10,000 tons were mined on the island of Binton. By 1940 annual production had reached 275,000 tons, which at that time represented somewhat over 6 percent of world production. Production after the war rose rapidly, so that in 1948 it had reached 400,000 tons. Between 1951 and 1955 the average annual production was 261,000 tons and between 1955 and 1960 the average had increased to 303,000 tons. In more recent years there has been a steady increase, with production reaching 701,255 tons in 1966. In 1965 the government signed a contract with Japan to furnish 1.9 million tons of bauxite to Japanese aluminum refineries over a three-year period.

S. H. Patterson (Patterson 1963) has calculated the total bauxite reserves for the world at 5,760 million tons and marginal to submarginal resources as 8,740 millions of tons. His estimates for Indonesia were 25 million tons of reserves and 10 million tons of additional marginal to submarginal resources.

Virtually all the Indonesian production has come from the island of Binton, where the ore is aluminous laterite, formed by the intensive weathering of aluminum-rich rocks under humid tropical conditions. It is reasonable to expect that conditions favorable for the development of such laterites have been met in other parts of the archipelago. Particularly favorable areas should be in the "tin islands" and in parts of Kalimantan where very little geological investigation has been carried out.

NICKEL

Commercial deposits of nickel fall into three categories: sulphide ores, nickel silicate ores in iron, and nickeliferous iron ores. The potential ores of Indonesia are of the latter two types. Both are the result of laterites weathering in tropical zones of serpentinized peridotite or other ultrabasic rocks. As may be seen from production figures (Table 7:2), there has been a steady increase in production for the past several years. It has been coming from Mantang and Lemo islands and Pomalaa in southeast Sulawesi. Recent estimates of reserves in the Pomalaa area indicate 40 million tons of ore containing 1.5 to 2.3 percent nickel with .005 percent cobalt (*Minerals Yearbook* 1965). There are also large deposits in the mountainous country in the vicinity of Lake Towuti in central southeastern Sulawesi. These are nickeliferous iron ores which have an iron content averaging 49 percent and an indicated nickel content of around 1 percent. Probably reserves in this region total over one-half billion tons. There are also lateritic nickeliferous iron ores in southeast Kalimantan. Though grades are uncertain, it is likely that large reserves exist in this area.

There are also serpentine and basic igneous rocks occurring in many parts of the little-explored area of West Irian, as well as in other islands of the country, which may lead to further discoveries of valuable nickel reserves. Though the nickel sulphide ores of Canada, which have dominated production from non-Communist countries for years, will probably continue to do so, an expanded market may be expected for Asian ores to be utilized within the region. Current Indonesian production is going to Japan.

GOLD AND SILVER

The production of gold and silver in Indonesia has never been large when compared to world production, but it can be of considerable economic importance in the national development program. Total recorded production of gold between 1900 and 1940 was slightly in excess of 3.25 million troy ounces. Silver production in this same period was approximately 32 million troy ounces. In recent years the only production of gold of significance from an identifiable area has been from the Tjikotak Mine in West Java. This government operation reported production of 6,750 troy ounces of gold in 1965. However, production figures as shown in Table 7:1 represent government output only, and private production by small unorganized producers may be as much as 30,000 troy ounces per year (*Minerals Yearbook* 1965).

The mineral map (Figure 7:1) shows a number of known occurrences of both placer and primary gold and silver ores in most of the larger islands of the archipelago. However, known occurrences which have yielded significant production have been limited to Sumatra and West Java. The numerous localities where mineralization is known to occur can only be taken as an encouraging sign that there are many localities where careful prospecting is likely to uncover new sources of these elements. There is also a possibility that considerable gold production may be realized as a byproduct of offshore tin dredging operations.

The greater part of the Barisan Mountains of Sumatra has not been explored in detail. Large areas of western and southern Kalimantan should be subjected to detailed exploration. Central Sulawesi is an almost unknown region regarding mineralization. The important gold district of Bulolo in eastern New Guinea indicates that the western part of the island has potential.

An agreement was signed in 1964 with Dutch interests, allowing resumption of gold mining in the Meulaboh area of North Sumatra where operations were forced to close many years ago (*Mineral Yearbook* 1964, p. 1185).

COPPER

As may be seen from the mineral-resources location map (Figure 7:1), there are numerous occurrences of copper mineralization on the various islands. None to date has proven to be of major significance. However, it is difficult to imagine that, with the wide distribution of copper occurrences, there is not some economically significant deposit within the region. Yugoslavian surveys in the Sankoropi area of South Sulawesi indicate minable ore which may soon be developed. In 1967 an

American company was engaged in a sizable exploration program for copper in West Irian, where several (though not proven commercial) occurrences are known.

LEAD AND ZINC

These two elements so frequently occur together and under the same geological conditions that they are treated here under a single heading.

The islands of Indonesia have never produced these metals in quantities of any significance. Inspection of the resources map (Figure 7:1) indicates that there are many localities where lead- and zinc-bearing minerals (principally galena and sphalerite) are known to occur, but the deposits have thus far proven to be small and unfavorably located with respect to transportation. The important world sources are from relatively low-grade large deposits which lend themselves to massive mining operations. Currently known mineral information about the area indicates that, should there be any appreciable increase in the recovery of these metals, it will be as a byproduct of other mining activities, such as for gold, silver, and possibly copper.

MANGANESE

Manganese ore production in Indonesia dates back as far as 1918, but it has not been large. Known deposits have proven to be small. The manganese occurrences are formed from secondary concentration of sediments or volcanics which have been acted upon by groundwater. Being small, the deposits are difficult to prospect. Production data shown in Table 7:1 shows a marked drop in the 1964 and 1965 production over previous years, resulting from the fact that only one of the four producing mines of the country was in operation in 1964 and labor difficulties were encountered. Though new production may result from future mineral exploration programs, there is little geological basis for expecting a sharp increase in manganese recovery.

SULPHUR

All the known sulphur deposits of Indonesia are associated with volcanic activity and are the product of sulphataric action in craters or on the slopes of volcanoes. Production has never been large and known reserves are small. It appears unlikely that deposits will yield sufficient amounts to compete in the world market, but steps need to be taken to produce as much as possible for domestic consumption, since the sulphur-consuming industries are now forced to rely almost entirely upon imports.

MISCELLANEOUS MINERAL SUBSTANCES

There are several mineral substances which are currently being produced in limited quantities or have had some past production history. Among these are phosphate rock, iodine, kaolin, clay, pumice, asbestos, asphalt rock, salt, cement, soda ash, limestone, and various other rocks for building stone and aggregate purposes. Several of these will undoubtedly play an important role in the total economic development program. An expanded exploration and exploitation effort is a necessity if these mineral resources are to contribute significantly, as they must, in the nation's development. Such an effort is likely also to uncover some substances which currently have no known occurrence in the islands.

This general appraisal of mineral wealth indicates that increased production is reasonably assured for a number of minerals and that for several of them it probably can be accomplished in a short length of time. These include petroleum, natural gas, tin, and nickel. The possibilities of new discoveries with an expanded exploration and exploitation program and the potential inherent in an advancing technology may well assure the replenishment of some depleting reserves. Structures, roads, and machines are built largely from mineral products, and the energy to power the machines is obtained from minerals. Mineral supply outlook must be a major national concern if a sound and prosperous economy is to be developed.

SELECTED REFERENCES

Beltz, E. W. 1944. Principal sedimentary basins in the East Indies. *Am. Assoc. Petroleum Geologists Bull.,* Vol. 28, no. 18:1440–54.

Brouwer, H. A. 1926. Oil provinces in the Netherlands East Indies. Pan-Pacific Sci. Cong. 2d, Melbourne and Sydney, 1923, *Proc.* 1: 1280–84.

Dalton, Howard W., and Humphrey, William E. 1966. *Am. Assoc. Petroleum Geologists Bull.,* Vol. 50:1775–77.

De Sitter, L. U. 1941. Facies analyse. *Geologie en Mijnbouw,* no. 8:225–37.

Dufour, J. 1957. On regional migration and alteration of petroleum in South Sumatra. *Geologie en Mijnbouw* (Nieuwe Serie), Vol. 19:172–81.

Economic Commission for Asia and the Far East. 1962. Oil and natural gas map of the Far East. Lake Success, N.Y., United Nations Publications.

Habitat of Oil, a symposium. Am. Assoc. Petroleum Geologists. Tulsa, Okla., 1958.

Ismet. 1962. Explorasi minjak di Indonesia. Madjalah Ikatan Ahli Geologi Indonesia (Bandung, Indonesia). Vol. 1, no. 1: 21–28.

Kaufmann, G. F. 1951. The tectonic framework of the Far East and the influence on the origin and accumulation of petroleum. World Petroleum Cong. 3d, The Hague, 1951, *Proc.*, 1:87–118.

Mallory, W. W. 1963. Analysis of petroleum potential through regional geologic systems. *Am. Assoc. Petroleum Geologists Bull.*, Vol. 47, no. 5:757–76.

Minerals Yearbook, 1964, Vol. 4. U.S. Bureau of Mines, U.S. Govt. Printing Office, 1965.

Patterson, S. H. Article 41 in U.S. Geological Survey Prof. Paper 475–B. P. B. 158–B. 159, U.S. Govt. Printing Office, 1963.

Schaub, H. P., and Jackson, A. 1958. The northwestern oil basin of Borneo. In *Habitat of Oil,* a symposium. Am. Assoc. Petroleum Geologists, pp. 1330–36.

Schuppli, H. M. 1946. Geology of oil basins of the East Indian archipelago. *Am. Assoc. Petroleum Geologists Bull.,* Vol. 30:1–22.

Sigit, S. 1958. Oil map of Indonesia. Bandung, Indonesia, Direktorat Geologi Republik Indonesia.

Umbgrove, J. H. F. 1933. Verschillende typen van Tertiare geosynclinalen in de Indischen Archippel. *Leidsche Geol. Mededeel.,* deel 6:33–43.

Van Bemmelen, R. W. 1949. *The geology of Indonesia.* The Hague: Martinus Nijhoff. Vols. 1a, 1b, 2.

Von Steiger, H. G. 1922. Resultaten van geologisch-mijnbouwkundige verkenningen in een gedeelte van Midden Sumatra. *Jaarb. Mijnw.* 1920, Verh. 1:180–86.

Weeda, J. 1958. Oil basin of East Java. In *Habitat of Oil,* a symposium. Am. Assoc. Petroleum Geologists, pp. 1359–65.

———. 1958. Oil basin of East Borneo. In *Habitat of Oil,* a symposium. Am. Assoc. Petroleum Geologists, pp. 1337–46.

Weeks, L. G. 1958. Habitat of oil and some factors that control it. In *Habitat of Oil,* a symposium. Am. Assoc. Petroleum Geologists, pp. 1–61.

Wennekers, J. H. L. 1958. South Sumatra basinal area. In *Habitat of Oil,* a symposium. Am. Assoc. Petroleum Geologists, pp. 1347–58.

World Oil, Vol. 163, No. 3, 1966. Houston, Tex.: Gulf Publishing Co.

World Oil, Vol. 164, No. 3, 1967. Houston, Tex.: Gulf Publishing Co.

World Petroleum Report, 1967. New York: Mona Palmer Publishing Co.

Zwierzycki, J. 1922. Geologische overzichtskaart van Ned. O. Ind. Archippel–Toelichting by blad VII. *Jaarb. Mijnw.* 1919, Verh. 1:72–129, 230–49.

Part III Man and His Determination: Human Capital

CHAPTER 8

Catharine S. Rose and Paul György **Malnutrition in Children in Indonesia**

It is no mere sentimentality to think of bright and healthy children as one of the finest natural resources of any country. These, in the long run, are the beneficiaries and guardians of our technology, and their optimum upbringing, even in terms of national development, is a matter of proper concern.

In Indonesia, as in most underdeveloped countries, the nutritional situation is poor. Corrective efforts have not kept up with the problems of rising population. Some benefits have been obtained through small and large projects of the national government and with foreign assistance, but the accomplishment has often fallen short of what was hoped, and the benefits, if any, were only temporary. Unfortunately, one must attack on many fronts at once. Improvement in nutrition will come only as one phase of a program that includes increased agricultural production, better water supply, development of home industries, and all the other ingredients of successful rural reconstruction. Not least, the rapid rise in population must be checked or, work as hard as we can, we may find ourselves drifting backwards rather than moving ahead.

Good nutrition requires the right foods, and understanding of what is proper nourishment. It is useless to tell people they should eat eggs if they have no money to buy them or, if they have a few chickens, must sell eggs to obtain the rice which they need even more. An all too common attitude toward nutrition is one of *laissez faire:* that teaching nutrition is unnecessary or foolish; that people, given enough food (or money), will be well nourished. This is, of course, a fallacy. Many traditional food habits do not provide proper nutrition. People of relatively good income in Indonesia are not all well nourished, and children, particularly, are not given proper food. Many do not realize the need for higher protein and protective foods, and, even if they can afford eggs, fish, or other foods, do not use them in sufficient quantity.

Most acute is the problem of the preschool child. This age group, which represents the future of the country, is most vulnerable. Damage during these critical years may prevent full development both of physical and mental potential. Whether, or at what ages, this damage may be irreversible is still obscure.

Nutrition and Growth of Preschool Children

For the first few months of its life, the infant is breast-fed and well nourished, at the expense of the mother if necessary. When the mother's milk is no longer sufficient, the food supplements are liable to be starch gruels, insufficient in amount and even more inadequate in protein. The infant which starts its life at a size equal or almost equal to that of western children soon drops off in both height and weight. We all have a mental picture of the malnourished child: drawn old-looking face, thin and wizened. This is the extreme case; the starved child is very rarely seen. If you, as a foreign visitor, come to an Indonesian village, the children who crowd to look at you appear healthy enough, and most of them seem not too thin. It is only when you ask the age that you realize that you were underestimating by two or more years. The term "nutritional dwarfs" has been applied to these children. They, not the children with kwashiorkor, are the typical undernourished children.

Figure 8:1 shows the median height and the third and ninety-seventh percentiles, which enclose an area including all but the tallest 3 percent and shortest 3 percent of a group of boys studied at the University of Iowa. These are commonly used as an "American Standard." The lower line is the average height of Djakarta boys as measured by De Haas and his associates about 1935. These data are generally used as the "Indonesian Standard." The average height is below the third percentile of the American boys. The pattern is similar in underdeveloped countries all over the world. Data from Burma, Jordan, Thailand—all agree closely with those from Djakarta. The role of genetics in this picture appears to be minor. We know that the American people have grown taller over the past century. The changes in Japan are far more striking. In Figure 8:1 the points indicating the height of Japanese boys in 1900 fall almost exactly along the line of the Djakarta standard. By 1960 there was an increase of about 5 cm at 6 years and 9 cm at 12 years of age, repairing a deficit of one up to almost two years.

In Figures 8:2 and 8:3 the physique and development of the Indonesian child has been compared with that of the American, utilizing the Wetzel Grid. These charts have been designed to take into account different birth weight and body structure in estimating an acceptable rate of growth. In body build this average Indonesian child is generally within the acceptable limits for the American child. When one looks at the "developmental level" which indicates the rate of growth, the Indonesian children move slowly and at 3 years are the size of the average American child of 18 months. After 5 years of age the developmental line lies along that of the lowest 2 percent of the American children, and the 12-year-old is the size of the average American child of 9½.

Survey of Nutritional State of Javanese Children
Our own height-weight data (Figures 8:4–8:7) were obtained in two areas of Java. In Central Java we had measurements on over 1,000

FIGURE 8:1

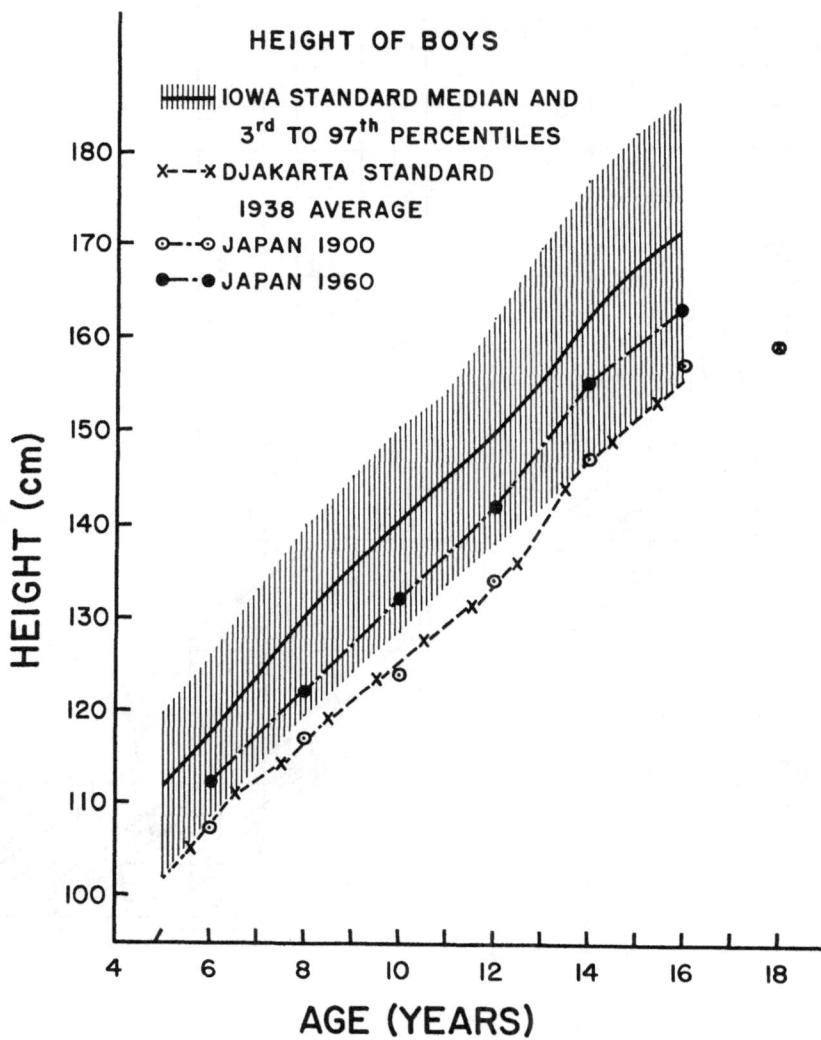

HEIGHT OF BOYS

FIGURE 8:2

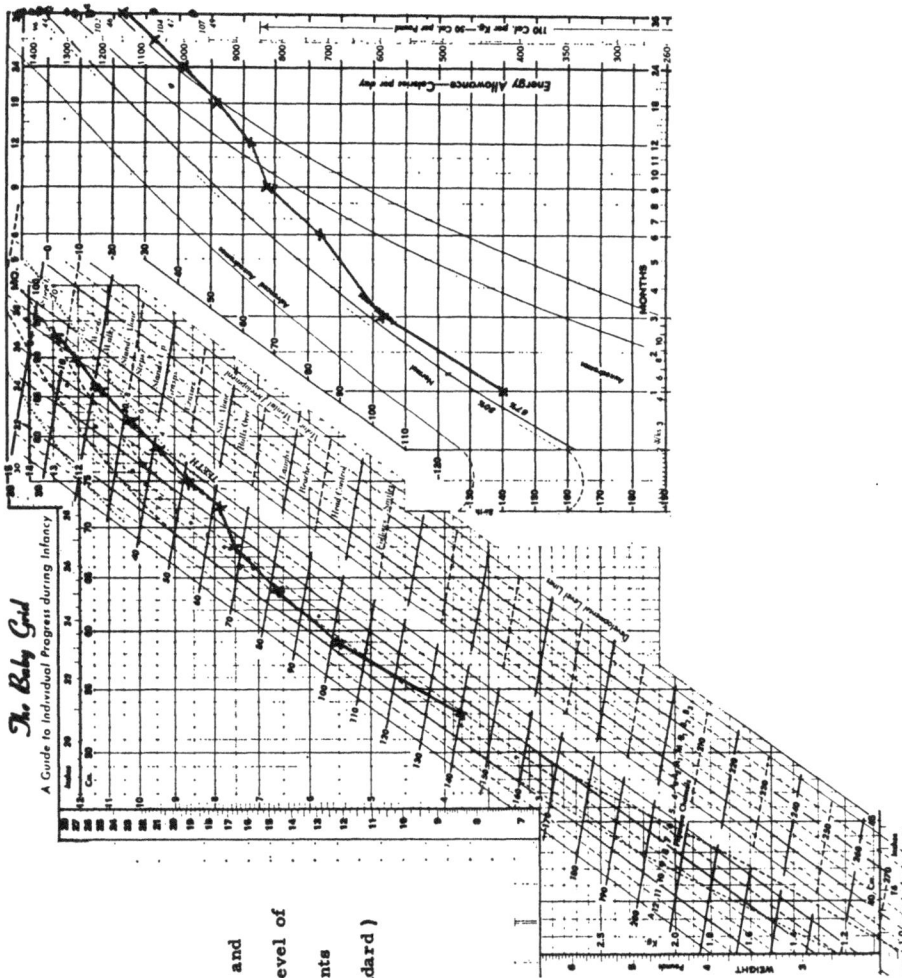

Height, Weight and
Development Level of
Indonesian Infants
(Djakarta Standard)

The Baby God
A Guide to Individual Progress during Infancy

FIGURE 8:3

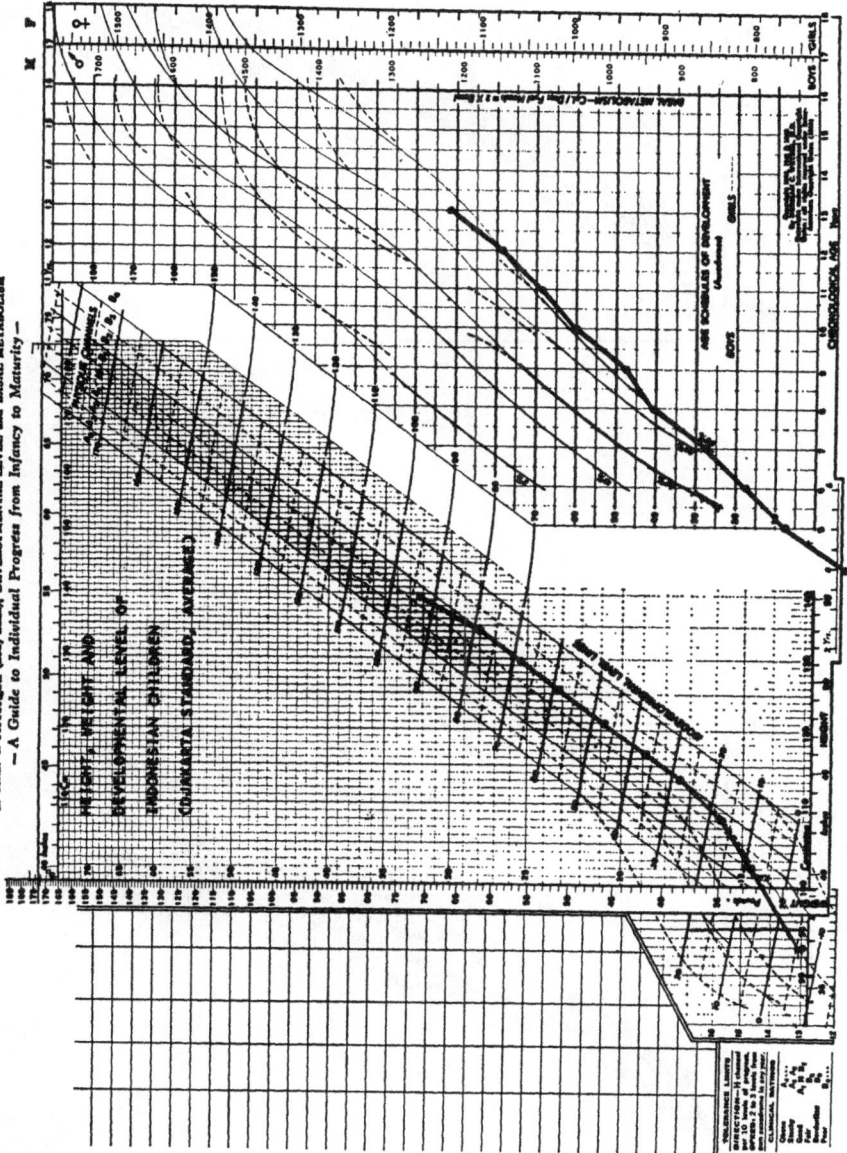

FIGURE 8:4

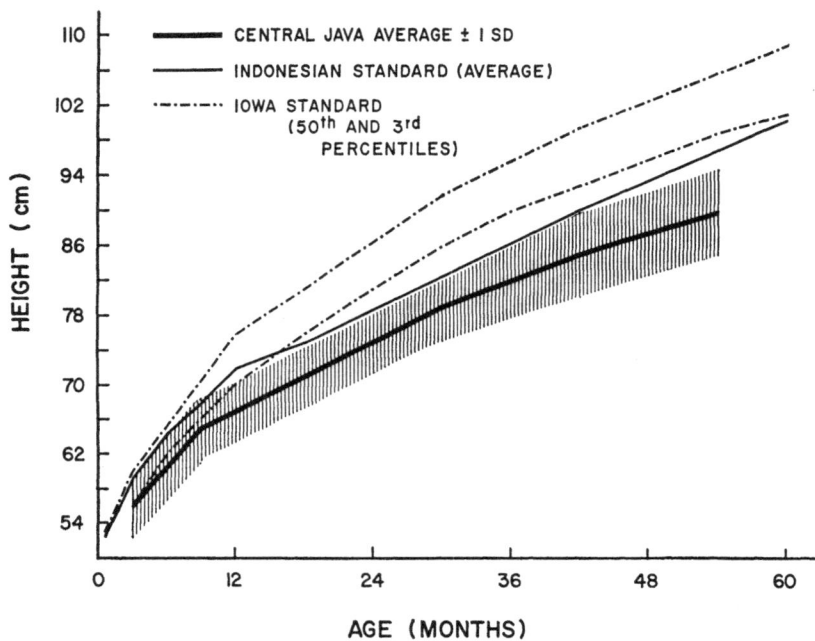

FIGURE 8:5

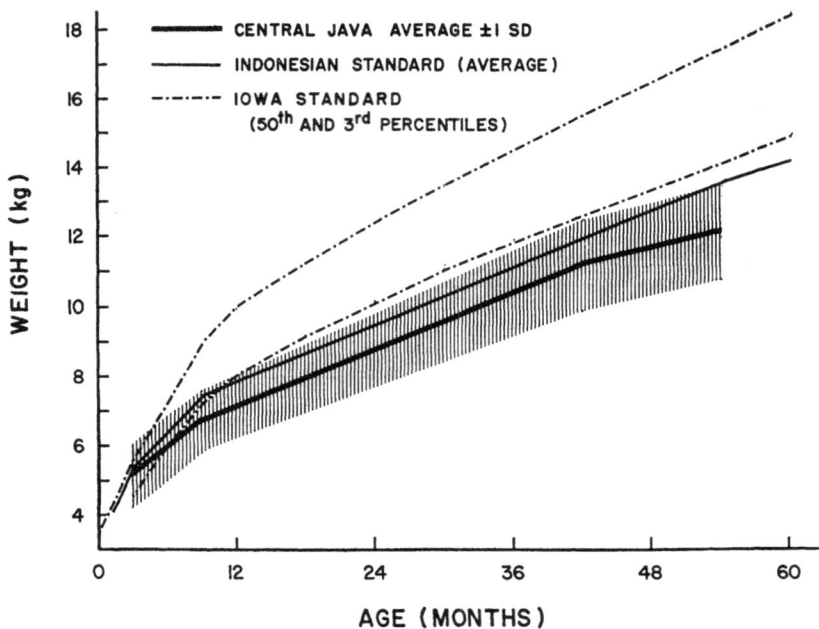

FIGURE 8:6

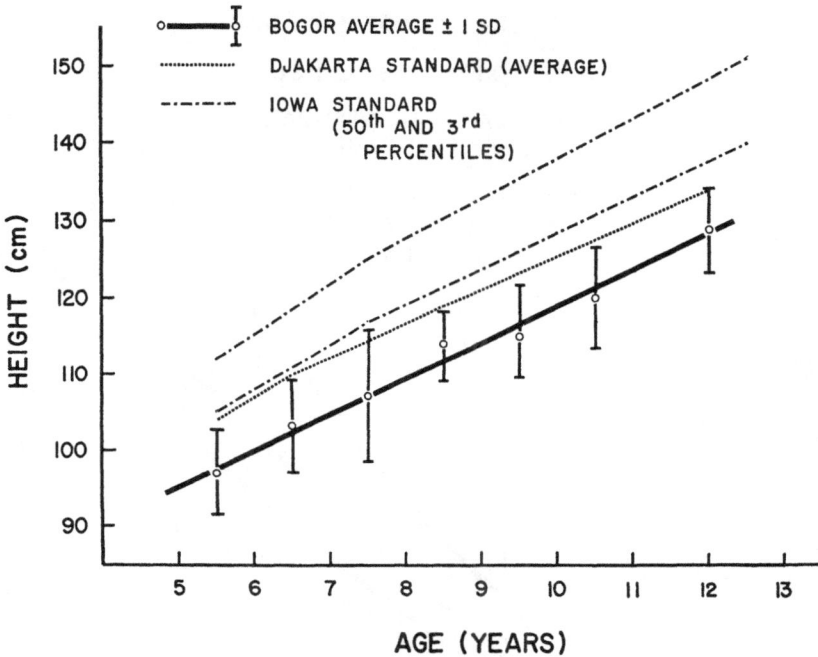

preschool children from five villages near Semarang. In Bogor we studied a smaller group of 5- to 13-year-old children. In both cases we found the same pattern which has been described, but with growth slower than that of the children studied in Djakarta. In Central Java the children were smaller than the Djakarta standard even as infants, and at 5 years were one full year behind in both height and weight (1½ years behind the Iowa third percentile). The Bogor children, from low-income families, were about 1½ to 2 years behind the Iowa third percentile during the 6- to 12-year-old period, or about the size of a group of American children 3 to 8 years old.

The project in Central Java, which was carried out in cooperation with the Nutrition Section of the Department of Health in Central Java and with the help of the United Nations International Children's Emergency Fund (UNICEF), had as its purpose a longitudinal study of the growth and health of preschool children, with concentration on the problem of vitamin A deficiency. The five villages had a total population of about 12,000, of whom 15–21 percent were preschool age children.

We found that the general development of the children, like height and weight, was somewhat retarded in comparison with western values:

FIGURE 8:7

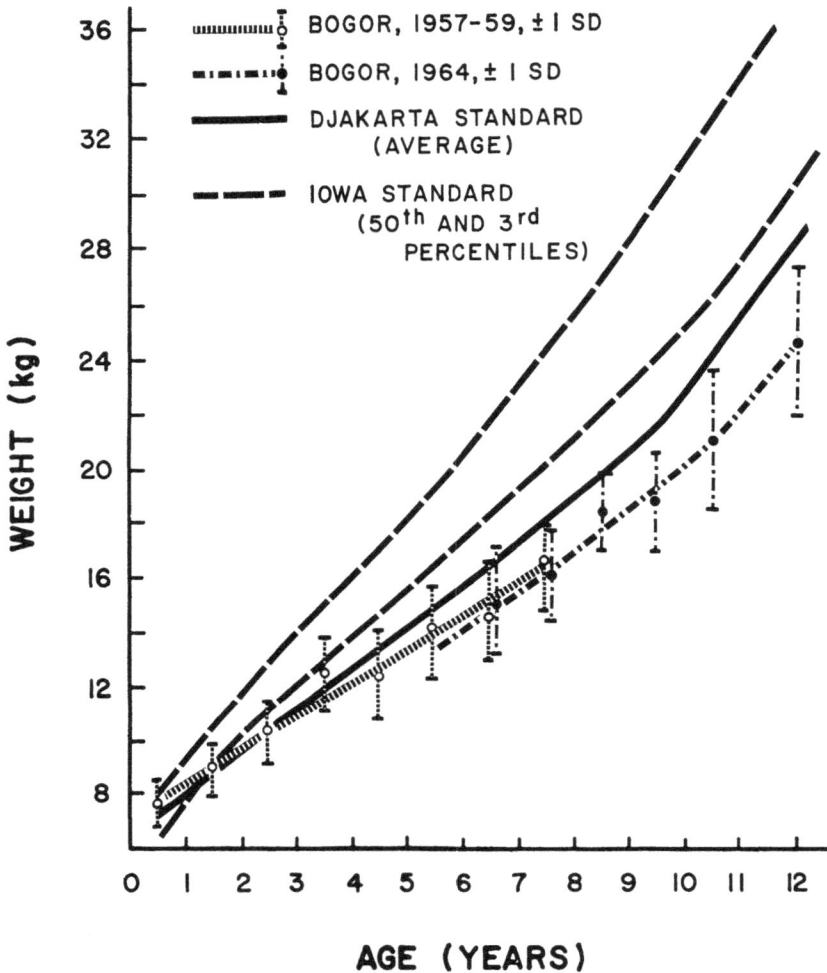

age of sitting unaided, walking, eruption of teeth, etc. Other signs went along with the thesis that these children were not "starving" but were undernourished and "adapted" to some extent to the poor food intake. Serum albumin was a little low, but mostly in the normal range. The same was true for hemoglobin levels. A rather large number of children had enlarged liver, but it was of the mildest degree. Thanks to the malaria program, there was no evidence of malaria in the children of any of the villages and, gratifyingly, very low incidence of tuberculosis as measured by the tuberculin test. As was to be expected, a large proportion of the children had intestinal parasites.

The death rate of the children was high. Our data included only the total number dead in each family, not cause or age of death. In one village, 96 children under one year of age were examined. Seventeen of these were the first child. The other 79 mothers had given birth to 2–10 children, a total of 361. Of these, 87, or 24 percent, had died. In only 3 of 21 families with 6 or more children were all of them living.

Vitamin A deficiency which, in its acute clinical manifestation, causes night blindness and more serious eye damage which frequently results in blindness, is widespread throughout Indonesia. It has been best documented recently by the work of Oey Khoen Lian in Central Java and by Teng Khoen Heng in Bandung. Oey Khoen Lian has stated that the eye disorders related to vitamin A deficiency are the largest single cause of blindness in Central Java. Neither the problem nor recognition of it is new. Both were discussed in prewar literature, and remedies suggested: another example of the gap between what is known and what is done. The most susceptible age is early childhood. The major source of vitamin A in the Indonesian diet is carotene which is the precursor of vitamin A, a "provitamin" which is present in green leaves and yellow fruits and vegetables. Children usually do not consume these in large quantity. Another natural source of the provitamin is red palm oil (RPO), the color of the oil being due to the carotene it contains. Areas of Africa where this is the common cooking oil are free of symptoms of vitamin A deficiency. The oil palm is grown extensively in Sumatra and West Java but not in Central Java. Through UNICEF we obtained RPO which was distributed in two villages as "vitamin medicine" for the 1- to 5-year-old children. The effect of the treatment was studied by the eye team under Dr. Oey Khoen Lian and by biochemical measurement of serum carotene and vitamin A levels. There were two control villages. One of these had been selected by the Ministry of Health nutritionists in Semarang for education in nutrition and homemaking. The children in this village received no supplement. Since the children in the treated villages were receiving 4 ml of oil daily, which with their low food intake might influence nutrition irrespective of its carotene content, children of the second control village were given decarotenized palm oil. Removal of the carotene is the first step in making margarine or soap from the oil.

In the preliminary examinations (Table 8:1) we found every evidence of vitamin A deficiency. Clinical eye symptoms were observed in up to 7 percent of the children in the villages. Almost 75 percent of them had serum vitamin A below the "acceptable" level suggested by the Interdepartmental Committee on Nutrition for National Defense (ICNND), and a very large percentage were in the "deficient" range— with values of the same order as those found in children coming to the eye hospital in Semarang with clinical symptoms of vitamin A deficiency.

Table 8:1 Serum Vitamin A Levels, Central Java

		No. of Cases	Average μg/100 ml[2]	Vitamin A (% of subjects)			Xerophthalmia (% of subjects)
Village				Def.	Low	Accept.[1]	
Gunung Pati	Before	138	14.7 ± 0.61	20	57	23	7.3
(RPO)	After	171	19.4 ± 0.58	12	46	42	2.0
Sugihan	Before	155	14.8 ± 0.48	12	59	29	2.4
(RPO)	After	133	19.7 ± 1.0	8	36	56	3.1
Lemah Ireng		190	17.1 ± 0.51	5	63	32	0.0
("Education")		73	15.7 ± 0.86	16	52	31	1.2
Kedung Pane Decolorized	Before	109	13.0 ± 0.64	31	57	12	3.5
Palm Oil	After	50	13.0 ± 1.44	32	48	20	1.9
Xerophthalmia (Eye Hospital, Semarang)		226	8.8 ± 0.61	68	23	9	

[1] ICNND Classification
[2] Micrograms per 100 milliliters (the equivalent of 1/1000 of a litre).

TABLE 8:2 Serum Vitamin A in Relation to Height and Weight

Height*	Number of Children	Vitamin A	
		Mean (μg/100 ml)	% of Values > 15μg
< 90	64	13.2	35
90–94	201	15.4	54
95–99	310	16.0	55
>99	109	16.6	72
Weight*			
<70	27	12.9	26
70–79	84	14.9	49
80–89	197	15.6	52
90–99	224	16.8	60
>99	152	16.5	60

* Expressed as percent of Djakarta standard.

These low values of vitamin A in serum do not necessarily indicate incipient eye damage, but they do indicate susceptibility, with the possibility of acute symptoms being precipitated by infection or some other stress. We observed also a distinct correlation between the vitamin A nutrition as indicated by the serum vitamin A levels and the height and weight of the children (Table 8:2). In spite of problems in distribution of the

RPO to the village and within the village, there was clear evidence of a beneficial effect in the blood vitamin A figures, in average and in distribution as compared with the control villages (Table 8:1). For political reasons the project had to be discontinued after less than a year and a half. Because of this and the small number of acute clinical cases, clinical improvement was not clearly statistically significant, although the decrease in the number of cases in Gunung Pati was impressive.

The Bogor children were of interest because their nutritional status had been studied earlier, 1957–1959, by Blankhart and his associates at the Academy of Nutrition. There were 113 of these children, from 54 families. The parents were low-income employees of the Agricultural Institute and the Academy of Nutrition. According to the original study, 17 of the children had a history of night blindness between the ages of 2 and 4 years. This was associated in most cases with other signs of vitamin A deficiency and with severe illness and/or malnutrition. Twenty-nine children were listed as malnourished but without clinical signs of vitamin A deficiency, the remainder as healthy. In the first examination the children were rated clinically and food intake was studied. The second study in 1963–1964 included, in addition, biochemical and mental tests, and electroretinography. The mothers were examined by the physician and blood tests were made. It should be remembered that none of the children were "sick." They were brought for examination purely for the purpose of this investigation.

TABLE 8:3 Height and Weight of Bogor School Age Children in Relation to Nutritional Status (expressed as % of Djakarta Standard)

Nutritional Status (1957–1959)	Height	1964	(Number of Subjects)	
	<90	90–94	95–99	>99
Vitamin A Deficient	5	9	3	0
Malnourished	6	14	6	3
Healthy	2	10	20	10
	Weight	1964	(Number of Subjects)	
	<80	80–89	90–99	>99
Vitamin A Deficient	6	9	2	0
Malnourished	9	11	8	1
Healthy	5	17	12	10

Pertinent data are summarized in the tables. Physical stature, clinical score, serum vitamin A and carotene: all are most favorable in the original healthy group, poorest in the group with clinical manifestations

TABLE 8:4 Clinical Condition Related to Early Nutritional Status

Nutritional Status	Vitamin A Deficient	Malnourished	Healthy
Number of Subjects	17	29	44
Clinical Score	3.9	4.5	5.7
Serum Vitamin A	15.5 ± 1.4	18.2 ± 1.2	10.6 ± 0.9
Serum Carotene	.29 ± 3.4	44 ± 3.6	52 ± 4.4
Serum Albumin	3.8 ± 0.11	4.2 ± 0.08	4.2 ± 0.06

of vitamin A deficiency in 1957–1959 (Table 8:3). Vitamin A of the mothers was significantly higher than that of the children (Table 8:4). Serum vitamin A was measured in a small group of children from a higher economic bracket in Bogor. The level was definitely higher; all values could be considered as satisfactory. These children also were slightly above the average height and weight of the Djakarta standard (Table 8:5).

TABLE 8:5 Vitamin A, Mothers and Children

	Vitamin A (μg/100 ml)			
	<10	10–19	20–29	>29
Mothers	1	12	19	15
Children*				
Healthy	0	19	17	4
Malnourished	3	14	11	1
A-deficient	1	12	4	0

* Classification 5 years earlier.
Significance of difference: Vitamin A $<$ 20/Vitamin A $>$ 20
Mothers/all children, p $<$ .005; Healthy children/A-deficient
children, p $<$ .05

The electroretinogram, an electrical potential measured at the surface of the cornea, was studied because there have been indications that it might be used as a criterion of past or present vitamin A deficiency. It was found that in the 5- to 9-year-old group there was a lower response in children with low serum vitamin A (Figure 8:8). This was not true in older children. However, older children with a past history of clinical deficiency gave the low response. This indication of a long-lasting effect of low vitamin A levels was corroborated by the finding of a lower potential in Thai soldiers, whose diet at the time of test was entirely adequate in vitamin A, than in American soldiers in Thailand.

FIGURE 8:8   Electroretinogram of Children 5–9 Years Old

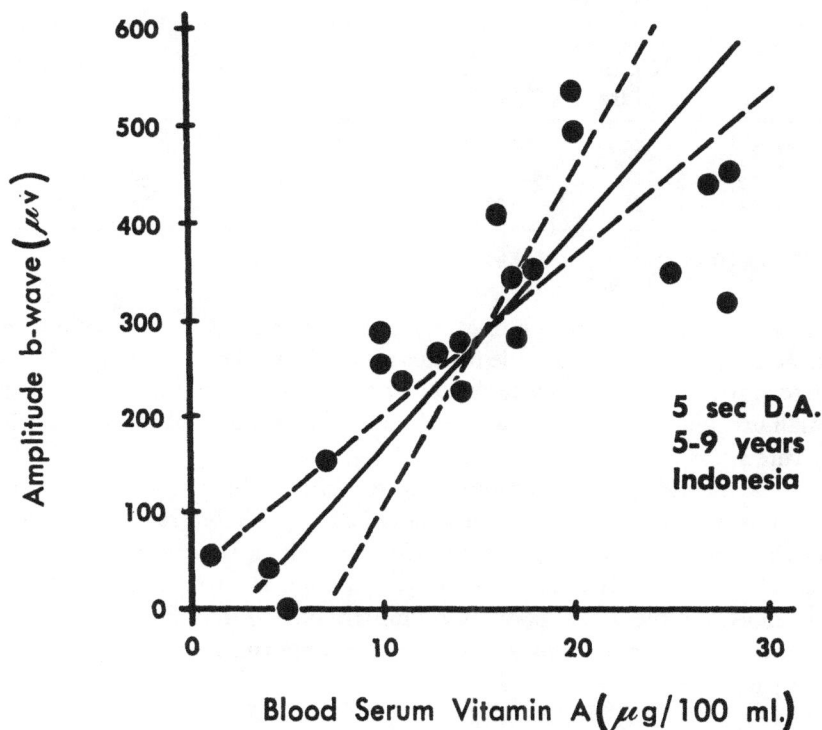

Recently there have been a number of reports of the effects of malnutrition on the development of the brain. It has been claimed that undernutrition in infancy may cause irreversible damage and prevent the child from attaining its full mental potential.

It is well recognized that no test of intelligence is completely independent of the experience and cultural background of the subject. The Goodenough test, which involves only the drawing of a human figure—and with no requirement of artistic merit—is the test which has proved most satisfactory in this respect. The values found for intelligence quotient indicated that nutrition did have a strong influence on the intelligence of the children (Table 8:6). The children who had shown symptoms of vitamin A deficiency were most retarded mentally. The distinction between the malnourished and healthy groups was not as marked. Using present clinical condition or present height and weight as criteria of nutritional status, the same trends were found.

From every angle studied, the children who were vitamin A deficient when first examined were in the poorest condition five years later. It

TABLE 8:6 Stature and Serum Vitamin A of Children of Higher Economic
Level in Bogor

Age	No. of Children	Height	Weight	Serum Vitamin A
		% of Djakarta Standard		$\mu g/100$ ml
1–5	13	105 ± 1.5*	115 ± 4.7	
				22.9 ± 1.8
5–12	16	102 ± 1.0	108 ± 2.1	28.5 ± 2.2

* Standard Error

is not suggested, however, that there is evidence that the vitamin A
deficiency *per se* is responsible for this result. The deficiency symptoms are
frequently precipitated by infection or other illness in conjunction with
malnutrition and indicate that the child has been subjected to particularly
severe stress.

Although the observations seem to indicate that early malnutrition
extends to a later age and the originally healthy children remain continuously in better condition physically and mentally, it is not yet permissible
to relate these differences to early irreparable damage. These children
remained in the same poor environment during the five-year period
between the examinations and had no real opportunity to overcome the
early damage.

Food Intake Studies

We did not attempt a survey of the food intake of the children
studied in Central Java. At the time of the clinical examination the
mother was questioned about what the baby ate, and in spite of vague and
sometimes conflicting answers, certain general conclusions may be drawn.
Additional information was obtained from nutritionists in the area. All
children are breast-fed for at least one year, and a very large percentage
for two years, the proportion decreasing after that time. Supplementary
feeding may be begun after 3–5 months, but not in large amount. The
first semi-solid food is porridge, usually of well-cooked rice. As soon as he
shows a willingness to hold it, the child may be given a piece of boiled or
fried cassava. In some cases this may be the only supplement. Only after
one year are such foods as beans, eggs, or fish added to the porridge or
rice, and the amounts even then are small. Young children 1–2 years old
most frequently receive *tempe* or *tahu,* preparations from soy beans. Fish
is given for the most part as dried, salted fish for the taste of the salt only.
Eggs and meat are almost never given, or at most once or twice a month,
because of the expense. It is not generally considered that children need
fat. Except occasionally, milk is not available for very poorly nourished

children. Vegetables and fruits (except banana) are not part of the traditional food pattern for infants. It may be of significance that the questionnaire drawn up by the Indonesian physicians for our study requested detailed information about milk, beans, and other protein sources but did not ask about fruits or green vegetables.

TABLE 8:7 I.Q. of School Children (Bogor) Related to Nutritional Status

		No. of Children	Intelligence Average	Quotient % of Values above 80
Clinical Evaluation, 1958				
Vitamin A Deficient		12	63 4.1*	9
Malnourished		19	77 4.0	31
Healthy		33	82 2.7	55
			(p < .01)	(p < .02)
Height, 1964 % of Djakarta	<95	31	72 ± 3.0	24
Standard:	95+	34	84 ± 2.9	55
			(p < .01)	(p < .05)
Weight, 1964 % of Djakarta	<95	47	73 ± 2.0	33
Standard:	95+	18	85 ± 4.8	59
			(p < .05)	(p ± .05)

* Standard Error

In the Bogor study a complete dietary survey was made in each home. A student recorded the food intake of the children and their mothers over a five-day period (Table 8:7). It was apparent that most of the children had a low food intake and there was deficiency of protein, particularly of animal protein. The amount of food consumed did not increase with increasing age of the child nor was there any difference in intake between those classified as healthy or malnourished, in either the first or second examination. The average intake was 1,110 calories per day, with about 85 percent of the total furnished by rice. Vitamin A intake was very low. Most of it was supplied by green vegetables, with small amounts of maize, sweet potatoes, or fruit. Intakes ranged from almost 0 to 4,900 units per day, with a mean value of 695 units. The median was even lower, 445 units.

We did not measure the food intake of the fathers. On the basis of the data of others, it was probably considerably higher than that of the rest of the family. As far as the mother and children were concerned, food seemed to be rather evenly divided. Calorie and protein intakes of the mothers were only a little higher than those of the children (and grossly inadequate considering that many of them were pregnant or lactating or both). Only with respect to vitamin A was the situation different, the intake of the mothers being about three times that of the children. The child had his full quota of rice and fish, but his portion of cooked green vegetables was apt to be smaller, and the salad of raw cassava or papaja leaves he frequently rejected altogether. Twenty mothers had an entirely adequate intake of over 2,000 units per day, with an average of 4,400. The average for their children was 1,100 with only seven having more than 2,000 units. In a dietary survey in Pelabuanratu it was observed that for the most part the children 2–5 ate the same food as the mother. The only category where there was a marked difference was "green leafy vegetables": two-thirds of the mothers ate greens, one-third of the children.

The nutritional condition observed in the small segment of the population studied is representative of the largest part of the Indonesian population. The villages we saw were typical, possibly somewhat above average, since for the purposes of our project it was necessary to have good village records and an efficient local administration. All the villages were on or near a paved road. Several raised vegetables or fruit for the city market or had local industry with goods for sale; one was a suburb of Semarang, with many of the men employed in the city.

PROPOSALS FOR IMPROVEMENT OF NUTRITION

Nutrition of Adults
For adults the remedy, in simplest terms, is more food. The caloric intake of the women in Bogor was very little above the basal metabolic requirement calculated for their height and weight. (See Table 8:8.) (Even allowing for rather large errors in estimation of intake and for "adaptation," physiological and social, to chronic low food intake, calculations of this sort are very discouraging.) Eating 50 percent more of the same food would give a fairly adequate diet, although obviously capable of improvement.

Increasing the available food without depending on imports will require more extensive utilization of crops other than rice, if possible those with higher protein content than rice (certainly not cassava!). This can be accomplished more rapidly than increase in available animal foods. In this category, fish, both ocean and fresh water, appears to be the most promising approach.

Nutrition in Indonesia will continue to be based on rice. It almost seems that the words *food* and *rice* are synonymous. It is nice to have something to go with the rice, and other things make very good snacks but they are of relatively little importance. The idea of a single basic food is deeply ingrained. A frequent question is "What is your basic food in America?" Actually rice is a very good food. A man may consume 75 to 80 percent of his calories in rice and be well nourished if the rest of the diet is chosen with some judgment. The problem is the emotional attitude toward rice, the feeling that nothing can substitute for it, and that if there is a shortage and the price is high you subsist on too little rice rather than eat something else. This could be seen when the effort to popularize maize was initiated. People just did not want to use it, even when the price was less than half that of rice. On the other hand, steamed or roasted ears of ripe corn were a popular snack, and in some parts of Java maize has been the staple food for many years.

TABLE 8:8 Food Intake Study—Bogor

	Age	Calo-ries	Protein Total/Animal (g)	Fat (g)	Ca (mg)	Vit. A IU
Children (1964)	5–12	1110	29/5.0	12	190	695
Mothers (1964)		1190	32/5.5	13		2200
Children (1957–1959)						
Healthy	2–4	950	25/*			1625
A-deficient +						
malnourished	2–4	845	25/*			935
FAO	1–3	900	26/16	27	540	1000
(Recommenda-						
tion for trop-	4–6	1200	34/20	34	540	1400
ical area)	7–9	1500	40/24	40	540	1800

* Not known.

Corn should provide a valuable second staple in Indonesia, allowing a second crop per year or higher yield per acre than rice in some areas. In Indonesia in 1964, the corn year, one could see some of the problems of introducing a new food. The agricultural groundwork had been laid, suitable seed had been distributed, and corn could be seen growing throughout central and eastern Java. To the North American, corn suggests cornmeal mush, scrapple, cornbread, and hominy. Indonesians are not used to the texture of the mush; in general they do not have ovens and are not bread-eaters. When the government worker received corn as part of his food ration it was in the form of *beras djagung,* which is coarsely ground to resemble rice. But this *beras djagung,* unless it is cooked longer than rice, is apt to be tough or scratchy—and longer cooking takes fuel, which is expensive. It was probably a mistake to make snacks of the corn, as was done in investigating ways in which it could be cooked. That put it in the class of extras, with its chief value as an auxiliary staple. People also became interested in "maizena," which was on the shelves of the shops. One might assume that this was cornmeal; actually it was corn starch, containing no protein and much more expensive than the ordinary cassava carbohydrate. Even those who were working very conscientiously on the project still regarded the corn as a very inferior substitute for rice and had no particular inclination to eat it themselves.

This is not meant to suggest that new ideas cannot be introduced; such innovations do, however, require time, patience, and imagination. Surely, when maize is the chief food in Wonosobo, people in Semarang sixty miles away will learn to use it. When dried milk was first furnished to Indonesia a few years ago, it was hard to persuade people to try it. Now it is in demand. In Bogor the mothers were pleased to receive a package of milk when they brought the children for examination for our project. Consumption of fresh fish is increasing where inland fishponds have been established. In Pelabuanratu, despite old taboos against fresh fish for children, over one-third of the children between one and two years of age were given this food, and almost all of those over two.

Nutrition for Preschool Children

Immediate steps are urgently needed for this group; these steps can be outlined clearly and offer promise of achieving results within a reasonable time.

Fortunately, almost all Indonesian children are breast-fed. Their need comes when they require supplementary food (at about six months). The mothers must be convinced that they need more supplement earlier. Rice porridge is good, but the protein content of rice is only 7 percent, and it can hardly be consumed by a small child in sufficient quantity to give him as much protein as he needs. Beans are much higher in protein. Soybeans have the best protein in quality and quantity (five times as much as rice on an equicaloric basis). It would not require much change in food purchase or preparation for the mother to increase several-fold the amount of beans in the *sajur*[1] and to be sure that a generous quantity of them was mashed with the baby's rice. *Tempe* (fermented soya) is served frequently but not to the baby. The same is true of greens. A mother who is already giving fresh fish to her older children would not be averse to giving it to the baby under one year if the value was explained to her. Sweet potatoes are acceptable and could be recommended instead of cassava for the infant's snack. Papaja could be upgraded. Very few villagers eat it except unripe as a vegetable. These suggestions have in common the use of readily available foods, fairly cheap and not requiring elaborate preparation.

The nutritionists who visit the village have recently applied the same principle in the villages. They limit their "nutrition education" to a very simple (and lively) demonstration of the preparation of *nasi tim*[1] as a food for children. To the rice was added any protein food locally available (and it was explained that any one of several would be suitable) and some greens (in this case also, ones known to be most used in that village). For the youngest infants the mixture was mashed to a gruel, for the older, left as a thick porridge. It is pointless to talk to village women about grams of protein or international units of vitamin A, but they certainly can understand that beans, fish, meat, or egg help make the baby strong and that all sorts of green leaves and yellow foods like sweet potato, carrots, papaja (or RPO) will keep him from being night-blind.

Steps for Implementation of Plans for Improved Nutrition

For success in changing or improving conditions in nutrition or any other aspect of the life of a country, there must be active participation of the national government, recognition of the needs, and earnest and enthusiastic guidance and support—a "sky" view. There must be appraisals of present conditions (nutrition surveys, etc.) and similar followup studies for evaluation of the effectiveness of programs undertaken. Neither of these answers the question of how to promote and maintain progress and interest at the community or individual level. They do not have the "land" view.

Maternal Child Health Centers have expanded rapidly in number but they see chiefly sick children. In three of our villages, 50 percent of the children under one year of age, and in the other two villages, 90 percent, had never been to a Health Center. Only about one-half of those who had attended the Center had maintained what could be considered as adequate contact. The number who maintained any contact after one year was even smaller: 1–10 percent. These were the figures reported. One suspects that the actual number may be even smaller. At a meeting attended by 100 women in Gunung Pati where the MCH Center happened to be in the village, not one had ever taken her child to it. In many cases the Center is several kilometers from the village, and it is understandable that a mother would take her child only if he was obviously ill. The staff members of the Health Centers work very hard and can hardly be expected to take over the whole problem of nutrition in their area.

Nutrition education has reached only a limited audience. The visit of the mobile kitchen would be an event and would attract a good crowd, but it was a one-time occurrence, many would be unable to attend, and with no followup many originally interested would drift back into the old habits. A nutrition education program tried out in Lemah Ireng drew only a small number to the weekly meetings, about fifteen to twenty women at most. Some of the projects—planting of trees, design of a better stove—did reach others beyond the participating group. The seminars held in different sections for special groups such as agricultural leaders, local midwives, teachers, and LSD[2] members were probably more effective, but were still one step removed for the villagers themselves.

It is not enough that people be told, or even shown, what it is good for them to do. There must be continuing encouragement and help. Only in this way can they be conditioned to new ways. Someone vitally interested in furnishing this encouragement and help must live with them in their villages. The need for this type of person can best be satisfied by national and international volunteers. Dedicated and intelligent, they may take the lead in specific projects and be active in all aspects of village life.

It is planned to institute programs for improvement of nutrition in Indonesian villages, not as isolated projects but as part of a multiphase approach to rural rehabilitation. At first, food supplements from outside sources will be used, but they will not be regarded, or presented, as an ultimate solution. Increased production will be encouraged, so that local products will be available and people can take pride in no longer being dependent on donated materials.

The volunteers are an integral part of this program. Their connection with the food supplementation program will serve as an introduction in the village. They need not, and should not, be experts, but they should be intelligent, active young people whose enthusiasm can promote progress in many fields. They can introduce new ideas and can help in the realization of ideas of the residents by asking the right technicians for advice and assistance for a home industry or new agricultural venture. A successful program in one village will be talked about and lead to similar attempts in neighboring communities.

It is only by this grassroots approach, with active participation of the community, that progress will come. Indonesia, with its strong social structure and tradition of *gotong rojong* (mutual aid) is a promising field for this type of program.

REFERENCES

Most of the data reported are from a series of papers published in the *American Journal of Clinical Nutrition* (Vol. 20, No. 12, December 1967).

1. Liem Tjay Tie, Oey Khoen Lian, Thio Wie Liong-Ong, and Rose, C. S. Health, development and nutritional survey of preschool children in Central Java.
2. Oey Khoen Lian, Liem Tjay Tie, Rose, C. S. Prawirenagara. D. D., and György, P. Red palm oil in the prevention of Vitamin A deficiency: A trial on preschool children in Indonesia.
3. Lauw Tjin Giok, Rose, C. S., and György, P. A study of the influence of early malnutrition on some aspects of the health of school age children.
4. Genest, A. A., Djoko Sarwono, and György, P. A preliminary report of the Vitamin A blood serum levels and the electroretinogram in the 5–15 year age group in Indonesia and Thailand.
5. Pek Hien Liang, Tjiook Tiauw Hie, Oey Henk Jan, and Lauw Tjin Giok. Evaluation of mental development in relation to early malnutrition.

Other Reports on Nutrition and Malnutrition.

1. Blankhart, D. M., Tarwotjo, I., and Soetadi. 1960. Measured weaning patterns in Indonesia. Berita Dep. Kesehatan R. I., 9:18.
2. Blankhart, D. M. 1963. Individual food intake of 2–4 year old children in relation to night-blindness and other deficiencies. *Proc.,* VIth International Congress Nutrition, p. 590, Edinburgh.
3. Lauw Tjin Giok, Tartwotjo, I., Djokosaptono, and Rasidi, R. 1962. A study of the nutritional status at two economic levels in Tjiwalen and Amansari villages of West Java. *Proc.,* Sec. Nat. Congress Sciences, Jogjakarta.
4. Lauw Tjin Giok, Tarwotjo, I. Djokosaptono, and Hermana. 1965. A Nutrition study of fisherman families at Pelabuanratu, West Java. *Paediatrica Indonesiana,* 5:556.
5. Mitchell, H. S. 1962. Nutrition in relation to stature. *J. Am. Diet. Assn.* 40:521.
6. Oey Khoen Lian. 1962. Efforts toward preventing blindness in Indonesia. *J. Indon. Med. Assoc.* 12:72.
7. Poorwo Soedarmo. 1964. Food and nutrition policies in Indonesia. *Paediatrica Indonesiana* 4:67.
8. Ramos-Galvan. 1966. *Homeorrhesis as a phenomenon of adaptation to calorie-protein deficiency.* WHO/FAO/UNICEF Protein Advisory Group, Geneva.
9. Teng Khoen Heng. 1964. Ocular fundus changes in hypovitaminosis A. Thesis, University of Djakarta.
10. Tarwotjo, I., and Suhadi Hardjo. 1965. The role of fish in the Indonesian child diet and methods to improve traditional fish processing. *Paediatrica Indonesiana* 5:578.

Standards of Height and Weight

Iowa Standards: Publications from the Institute of Child Behavior and Development, State University of Iowa, Professor H. V. Meredith.

Wetzel, N. C. 1943 and 1946. Assessing the physical stature of children. *J. Pediat.* 22:329, 29:439.

Indonesian Standards

De Haas et al.: Gen Tschr. v. Ned.-Indie 77:3207, 1937.
 Gen. Tschr. v. Ned.-Indie 78:3309, 1938.
 Maandschrift voor Kundergeneeskunde *15*:167, 1947.

Miscellaneous

ICNND. Manual for Nutrition Surveys. 1957. Washington, D.C.: U.S. Government Printing Office.

Calorie Requirements FAO of the United Nations. 1957. FAO: Italy.

[1] *Sajur:* a soup-like vegetable mixture served over rice. *Nasi tim:* a mixed dish with boiled rice.
[2] *Lembaga Sosial Desa:* Village Social Committee.

CHAPTER 9

John S. Wellington   **Medical Science and Technology**

The introduction of Western medicine to Indonesia preceded any local educational efforts by nearly 250 years. During the centuries prior to the coming of the Europeans, Hindu, Arabian, and Chinese medicine had been practiced in various parts of the archipelago, and remnants of all these systems are still to be found today (de Langen 1938). The ships' surgeons on Dutch trading vessels, which began to arrive in Indonesia about 1600, established land-based hospitals for the medical care of sailors, most of whom suffered from scurvy. For the next 300 years, medical care in Indonesia was provided mainly for the Dutch colonists, with Indonesians being left largely to their own devices.

A government medical service was first organized in 1807 by Governor-General Daendels as a part of his plan for extensive renovation and expansion of the army, and this service remained under military direction for more than 100 years.

Medical education for Indonesians began in 1851 with the founding in Djakarta of a medical training course for Javanese boys at the military hospital, entirely under military supervision. The teaching consisted of lectures in the Indonesian language, which the students copied in their notebooks, and of practical work with patients in the hospital and clinic. The training related mainly to vaccination. During the next seventy-five years this school averaged less than eight graduates per year. By 1900, the Doctors Djawa, as the graduates of this school were called, had begun to play a more active role in medical care, but they were not yet on an equal footing with their European colleagues in professional affairs.

In 1913 medical education was revised and expanded. A second medical school was established in Surabaja, and both the new and old schools were made independent of the military service. The length of the medical course was increased to seven years to allow emphasis to be placed on physics, chemistry, botany, biology, Dutch, and German in the first year. Students had six years of primary school and three years of preparatory instruction before starting the medical course. Students of all races were admitted. Construction was begun on the laboratories, classrooms, and the teaching hospital, still in use in Djakarta.

Medical science and technology progressed more rapidly in Indonesia with the worldwide development of the biological and physical sciences and their application to medicine in the latter half of the nineteenth century. Research bearing on tropical medicine and hygiene was carried out in the Central Medical Laboratory in Djakarta, the Pathology Laboratory in Medan, and the Pasteur Institute in Bandung.

With rare exceptions, the staffs of these laboratories, like those of the medical schools, remained Dutch, largely recruited by nomination of Dutch universities.

The fundamental purpose of the two medical schools was to train physicians for the Health Service. After 1913 the graduates were fully licensed for practice in Indonesia, but, without a degree from a Dutch university, they could qualify only for lower-paid positions in the Health Service. After World War I, pressures for the establishment of university education in Indonesia began to mount. Indonesia's first university-level institution for medical education, the *Medische Hoogeschool,* or Medical College, was opened August 16, 1927 (de Waart 1936). Higher education in Indonesia under the Dutch was intended primarily for Dutch students. This is borne out by the composition of the first ten graduating classes from institutions of higher education; between 1924 and 1933, of the 138 graduates, 86 were European, 41 were Indonesian, and 11 were Chinese (van der Wal 1963).

In 1942 the medical schools in Djakarta and Surabaja were closed by the Japanese occupation forces. The former was reopened in 1943 under the Japanese designation *Ika Daigaku* and continued to operate until 1945. Under this administration, most instruction was carried out by Indonesians who had previously functioned at no higher level than that of assistants, and most of the instruction was clinical teaching of students in the final two years of medical school. With the end of the war in 1945, the school was at first entirely in Indonesian hands. A year later, after the return of the Dutch and the start of the Dutch "police action," parts of the school were dispersed, one segment eventually reaching Jogjakarta, where it became the medical faculty of Gadjah Mada University. The Dutch established a "temporary" university in Djakarta; this reverted to Indonesian control in 1950 when the fighting stopped.

Few physicians were trained during the first hundred years of the medical schools in Indonesia. Between 1872 and 1935, the year the last students under the old system graduated, the STOVIA (School for Training Indonesian Physicians) in Djakarta had produced 551 physicians for Indonesia; between 1913 and 1935, the NIAS (Netherlands Indies School for Physicians) in Surabaja had produced 165 physicians, a total of 716 in more than 60 years (de Langen 1949).

From 1955 to 1962, additional medical faculties were established, including those at the following universities: Andalas, in Padang; Hasanuddin, in Makassar; Padjadjaran, in Bandung; Sriwijaya, in Palembang; Diponegoro, in Semarang; Sam Ratulangi, in Manado; and Udayana, in Denpasar (Perguruhan Tinggi 1965). Since 1962, a few more medical schools have opened under state supervision, including one in Malang and a second in Djakarta.

The gravity of the health problem faced by Indonesian physicians is indicated by the following statistics. In 1962 the mortality rate in Indoneisa was 21.4 deaths per 1,000 population. By comparison, in the United States and Europe it was 9 to 10 deaths per 1,000 (*Demographic Year-book* 1966). Infant mortality in Indonesia was about 125 per 1,000 live births, compared with 25 in the United States and 15 per 1,000 live births in Sweden.

The number of registered physicians in Indonesia at the beginning of the period of independence was 1,276; by the end of 1963 this number had reached 2,935 (*Public Health Care* 1964). Thus, approximately 1,650 physicians were graduated in fourteen years, most of them during the last seven or eight years of this period. In 1963 the population of Indonesia was estimated at 101,600,000 inhabitants. Thus there was one physician per 35,000 inhabitants. By comparison, in the United States the ratio was one physician per 780 inhabitants; in Japan, one physician per 930; in India, one physician per 5,000 (World Health Organization 1963).

In 1963 the Department of Health in Indonesia had 1,215 physicians, 2,838 midwives, 21,835 nurses, and 5,664 other health sciences workers in its employ. It operated 3,624 maternal and child health centers, 480 general hospitals (39,184 beds), and seven more central general hospitals (5,882 beds). There were also 27 governmental mental hospitals with 8,090 beds—a ratio of one bed per 12,500 population. (In 1962 the ratio in the United States was 1:260). Including all hospitals—public and private, general and specialty—the total number of hospitals in Indonesia was 930 and the total number of beds was 80,445; thus the ratio was approximately one bed per 1,250 population (Nugroho 1967). The ratio in the United States was 1:114 (*World Almanac* 1966). Calculations based on these statistics indicate five physicians per hospital, with none left over for teaching, research, administration, or service in the 4,700 polyclinics in the rural areas where most of Indonesia's population lives and works (*Public Health Care* 1964).

By virtue of its geographical location, size (both in terms of population and area), level of economic development, and its past and recent social and political history, health planning will assume special importance for Indonesia. Will medical science and technology be oriented mainly toward the same sort of mixture of service, teaching, and research with which we are familiar in the West? Will development follow the lines of disease-oriented research, stressing molecular approaches? Will attention be focused on social aspects of health care as it affects large numbers of people, or on the diagnosis and treatment of disease on an individual-by-individual basis? Just what direction will research take?

These are, in fact, the types of questions which the University of Indonesia asked the Curriculum Committee of the Faculty of Medicine at Djakarta more than a decade ago. Some of the answers were indicated in this committee's report (1960), approved by the faculty and forwarded to the Ministry of Education and Culture in 1955. This was a time when goals and programs which would affect many other Indonesian schools were being developed. The task of the committee was "to formulate a new program for the training of medical doctors which will be more in accordance with the present conditions and needs." The committee considered that the aim of medical education should be "for every school of medicine to graduate each year as many doctors as possible, doctors who are well qualified and who possess the knowledge and aptitude in accord with the needs of society." There was to be no compromise with quality of education, but it was stated that "our society, which is very short of doctors, is confronted with a heavy task of reconstruction and of development also within the field of health, needs doctors who are not only prepared to treat individual patients, but who have the knowledge and consciousness of science and public health measures, to effect the advancement of the health and security of the nation." These answers seem to indicate an intent to educate physicians who will be capable of carrying out rural and community health programs. Carrying out these programs requires that the physician be the key member of a team including medical assistants, nurses, midwives, health educators, nutritionists, sanitarians, and technicians of many sorts.

One of the programs intended to help in achieving these goals began in 1954. This was a cooperative project in medical education between the Faculty of Medicine of the University of Indonesia at Djakarta and the University of California School of Medicine at San Francisco. The project was financed by the United States International Cooperation Administration (ICA), the forerunner of the Agency for International Development (AID) (*Projects* 1966). Under the contract of affiliation, the University of California provided field staff to teach medical and premedical subjects as needed, and administrative support was available when required. Assistance was given in equipping departments for more effective teaching; purchases of books, equipment, and supplies were made with ICA funds, the field staff providing consultation and advice regarding the priorities and selection of these items. Appropriate departments on the San Francisco campus assisted in purchasing and shipping.

The field staff performed two major functions. In many instances they functioned as interim professors, carrying a large share of the departmental teaching and administrative load while their Indonesian successors were completing preparations to take over the job. Second, and probably more important, they advised and participated in the reorganization and development of teaching programs within the individual departments. All field staff members taught medical students and, in so doing, they also taught their Indonesian colleagues, expecially the junior department members.

The Curriculum Committee of the University of Indonesia Faculty of Medicine outlined the broad changes that were to be made in the curriculum. Courses were to be arranged so that first-year courses would provide a better foundation for those offered in the years following. Practical work was to be integrated with theories. Entering students were to be limited in number; criteria for admission were to be based on academic promise. Most important of all was stress on the development of a new philosophy of education, one that would encourage the student to think independently.

The field staff worked with their Indonesian colleagues in developing a more disciplined program for students. Prior to the affiliation, students often repeated courses, with the result that there were many students in attendance, but few graduates. For example: during the period from 1951 to 1954, out of a total of 1,478 first-year students, 289 failed, 971 withdrew, and 218 passed their examinations at the end of the year. If a student failed he could and often did repeat classes for two or three consecutive years.

Under the affiliation program, as part of the new curriculum, examinations were given on a fixed schedule rather than at the time the student determined. The number of students admitted was limited by the faculty and space available. The new criteria for selection of students contributed to a decrease in the rate of failures and the number of repeaters. Greater emphasis on clinical practice and less on theory was introduced at all levels. The number of courses was increased, but the total time for completion of work for the degree in medicine was reduced to six years. A detailed description of the old curriculum and the new one that replaced it was prepared by the University of Indonesia in 1960 (*Report* 1960). In the years of clinical training, greater emphasis was placed on direct observation and participation by the students. Supervised work in the wards and outpatient clinics became an important part of the curriculum. The principles of independent thought and study were fostered.

The project in Djakarta extended over a period of six years, from 1954 to 1960. This permitted the change in the six-year curriculum to be instituted in yearly steps, beginning with the class admitted in 1954. Remodeling of buildings, rearrangement of space, and some badly needed new construction took place during this time. A parallel program operated by AID provided for the selection and placement of advanced postdoctoral students for special training in the United States. The budget and administrative details were assigned by AID to the Education and Training Division of the U.S. Department of Health, Education, and Welfare. Members of the field staff advised and helped the Indonesian faculty to select candidates. The coordinator's office at the University of California San Francisco Medical Center helped to plan the placement of the postdoctoral trainees. A sample of these trainees was studied in 1967, a few years after their return to Indonesia (Wellington 1968). The rate of return to their teaching positions in Indonesia was high. Many of the trainees regarded their training abroad as an important and useful part of their academic background. Of thirty-three trainees interviewed in 1967, five felt that they had used only "a little" of what they had learned abroad; thirteen felt they had used "some," nine "quite a bit," and six "almost everything." The chief difficulty encountered after their return was a shortage of supplies. In addition, these trainees were concerned with the lack of autopsies, and sometimes they faced organizational problems and the resistance of colleagues to their new ideas.

As the time approached for termination of the contract with the University of Indonesia at Djakarta, the Faculty of Medicine of Airlangga University at Surabaja expressed a desire to start a similar program. Late in 1959 a program similar in most respects was begun at Surabaja; curriculum revision began with the class entering in 1961. However, the program was terminated prematurely in 1965 because of mounting instability in Indonesia.

The contribution that these programs made toward meeting Indonesia's immediate manpower needs is shown by the numbers of medical graduates. Between 1950 and 1958, 268 physicians were graduated from the Medical Faculty of the University of Indonesia, an average of 30 each year. Between 1959 and 1962, the first four years during which students from the new curriculum were finishing their medical studies, there were 566 graduates, an average of 141 per year, more than a fourfold increase.

It would be wrong, however, to conclude that this increase in numbers of graduates made an immediate impact on the medical services that could be provided to the people of Indonesia. There are two main reasons why this was not so. First, all the new graduates did not immediately enter the Health Service for assignment to hospitals and clinics. Many graduates were requested to remain at their university for postgraduate medical training in various needed medical specialties. Many who did remain became teachers, some in the expanding medical faculties at Djakarta and Surabaja, now designated as "feeder faculties," and others in the many new medical schools that sprang up in the late 1950s and early 1960s.

The second reason is found in the sheer magnitude of the medical manpower needs of Indonesia. Even as late as 1964 the Ministry of Health employed only 1,323 physicians, whose job was to provide health care for more than 100 million people (Nugroho 1967). The total number of Indonesian physicians at that time was not much larger than 3,000, including medical school teachers and military service physicians. The ratio of physicians to population was thus so low that even doubling the number of physicians would scarcely produce any very striking effect.

In order for Indonesia to make real headway in supplying medical manpower, it was necessary first to expand greatly the facilities for medical education. The growth of primary and secondary education in Indonesia since 1950 had resulted in providing the necessary number of students. Facilities for medical education at university level were required next, and the teachers for these facilities would have to come largely from the graduates of the expanded facilities at Djakarta and Surabaja. Moreover, it is not only physicians who are needed in larger numbers to staff the Health Service. Workers for all the allied health professions must also be trained.

At present, a maternal and child welfare organization is being established in each ketjamatan (subdistrict). The objectives of these organizations include aid in prenatal care and delivery inside or outside a hospital by an expert or a nurse-midwife. They also include care of the health of infants and children to six years of age, with emphasis on nutrition and immunization. Indonesia's 3,000,000 births each year require about 10,000 midwives if each midwife is to attend about 300 births per year. Since 1953, 21 schools have produced 1,720 assistant midwives (*Public Health Care* 1964).

Besides these, how many other health workers must be educated? More than two million provide for the health needs of the inhabitants of the United States, and the number is growing. Within a decade, health may well be the single largest industry in the United States. The Indonesian government has undertaken the responsibility, among others, of providing the basic structure for creating and maintaining a healthy society. Sketched in broad terms, this means providing the organizations and institutions necessary to maintain health, and providing the means of staffing them with suitable personnel at all levels.

In addition to the need for much larger numbers of health profession personnel, there is great need for and opportunity to undertake community health research. Subjects awaiting such investigation might include the following: How do culturally determined attitudes and traditional concepts influence the management of disease? What are the relative strengths and weaknesses of medical assistants, and how can the dangers involved in their development and utilization be avoided? What system of organization can best bring the benefit of modern science to every village and villager? How can health services be ruralized? What are the bottlenecks in providing health care? (Shortage of physicians; inappropriate training or distribution of physicians; shortages of medical assistants, buildings, drugs, equipment; failure to reach the rural consumer of health care with the program offered?)

Closely linked to medical needs are important problems relating to medicine and the other biological sciences. For example, there is the question of providing teachers of the biological sciences. The recruitment, preparation, and utilization of these teachers are of common interest to medicine and all the other biological sciences. Generally, in Indonesian medical schools these teachers are graduates of the Medical Faculty who, after completion of medical training, have added a period of training in one of the basic sciences. Could not some of these teachers be educated more thoroughly and more efficiently within science faculties? The trend elsewhere is toward teachers with Ph.D. rather than M.D. degrees for both premedical and preclinical science courses. Pooling efforts in training teachers for these subjects should be to the advantage of the fields of chemistry, physics, biology, and medicine alike.

A second link involves the relationship of man with his environment. It seems ill advised to consider the ecology of any system without including all the inhabitants of that system. Certainly man must be one of the most intrusive and disruptive, if not the most ubiquitous, forms of life in any ecosystem. Therefore, man would seem to be a proper subject to include in these studies. On the other hand, the study of nonhuman biological systems is basic to the understanding and control of much of human disease. Without fundamental and detailed knowledge of the life pattern of many types of mosquitoes, for example, the control of malaria or filariasis would not be possible. This research clearly must be done in tropical areas. In this instance, basic biological research has led the way to effective control of human disease.

A third link may be found in biomedical research. Fundamental (or pure, or basic science) research, usually of a type that is carried out in a laboratory, is the province of those whose interest lies in either human or nonhuman biology. The processes whereby the chemical substances within the cell nucleus control chemical processes within the cytoplasm are fundamentally of the same interest to all kinds of biologists. While it may not be appropriate or desirable for a developing country to undertake an ambitious program of such research, it is of great importance that some fundamental laboratory research, focused on the needs and conditions in Indonesia, be carried out in that country if the quality of both undergraduate and postgraduate teaching in medicine and biology is to be sustained. The reason for this is stated succinctly by Whitehead: "Do you want your teachers to be imaginative? Then encourage them to research"

(1949). It seems important that there be as wide an understanding as possible of the close connection of fundamental biological research to problems in human health.

REFERENCES

1. de Langen, C. D. 1938. Medical Training in the Netherlands Indies. *Medical Life* 45:23–31.
2. de Waart, A. 1936. *Het Indisch Geneeskundig Onderwijs in de Laatste 25 Jaren.* Geneeskundig Tijdschrift voor Ned.-Indië Feestbundel 1936, pp. 246–57. Batavia: G. Kolff.
3. van der Wal, S. L. 1963. *Education Policy in the Netherlands-Indies 1900–1940.* Groningen: J. B. Walters.
4. de Langen, C. D. 1949. Indonesia Before the War. IV. Medical Tuition in Indonesia. *Doc. Neer. et Ind. de Morbis Trop.* 1:215.
5. *Perguruhan Tinggi di Indonesia.* Djakarta: Departemen Perguruhan Tinggi dan Ilmu Pengetahuan, 1965.
6. United Nations. *Demographic Yearbook.* 1963.
7. *A General Outline of Public Health Care in Indonesia.* Department of Health, Djakarta, 1964.
8. World Health Organization. *World Directory of Medical Schools.* Geneva, 1963.
9. Nugroho. *Indonesian Facts and Figures.* Djakarta, 1967.
10. *The World Almanac and Book of Facts.* Harry Hansen, ed. New York: New York World Telegram and The Sun, 1964.
11. University of Indonesia. *Report on the Development of Medical Education at the School of Medicine.* Djakarta, 1960.
12. *Projects in Medical Education, 1954–1966.* Report of the Accomplishments under the University of California-Airlangga University Contract No. ICAc-1114, June 16, 1966.
13. Whitehead, Alfred North. *The Aims of Education and Other Essays.* New York: New American Library, 1949.
14. Wellington, J. S. 1968. Indonesian Physicians Studying Abroad. *J. Med. Educ.* 43:1183–91.

Ruth A. Boak   **Needs as Seen by a Visiting Professor**

In Indonesia the needs in medical science and technology are similar to those in many other developing countries in the world. Like other countries, Indonesia has gone through a period of accomplishments and mistakes from which it has learned to profit. Indonesia differs from some developing countries in that it has an overpopulation problem and has suffered from revolutions and political instability. Although wealthy in natural resources, Indonesia lacks development and is in need of immediate foreign trade, food, and financial and educational assistance.

From a background of two years in Indonesia as a visiting professor at Airlangga University, School of Medicine, I shall try to summarize some of the needs and difficulties which are encountered in medical care, public health, and medical education, and to suggest some ways to improve the medical sciences and to carry out programs of cooperation.

There are numerous fields in medical science and technology in which visiting professors and technicians may be helpful in Indonesia. In the same fields, Indonesian students would profit by opportunities for additional training abroad, for example, in the United States. Visiting professors can work more effectively if they are closely associated with Indonesian staff members who have returned from foreign study. Although Indonesian colleagues have gained competence in their work abroad, upon return to their positions in Indonesia they may be without the supplies and equipment which they have learned to use. This is likely to result in some discouragement, with the result that the value of the training is not immediately evident. If a well-seasoned visiting professor or technician is at hand for guidance and encouragement, to help find and use local supplies and substitutes, Indonesian staff will be better able to adjust more readily to the facilities at hand.

The selection of candidates for foreign study is very important. If one has drifted along in medical practice and used his university appointment as a means of staying in the city, he may not be in a position to accomplish what is needed after his return. The best-qualified candidate will have demonstrated ability to be a good teacher and will have shown interest in the investigation of some problem in his field. If he is a Medical School graduate, he may be expected to pass the ECFMG examinations before leaving Indonesia. These will evaluate his understanding of English, his general ability, and his medical training. Selection on any other basis will not assure the possibility of the future satisfactory professional service which is the purpose of the additional training provided. Extension for a second year of training should be granted only if satisfactory growth has occurred in the first year.

Professors or technicians who serve as visitors on Indonesia medical faculties are better qualified if they have previously had some satisfactory overseas experience in medical education. This gives them the necessary ability to adjust readily to new and different living conditions, which lack many of the comforts of home, and often require working without familiar equipment and supplies. They need to be familiar with substitute materials, to know what is available in the surrounding area, and to be courageously persevering. They should avoid interpreting their experience overseas as only a vacation. Indonesians are eager to work and learn, and these are qualities for which a visiting professor may and should set a good example.

If unable to adjust to Indonesian living conditions and to the requirements of the job, a visiting professor or technician should not remain longer than the first year. If an appointee is unsatisfactory, his departure would be better for the Indonesian faculty. However, for a visiting professor or technician who distinguishes himself by good work, there should be some bonus or extra incentive, at least in the form of encouragement to remain one or two years more.

In Indonesia there has been much equipment from abroad which was either discarded or not used because of some needed repair. It was practically impossible to find local repairmen with necessary skills or any local funds to encourage someone to determine why the equipment would not function. Sometimes the prevailing thought seemed to be "let's discard it and get a new one." Memory recalls one illustrative experience on this point. A number of new microscopes had been requested because fungus had attacked and reportedly ruined the lenses of those formerly received. Actually, the lenses had not been damaged but only needed cleaning.

A small group of Indonesian technicians with some mechanical aptitude could be sent abroad for study. For example, training would be possible at the U.S. Army–USAF Medical Equipment Maintenance and Repair Center—or at some similar school with a training program in the repair of all kinds of medical equipment. Skilled repair technicians, following special training, might be a nucleus staff for a center in Indonesia, which could, in turn, train repair technicians for other medical schools and hospitals. Technicians with such preparation could salvage a large amount of equipment, and could teach personnel in their schools and hospitals in the care of equipment.

It would be useful to have an inventory of all equipment and its location in each medical school and hospital, with a copy to be retained by the repair department of that school. This would prevent the nonuse in one department of equipment which another department needs. There is much lack of communication between departments within a medical school and hospital and with other institutions. The importance of equipment records is highlighted also by the memory of an occasion on which it was found that supplies which needed refrigeration had deteriorated because during certain political disturbances there had been no electricity for weeks. If complete records and accurate identification of equipment had been at hand, their supplies could have been saved by use of a kerosene refrigerator which was stored nearby but forgotten and overlooked.

There is great demand for medical technicians in Indonesia, and a training center is urgently needed to supply them for hospitals and medical schools. Such a center should, however, be planned to serve as a source of superior, well-trained technicians. A possible location might be at Bandung, where there could be a close relationship with the Bio Farma Institute. Students for such a center could be selected carefully and in terms of long-range plans for their efficient service and adequate pay. It is always discouraging to encounter a department with teachers, technicians, glassware washers, and janitors—all underpaid and all inefficient, absent, or on duty but overly fatigued from trying to supplement their salaries by outside work.

During hard times at Airlangga it was necessary to take contributions from the doctors and visiting professors to have the glassware washed, the laboratory cleaned, and to have the assistance of a technician. There were ample names on the list of these employed for such purposes, but the personnel were really of little help because of their incapacity to serve.

Foreign currency is necessary in Indonesia for the purchase of supplies such as spare parts for equipment, stains, biologicals, drugs, chemicals, media, and equipment which are not available within the country. For the purchase of local products such as alcohol, animals, feed, and various supplies, the medical schools and hospitals need local funds. In the absence of rupiah these local products have sometimes had to be paid for personally by staff members and visiting professors. Laboratory teaching, diagnosis, and research could not otherwise have been continued.

Rodent control is an important problem in the hospitals and medical schools, as well as in the entire country. There is great need for educational programs to eradicate rats and mice. Black rats are numerous in the buildings and destroy many of the supplies in the laboratories. There is the memory that it was practically impossible at times to keep experimental animals in the medical school laboratory because the wild rats ate the food and the animals. There has been a large rodent population for so long in Indonesia that it is taken almost for granted. There is fear of poisoning the rodents because the dense human population might ingest the poison. Rodent eradication efforts might indeed be carried out as a public health education program.

A good school of public health, closely associated with the medical school, would seem to be one of the greatest needs in education in Indonesia. Such a school could be a foundation for a future Institute of Public Health. Close association with the Bio Farma Institute in Bandung would be a great asset, because of its excellent work in supplying vaccines, toxoids, antitoxins, antisera, and antigens for the entire country. In addition, Bio Farma Institute acts as a reference laboratory and carries out many research programs. By locating a School of Public Health in Bandung, where the Medical School and Bio Farma Institute are already established, a great center for research, medical training, and postgraduate training in medicine could some day become a reality.

Several educational programs could be undertaken at such a School of Public Health, and some of them are listed below.

a. *Immunization*—An immunization program for the prevention of smallpox, tetanus, diphtheria, typhoid fever, and cholera is acutely needed in Indonesia. Each year great numbers of preventable deaths occur from these diseases.

b. *Sanitation*—Extensive sanitation and health education programs could be planned and undertaken to provide safe sources of drinking water and appropriate sewage disposal. At present, most Indonesian communities are deficient in these facilities. In a paper presented at the International Conference on Water for Peace, Dr. Richard A. Prindle, Director of the United States Public Health Service Bureau of Disease Prevention and Environmental Control, stated that more than ten million people die every year in the developing countries of the world because of bad water. A reason for neglect of water projects lies in the greater popularity of "more glamorous" projects.

c. *Population Control*—Educational programs in population control are essential in Indonesia, which has such a dense population that it is impossible to produce sufficient food for a good level of living. As medical care, prevention of disease, and sanitary programs are undertaken, the dense-population problem will become even more acute. It is encouraging that open, official support of large-scale family planning projects has been announced by the Indonesian government.

d. *Rodent and Mosquito Control*—The need for rodent control has been mentioned above in its relation to medical education. Rodent control programs are also very important to the health and welfare of the people. Rodents not only spread plague, leptospirosis, and salmonelloses, but they consume tons of food which is badly needed by the human population, and they destroy vast quantities of supplies. Mosquito control is, of course, essential to prevent malaria, dengue fever, and numerous anthropod-borne virus diseases.

e. *Hospital Administration*—Education in hospital administration is another severe need because most of the hospitals are poorly managed. Hospital sanitation is poor, and patients often are not protected from flies and mosquitos. Medical records systems are absent; living facilities and food for residents and interns are rarely available. Supplies are inadequate, and there is a great overcrowding of patients. Lack of sufficient funds to run the hospital is a common complaint, and a general need for trained hospital administrators is apparent.

f. *Diagnostic Laboratories*—Lack of diagnostic laboratories in hospitals is common; they are not available even in teaching hospitals. Usually blood counts can be done and a small amount of chemical analysis is possible, but serological and bacteriological work is not possible. Thus, a doctor is greatly handicapped in the diagnosis and treatment of patients. The proposed School of Public Health could train not only technicians for diagnostic laboratories but also directors for the laboratories.

g. *Health Educators*—Health-educator training should be an important department in the school. Health educators could assist in programs to promote popular understanding of disease prevention, immunization programs, nutrition, sanitation, and parasite control.

h. *Epidemiology, Medical Statistics, and Public Health Nursing*—The School of Public Health should be prepared to train doctors for the degrees of master and doctor of Public Health.

i. *Tuberculosis*—Programs for the control and prevention of tuberculosis are very important because of wide prevalence of this disease in Indonesia. Poliomyelitis and measles immunization programs should be planned for the future.

The proposed School of Public Health should encourage and carry out research on diseases and their prevention. Great opportunities for visiting professors would be available; no doubt such a school would attract some of the best investigators and teachers in the world. It might very well be considered also as a training center for teaching staff from all of the other medical schools in Indonesia. Special postgraduate courses could be presented at various times during the year, and some members of the medical schools would be encouraged by the opportunity to attend.

Medical Schools
Prior to 1946, there was only one Medical School in Indonesia, but since then fourteen others have been established. Some are still in the planning stage; some are active, but offer only preclinical training.

There has been a natural tendency in the medical schools to accept more students than can be trained with available funds, equipment, and personnel. Almost without exception, a staff member's primary occupation is private practice, which is a necessary source of income for him and his family. Often a faculty member is too tired to teach effectively. Most students are eager to learn and carry out their assignments very well, though there are a few who may have neither the ability nor the desire to become doctors. Unfortunately, these inferior students have been allowed to repeat the academic work for the year that they have failed. This is a continuing burden on staff and facilities, and those who fail should be allowed to repeat no more than once—and then only in unusual and extenuating circumstances.

In the past, there has been a tendency to assign failing grades to a large number of medical students; this may, in part, reflect poor teaching methods. When a student fails in medical school, it is a great economic loss to him, the school, and the community. Also, long delays in the completion of oral examinations are a great loss of time, both to the student and the teacher, and often give unfair estimates of the student's knowledge.

The emphasis in medical education should be to produce quality rather than quantity and to improve the existing medical schools rather than to attempt the establishment of more schools before the economy of the country is ready to support them. In the meantime, postgraduate training programs are needed to update the knowledge of the present practicing physicians. The programs which have been suggested above in the discussion of Public Health could do much to improve the practice of medicine and the health of the Indonesian people.

Medical Assistants

Until enough physicians are available for the medical care of the population of Indonesia, medical assistants or aides could be trained to assist the physician and work under his supervision in the care of minor illnesses, minor injuries, immunization programs, etc. This type of assistant would be similar to the medical corpsman in Armed Forces units. Their training could be accomplished in one or two years at a center designated for this program. The use of medical assistants in other countries of the world, of course, has had both good and bad results. If they are well trained and properly supervised by physicians, they can be very valuable and greatly increase the medical care which a physician can give to a community. However, if a medical assistant goes beyond his ability or is not supervised by a physician or assumes the title of doctor, he may be more detrimental than valuable. Poor medical care can be worse than no medical care.

CHAPTER 10

Francis E. Dart **Science Education in Developing Countries**

An American professor who had watched satellites cross the night sky over Java thought that this paper—which begins with an anecdote of a satellite viewed from Nepal—might be as relevant to problems of science education in the former as in the latter place.

I have not worked in Indonesia—the only exception among those who have written papers for this seminar—but was invited to participate —and was encouraged to accept—on the ground that, pending research in Indonesia, it is useful to examine for adaptive reflection in that country what may have been learned from observation in other developing nations. This paper does not derive from experience in Indonesia; it is a paper only about Nepal. The issues it presents, however, have major importance in both of these countries—and in several others. In the text below appropriate references to Indonesia have been inserted at the behest of seminar participants who know education in that nation.

I

One evening not long ago I stood in the Nepalese town of Panga talking with a group of its citizens. For two hours or more I had been inquiring about their views of nature and man's relation to nature, and our discussion had ranged widely over the world of familiar phenomena from rice planting to cosmology, from rainbows to moon and planets. As I was about to leave, we stepped out into an enchantingly beautiful night. The houses across the square and the temple at its center were silhouetted against a brilliantly jeweled, velvet black sky. Here and there a little mustard-oil lamp offered a flickering challenge to the darkness, but there was no glare of street light or neon sign. Now and then a child's voice or the murmur of a conversation somewhere accentuated the quiet of the night, but there was no sound of vehicles or sirens or other machines of civilization, and we stood silent ourselves a while enjoying the night. As I turned to leave, a bright "Echo" satellite appeared from behind the pagoda and swept in a slow silent arc across the sky, and we watched it for several moments before I took leave and departed for my lodgings in the city.

No mention had been made of the satellite (almost as if by agreement not to push our view too far), but I was wondering what they were thinking while we watched it, and I supposed that they were wondering about my thoughts. I had gone to Panga seeking information only, without any intention of imposing my own ideas, and the men and women there had accepted me and responded to my questions in that spirit. Yet inevitably, when very different views of reality meet, the confrontation takes on overtones of comparison and, in the mind at least, of persuasion, and so I found myself wondering whether they saw in this satellite the inexorable approach of a new age even to Panga. I wondered whether they might be admitting to themselves this visible evidence of a new cosmology.

As I came to appreciate later, it is very unlikely indeed that their thoughts were of this sort, or even that theirs and mine intersected at all. To me this satellite, this manmade moon, stands as irrefutable confirmation of our understanding of the solar system, even of the whole cosmology derived from Newtonian mechanics. It represents a powerful link between man and universe, forged by men like Galileo, Kepler, and Newton, and now dramatically confirmed for anyone to see. To these men and women of Panga, the satellite is only a machine. Like an airplane or a jeep, it is ingenious and expensive, possibly useful to Americans, but it bears no conceivable relation to the moon, which is a deity. It has nothing to do with the larger universe and it does not concern them.

I recall this incident here because it has both a real and a symbolic bearing on most of what I want to present to you in this paper. Geographically speaking, Panga is not very remote any more. Starting from this campus one can easily reach Panga in two days of plane and foot travel. Intellectually it is considerably farther, for it involves a long journey across cultures or backward through several centuries of our own. Because a journey across continents or oceans is so easy, we tend to forget the real distance that separates us from the developing countries, and then assume that the intellectual journey, too, will be easy. We may be dismayed to find that the airlines do not schedule this trip, which is, in any case, not covered by a tourist visa.

Of course, many developing countries, such as Indonesia, have already come part way to meet the West, and so already possess some of the western material or intellectual gadgets familiar to us here. It often enough develops, however, that here *they* are playing the part of tourists: visiting, collecting intellectual curios, learning some new words while perhaps finding the true accent hard to master. In fact, this may make them seem nearer than they really are.

Let us be more specific now in delimiting our subject matter. A major aspect of the great revolution that is so profoundly affecting the "developing nations" consists of what is often termed the scientific-technological revolution. It is bringing to most of the world a new and greatly expanded control over man's environment. Control of disease, management of large-scale water resources, production of power, the development of oil and mineral resources, and of agricultural technology or new means of communication and transportation—all are examples of the expanded ability to control and utilize the natural environment. It is also bringing new knowledge, new ways of thinking and of learning, and new criteria of validity or relevance to peoples whose ways of thinking have been traditional and relatively static over long periods of their history. This latter aspect, the scientific part of the revolution, is slower and more difficult than the technological business of new tools and skills needed to operate them. It is much more difficult to introduce new ways of organizing observations of nature or new criteria as to the importance of such observations.

Yet the two are intimately interrelated. In the long run, nations that want to develop a viable "Western" technology of their own will need also to develop a "Western" science of their own.[1] Nearly all the developing nations are fully aware of this, even though they do not all appreciate the magnitude of the problems involved. Nearly all of them need and intend to become scientifically as well as technologically autonomous and self-sufficient. Science education, then, will play a pivotal role in their long-range development. We wish to consider their capabilities of carrying out that role.

II

Science education in Indonesia, and in all the developing countries of Asia or Africa, is, of course, only part of a more general formal educational system which was introduced as a foreign import by European colonists and missionaries. This whole system of education, which now largely replaces or supersedes earlier indigenous school systems, was introduced by foreigners intending to provide training for future colonial civil servants or to replace a "heathen" culture with a more "enlightened" Christian one, and in such an undertaking they saw little need to accommodate the new school systems to the traditional ways of the native people. In fact the schools were, in many societies, although less so in Indonesia, intentionally subversive of the indigenous culture, which they were expected to alter and improve. This, together with the fact that in the beginning many colonial schools were established for the children of European colonial officials or missionaries who would normally complete their schooling in Europe, led to colonial school systems that were close copies of some European prototype in both organization and curriculum. In Indonesia, the prototype was Dutch.

These "European" schools in Asia and Africa, British or French or Dutch in origin, have been modified only very slightly in the years that have led to independent nations, where once there were subservient colonies. The changes that have been made were too often forced by inadequacy of personnel or lack of finances, producing as a result schools of lower quality which still follow essentially their original pattern, and where they seem to be really different from an European counterpart, it is likely to be because the latter has moved ahead with the times.

These schools badly need to become truly indigenous and self-sustaining, adapted to the needs and ways of learning of the people who support them and attend them, and with no need to apologize for being different from a foreign system, if being different means serving their own people more effectively. This view is well recognized by educational leaders in Indonesia, and it is a guiding principle in educational development there. Of course, Newton's laws may be the same everywhere, but their place in society and the best ways of teaching or learning them may differ from one place to another. In a few countries moves leading in this direction are beginning to be considered. They are still very tentative, at least insofar as science education is concerned, but they may very well signal a major shift in emphasis soon to come. The following are suggestions toward making science education more nearly indigenous, even though science itself is principally Western in origin.

III

Let us consider first the most elementary levels of education, from early childhood through primary school grades. These begin with informal imitative play. A man in a small jungle settlement in Indonesia is splitting bamboo to make a mat when his three-year-old son picks up a knife and begins hacking at one of the pieces of bamboo. A woman weaving a basket gives her small daughter some of the basket material to "play" with. An American mother working in her kitchen gives her child a spoon and a saucepan. This is the world's largest and best school system. It has more students and more teachers than any other; it enjoys a more favorable student-teacher ratio, and has more class hours than any other; and it is by far more effective than any other school system known. Here the most basic attitudes and concepts are learned and a world view is developed. Here children learn how to ask questions or even whether to ask questions at all; here they learn how knowledge is sought, verified, and depicted; here they gain an inkling of the place man occupies in the universe and what manner of universe it is.

When the first formal schooling is added to this informal instruction, it makes a profound difference whether or not its teaching is consistent with the informal or opposed to it. This becomes a matter of considerable importance where a foreign system of thought is to be taught by means of an imported school curriculum, as is the case with science in so much of the non-Western world.

In order to assess this more exactly, a colleague and I interviewed children and adults in several Nepalese towns and villages, asking questions about familiar phenomena of nature.[2] Our questions were of three types, intending to learn:

(1) How the respondents account for various commonly experienced phenomena such as rain, lightning, thunder, fire, earthquakes. "How do you account for rain?" "Where does the rain water originate?" "What do most people in the village think about rain?" "What makes an earthquake?" "What is a rainbow?"

(2) What attitudes respondents hold about the control or manipulation of such phenomena. "How can rainfall be brought about or prevented?" "Is it appropriate for men to influence the rain?" "Is there any protection against lightning or thunder?"

(3) What are considered to be the origins of knowledge about nature and what are the accepted criteria of validity of such knowledge. "How were these things (about rain, etc.) learned?" "How does one know if they are true?" "How might new knowledge about such things be obtained?"

With very few exceptions, we were given both a "folk-oriented" or "myth-oriented" and a "school-oriented" explanation of a given phenomenon within a single interview, sometimes by a single individual. Surely similar explanations would be heard in Indonesia. Thus to account for earthquakes, one of a group of four Chetri boys said, "The earth is supported on the back of a fish. When the fish grows tired it shifts the weight, and this shakes the earth." All agreed, but another added, "There is fire at the center of the earth. It seeks to escape and sometimes cracks the earth, causing an earthquake." All agree to this as well.

This pattern is repeated again and again; thus, "The deities break vessels of water in the sky causing rain." And "The sun evaporates water from the sea, producing vapor which is cooled by the mountains to make clouds and rain." Again, "Lightning comes from the collision of clouds." And "Lightning comes from the bangles of Indra's dancers." Or "It rains only in the summer (monsoon) season because we need the rain then. In winter we do not need rain." And "It rains in the summer because the sun is hotter then and causes more evaporation."

Surprising is the fact that each group nearly always gave both types of answers illustrated above, and all members generally accepted both. Of course there is nothing unusual in the thought that a given phenomenon may result from either of two different causes, and hence that in general each of these causes may be accepted as potentially valid. However, here the two types of "causes" offered appear to be qualitatively different ideas of nature. It is as difficult for us to accept both as real alternatives as it is to accept them as simultaneously true.

The contradiction is far more apparent to us, however, than to our respondents, who showed no discomfort over it, a fact which serves as a warning to the science educator that all is not as it appears on the surface.

The philosophies and literature of Asia make use of paradox a great deal, and to Asians, contradiction may be more intriguing than disturbing. We should not, therefore, discount the possibility of very deep-rooted patterns of thought now limited to the "either-or" logic underlying Western science. However, a much simpler explanation might also be considered. Much of the teaching and learning in Nepalese schools involves rote memory only and demands very little understanding or conceptualization. It is quite possible that the way in which early "scientific" concepts are taught in school combines with a tradition-oriented home environment to produce no necessary distinction between myth and science. In any case, this dual view of nature is a matter that needs to be considered in the planning of revised science teaching methods.

When our Nepalese informants were asked to give the source of their knowledge about nature, they invariably said that it came from books and from old people. When we asked how the old people found out or how knowledge got into the books, they told us it came from earlier generations of old people or from other books. When we pressed for some ultimate source, most of our respondents said that these things had always been known, although a few of them referred to legends telling how some particular skill such as fire-building was given to men by the deities.

We went on to inquire how new knowledge, hitherto unknown to anyone, might be acquired, or how it might be sought. We were always told that such new knowledge is not to be expected. Even when we pushed this question so far as to call attention to such "new" discoveries as space travel or transistor radios, both of which are known about all over Nepal, it was held that such things were always known by someone or else that these are merely new applications of old knowledge. One very tentative exception was offered by a Limbu boy, who suggested that really new knowledge might sometimes come through dreams. We find it hard to believe that more probing would not reveal other exceptions, yet the predominant view is one that pictures human knowledge about nature as a closed body, rarely, if ever, capable of extension, which is passed down from teacher to student and from generation to generation. Its source is in authority, not in observation. Given this concept of knowledge, it is not surprising that the schools rely heavily upon rote memory. Memorizing would seem to be the easiest and most efficient way to deal with a closed and limited body of unvarying facts. There are also other well known and frequently criticized forces embedded within the formal educational system, which strongly reinforce this natural tendency.

American school children interviewed in Honolulu nearly always gave only one kind of explanation (a "school-oriented" one) of the same natural phenomena. They know and can repeat many "myth-oriented" statements about these phenomena, but they do not offer nor accept these as explanations of the phenomena. They invariably say that new knowledge is continually being obtained by means of observations or "research."

Science as the scientist thinks of it, and would like to see it taught, does not consist of a body of more or less isolated facts to be memorized, but of a system of empirically verifiable relationships between more or less abstract concepts. While the concepts are derived from the real world of phenomena, the relationships of science relate concepts, not real objects, and the theories of science are built around "models" which portray in abstract, often mathematical, terms a selectively idealized representation of the real world of phenomena. It is essential for the science student to learn to be at home, at some level of sophistication, with this process, which must surely appear even to the Western layman to be extraordinarily indirect. Much attention is given to this in the recently developed or improved science courses in the United States, which go to great care to give students systematic training and practice in skills of abstraction and inference, while striving to maintain contact with the real world by subjecting all conclusions to observational verification. Of course, informal learning plays a part in this process. The toys children manipulate, the games they play, the activities of adults that they watch and imitate, the conversations they listen to, all contribute to the attitudes and skills they develop. In everything the child does in school there is an echo of his environment at home.

How much more difficult science must be, then, for a child who lives in an Asian village or small town immersed in a very different environment with its own pervasive but non-Western influences. Here he lives close to nature in a direct, particularistic relation of planting and harvesting, with little or no abstraction and little need to generalize. Certainly his society or any society contains a great many abstractions, ranging from spoken or written language all the way to a very complex religious cosmology, but these are not all particularly useful in preparing the way for science, which wants to hold to a rather special and verifiable relation to nature. Thus, for example, every Nepalese child will be familiar with abstract representations of certain Hindu or Buddhist deities and heroes of religious myths and legends. Yet these are not subject to direct or even indirect observational verification after the manner of science, and they may not be conducive to a scientific approach.

As an indication of the effects of informal learning on children's readiness to use abstract "models," we asked our subjects to sketch rough freehand maps showing how to get "from your house to the school" (or some other well-known local landmark). A map is a fairly simple yet typical example of a scientific model. It preserves a verifiable one-to-one relation to reality, and yet it is an abstraction, useful for what it omits no less than for what it includes. It lends itself to great variety in the way a given reality is represented, and the relationships and inferences derived from it, while not totally unrelated to reality, nevertheless actually refer to the model and not to the real world. We believe that the maps which children or adults draw to represent a route or neighborhood well known to them will reveal with some accuracy their readiness to understand and use other scientific abstractions.

FIGURE 10:1. *Map drawn by 15-year old Limbu boy to show the way from his house to the school. In fact, the house and school are not on the same street or path.*

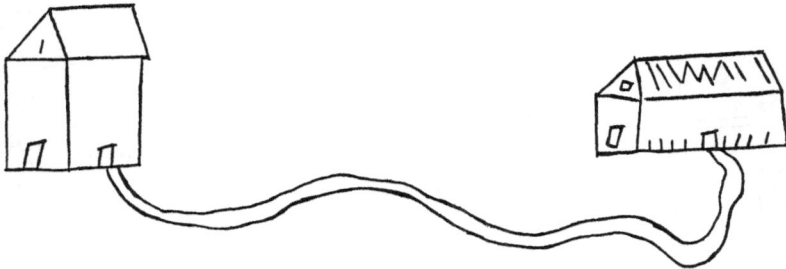

The "maps" we obtained are very similar to each other and to the example shown in Figure 10:1. Always they include a recognizable picture of the house and of the school connected by a line which seems to denote the process of going from one to the other, not the spatial relationship of one to the other. Thus, in the case shown, the two buildings in fact are not on the same street or path, but are separated by several street intersections and other landmarks which do not appear on the map. In contrast, Figure 10:2 shows a map typical of those drawn by American children in response to the same instructions. Here, both house and school are represented by abstract symbols, not pictures, and there is a clear effort to show spatial relationships and to provide needed spatial clues. The propensity of the Nepalese for making maps (whether verbal or graphic) which are sequential rather than spatial constructs is not limited to school children. In a land of foot-trails, where literacy is too low to justify road signs, it has been a source of consternation to more than a few travelers of western upbringing. We, too, in reply to our inquiries as we traveled, were given instructions or "maps" which, like a string of beads, list in correct sequence the places we should pass through without giving any clue as to distances, trail intersections, changes of directions, etc. Our interest is not in the accuracy nor potential usefulness of this different kind of model, but in the light it may shed on a way of thinking which may extend far beyond mere mapmaking. The villagers use no other kind of map; they do not use drawings in constructing a building or a piece of furniture—in fact, they hardly use drawings or spatial representations at all, and the lack of spatial models is very natural. The question remains, however, whether the teacher will have this in mind when he presents a model of a molecule or solar system.

FIGURE 10:2. *Map drawn by 11-year-old American boy to show the way from his house to the school. Note the wealth of spatial and directional clues.*

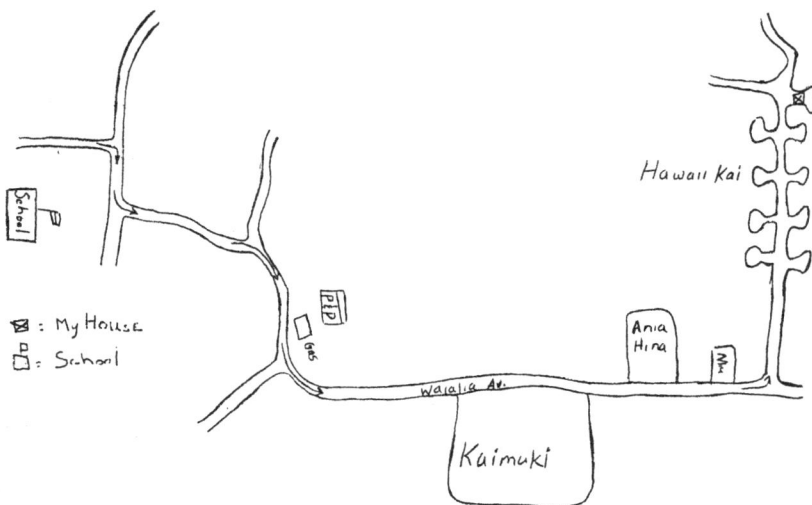

The foregoing observations suggest changes in method or content which might lead to easier and more economical as well as more effective teaching of science in Nepal. I believe that some of these changes will be found to apply more or less well in many other developing countries, and I hope that similar or more refined studies will be undertaken which will extend, improve, and corroborate these conclusions. For the present, let us limit ourselves to a few relatively clearly indicated changes that are capable of pilot scale introduction.

Preparation for Science

It is clear that the school-age boys and girls in the developing countries do not have the attitudes about nature and learning that are most conducive to science. Clearly too, they have not developed much skill in abstract representation or measurement skills which contribute not only to the manipulations of scientific experimentation but to their conceptualization as well. It is now well accepted that such attitudes and skills can best be developed relatively early in a child's school experience, well before the introduction of formal subject matter courses like chemistry or physics. I believe that a program of prescience instruction in the elementary grades, similar to those now under development in the United States,[3] will be both possible and desirable in Nepal and probably in other developing countries. This instruction may well follow the general guidelines that have been laid down for the American efforts, but it will need to be adapted to conform closely to the particular environment, needs, and available resources of the country and community where it is used, and it should start with the real or potential questions which children ask there. It involves questions of design and teacher training, but no difficult economic problems concerned with equipment or supplies, for local "phenomena" for observation are best and abundant, "laboratory material" will consist of leaves and pebbles, sunshine and seeds, and equipment will consist of pieces of bamboo and locally available utensils. Such a program can certainly present real phenomena and teach real facts, but its fundamental intent is to provide a basis of skills and attitudes, and a relation to nature, rather than facts as such.

Science as a Second Culture

I have noted the prevalence of a dual view of nature or reality which was especially striking because the two views expressed seem to us contradictory, although both were accepted simultaneously by our subjects. If this paradox is new in Nepal, it is certainly not new to the West. The same ambivalence has run through western thought at least since the early scientific revolution, and it is still with us. Yet, for the most part, we have been able to make our peace with the complementary worlds of matter and spirit, of objects and values. By careful delineation of boundaries, by conscious and unconscious compartmentalization, or reinterpretation, and a variety of intellectual nonaggression pacts, a reasonably secure and peaceful coexistence has been achieved, so that this particular dualism no longer poses serious problems for the scientist or student. Can others be helped to achieve or preserve a coexistence that does not violate their cultural values, as they try to assimilate our Western science and our scientific viewpoint?

I suggest as one step that science be presented as a "second culture," complementary to that already present rather than replacing it, and taught in the spirit with which a second language is taught—to be learned and used, certainly, but not to the exclusion of the student's native tongue. This will require a very different orientation from that commonly present in most Asian schools, or indeed in most Asian-American interaction, even if it does not mean great changes in school curriculum. I have noted that the attitude and often the intent of Western education has, in the past, been that of replacing a mistaken "primitive" or "decadent" civilization with a more modern and "better" one. This attitude tends to continue, even though colonialism is no longer a force behind it, and it tends to be particularly strong in science teaching, for science is taken to be the one really unique and powerful offering of the Western world. In fact, however, the purpose of education, whether in Nepal or elsewhere in Asia or Africa, is no longer that of destroying one civilization or even one set of ideas in order to replace it totally with something that is conceived to be better, and to proceed in that direction or with that implicit attitude is to create unnecessary difficulties along the way. An implacable either-or approach leading to a direct confrontation between traditional attitudes and a modern and very foreign approach to knowledge invites conflict both within the student's own mind and between him and his elders in the community. As has been seen too often, such a conflict results at best in a draw which alienates from one world without really admitting into the other. I propose to avoid or postpone this confrontation by starting early science instruction with simple observations of ordinary things and events, observations which stimulate and use the child's latent curiosity, which anyone can perform, and which demand no special or formal interpretation in cosmological or philosophical terms. Instead they will provide a foundation of skills, of attitudes toward observations, and of specific observations upon which a more formal knowledge of science may later be built. In doing so, I accept a complementarity of views as natural and perhaps as inevitable.

I am mindful of a seeming contradiction contained in this proposal. If extensive social and cultural changes are bound to accompany the introduction of science, it is wise to ignore this in the preparation for learning science. Of course, some kind of accommodation between the scientific revolution and the indigenous culture must and will eventually be reached if science is introduced at all. This is a complex matter which must evolve slowly within the Eastern cultures as it did within the West. Experience does not suggest that it will most easily be achieved simply by substituting one for the other, and particularly not during the school years, when children are so intimately immersed in the intellectual and physical environment of the village. It is important to them and to the village that they remain at peace there. Moreover, it would be well to base an eventual accommodation upon real science well learned, rather than on a set of memorized facts and formulas learned under stress.

Referring again to the analogy of language teaching, recent experience seems to show that the same attitudes and techniques used to teach English, say, to Urdu-speaking children, where no question of substitution or conflict arises, are most effective in teaching a standard English to children, in Hawaii or Harlem, for example, who speak a "substandard" dialect of English. It is easier for these children to learn standard English as a second language, free from the conflicts that arise from an attempt to substitute it for their own "incorrect" dialect, which of course, they continue to need in their own community.

Elementary Science Instruction

A detailed program of instruction in science is under development in Nepal, partly as a result of the observations reported above. It would be premature at this time to anticipate its final dimensions or content, but a few remarks may be made as to its hopes. Emphasis will be kept to an observational approach to phenomena that are already familiar to anyone or to those which can readily be produced by anyone, and a progression of skills and practiced experience will be built up, encompassing classification, measurement, generalization, inference, and quantification, leading ultimately to elementary but conceptually more or less sophisticated experiments designed and carried out by the students. The material will have some specific information content which is intended for later use, but not as the major emphasis and not for memorization. In addition to this observational material, some history of science will be introduced in essentially anecdotal form, with the intention of showing that the knowledge of "books and old people" is really a record of observations and interpretations made by real people. In addition to more or less familiar elementary experiments, there will be some that are intended specifically to meet special needs of children there in areas (such as the use of abstractions) for which their home environment has not given much practice. Examples would be: (1) A schoolwide "tic-tac-toe" contest or similar simple game of strategy, played at first with figures or boards and later with numbers alone. (2) A series of mapmaking exercises that start with a pictorial "map" of the school classroom and proceed through maps of the school or home neighborhood, and finally to very abstract representations, such as maps showing livestock population density. (3) A grid laid out with kite-string near the school, which gives each pupil a two-foot square section of garden or meadow for which he is to keep a complete inventory of plant and insect life and activity for a three-week period. This program is being developed and introduced with the help of American Peace Corps volunteers, who are in many ways ideal agents of educational change.

There is reason to hope that the new interest in better science teaching which has resulted from the American experimental curriculums in secondary school science will result in changes and improvements in Asia, and perhaps in Nepal, affecting the teaching of science at the secondary level. These courses, as well as other studies, place much emphasis upon observation and experiment as essential to better science instruction. I hope that a program such as this one at the elementary levels will provide a useful preparation for these more formal course changes. In fact, I am willing to speculate that some such preparation will be found necessary if courses founded on the American curricular improvements in science are to maintain their original spirit and emphasis as they are adapted for use in other countries.

IV

Formal teaching of basic science courses usually begins at the middle school or high school level, and continues into the university. This is a period of acquisition of basic facts and techniques. Problem-solving skills as well as laboratory techniques stressing observation and measurement are learned at this stage, and a student begins to develop a considerable fund of scientific facts and laws which can be called upon to help meet a variety of more or less standard examination problems. Little, if any, research or independent work is attempted at this stage, and hence the student has very little opportunity to try himself out on an independent scientific project, and he may achieve a bachelor's degree without such experience, and frequently without having learned to use a library independently.

I shall have less to say about this middle stage of a scientist's education than I have already said about the earliest stages, partly because it is, in my judgment, less critical and more standardized than either the earlier or the postgraduate levels, and partly also because in most countries the middle levels of the educational system, from about seventh or eighth year through the bachelor's level, are very rigidly fixed by tradition and by bureaucratically determined bounds and hence are in practice the least susceptible to improvement. I will limit myself then to two observations.

The first has to do with the general student who does not intend to study science as a major subject. Following a pattern that has been abandoned in the West, many of the developing nations separate science students from others fairly early, with the result that nonscience students receive almost no instruction at all in science subjects, and where they do it tends to be in a very routine course stressing memorized facts and formulas. A course in real science for nonscientists—one that concerns itself with the conceptual bases of science, with what science can do and what it cannot do, with how the scientist decides what is true and what is false—such a course is almost nowhere offered and is usually not given serious consideration when it is suggested. Thus these countries deny themselves a powerful feedback to the village or town environment that will continue to shape the thinking of their children. The "nonscientists" who would take such courses if they were given include the village teacher and its political leaders, the father who works in the town as a clerk or civil servant, and an increasing number of professional and semiprofessional people who must have had at least some secondary or postsecondary education. In fact, a feedback link of the sort suggested here could be extended to reach even the village mother or peasant farmer to a limited but significant degree, if imaginative use were made of the adult education and literacy programs already available in most developing countries.

Of course there was a time when the teachers or classrooms and equipment for doing anything of the sort suggested above were simply not at hand, when it was nearly impossible to offer good science instruction even to science majors, and nothing could be spared for others. However, it is becoming increasingly difficult to sustain such an explanation.

Second, I want to take note of the various high school science curriculum improvement programs which started in the United States about ten years ago and are now arousing quite a bit of interest in many parts of the world. In this country they are producing a major revolution in the teaching of science, and it is not surprising that many of the developing countries wish to translate or adapt them. They should certainly be encouraged in this and also warned of some traps. These courses owe their success partly to their willingness to introduce very modern and quite sophisticated concepts right along with the "simpler" classical ideas of yesterday. They assume, and practice bears them out, that "new" concepts are not harder for students to learn and understand than "old" concepts (which are new to the student in any case). However, this may not be at all true of the science teacher who was trained in another way, is accustomed to the old way, and in fact may not himself be at all at home with the more modern concepts he now is to include. Teachers can be very conservative.

Another very important characteristic of the new courses is their spirit of direct inquiry. They are intended to involve the student himself in simple yet significant experiments in which he will be invited to search for meaning that is not pointed out in advance and to arrive at generalizations which he constructs and then tests himself. The experiments themselves and the equipment used may be rather simple, carrying little inherent glamour or prestige. It is the thought processes they stimulate that are important and not the skills of measurement involved. This spirit of independent (although actually guided) discovery is very foreign to most of the science laboratories or classrooms in the countries now proposing to adopt the new courses (let us freely admit that it was new to most American high schools too). It may, therefore, be a fairly delicate business to preserve the original spirit of these programs as they are transplanted into a foreign soil. In good teaching no less than in other endeavors, "The letter killeth, but the spirit giveth life."

V

So far we have considered science teaching at relatively elementary or intermediate levels, without raising the question of where the scientists themselves come from. It would be a mistake to suppose that the developing nations do not have first-class scientists working in their universities and research institutions. They do. But it would be no exaggeration to say that they have very few in comparison to their needs. It is also fair to say that practically all of these few come, as scientists, from abroad, for even those who are natives of the country will usually have completed several years of advanced graduate study abroad before being recognized as fully qualified scientists. In the long run, every nation that intends to become self-sufficient in science must be able to produce its own scientists. This will mean that it must strive to become self-sufficient in graduate study, sending students and also mature scientists abroad for enrichment and exchange of knowledge, but not in complete dependence upon foreign academic resources.

The community of scientists is thoroughly international in practically every respect. It holds to a common and fairly stable set of professional and academic standards, and no institution or country can inflate these without suffering a loss of standing. It is therefore very necessary that a nation intending to be self-sufficient in graduate study give a great deal of attention to the quality of its graduate institutions. The temptation and also the need to expand graduate-level education rapidly are great, and it is reasonable to expect that such an expansion, with high quality or without it, will be the next major educational undertaking in a number of countries. It is then appropriate for us, and for them too, to consider carefully what is involved in this critical step.

The graduate school, if it is to achieve its purpose, must be much more than an extension of undergraduate teaching. It needs to do much more than provide for the student one more set of facts and laws. It must go beyond this to make of the student a self-motivating professional scientist, with standards of quality and ethics which become self-generating and self-enforcing. The task of the graduate school, then, is to fuse knowledge and skill with judgment; it should be dealing consciously not with "students" but with future researchers, professors, and high-level administrators. It must also be the seat of real research, for a major portion of the basic research done in the country will and should be accomplished at its universities.

Serious obstacles stand in the way of achieving this objective, and somehow they must be overcome or circumvented. The cost and availability of equipment and library facilities may appear to be prohibitive, although this objection might seem less imposing if these costs are compared with the true costs of not developing quality graduate work. In any case, the costs are high and certainly must be viewed realistically. The existing academic environment, with its heavy emphasis upon lectures and examinations, is likely to prove unsuitable. Somehow a change of milieu must be achieved, a change to one that encourages intellectual inquiry for its own sake. The graduate student needs to feel himself part of a scholarly community engaged in research and the pursuit of knowledge, a community where ideals and standards are high, where understanding itself is the goal rather than a satisfactory examination mark, where, for example, a student or a professor can derive genuine satisfaction and enhance his status among his peers by proving himself to be wrong where he is in error. An atmosphere of this sort is not at all easy to produce, but it is of the greatest importance. Its achievement may very well be both more difficult and more necessary than the provisions of any arbitrary sum for the purchase of supplies. It is likely to require such changes as:

(a) Making faculty members full-time members of the academic community, fully paid by it, and fully loyal to it. A salary scale that requires a professor or lecturer to hold another job as well makes poor sense academically and economically.

(b) Deliberately inviting or creating the confrontation of ideas by encouraging intellectual controversy, by bringing to the university challenging visitors and by welcoming nonconformity and debate. Needless to say, debate and nonconformity will not always limit themselves to purely "academic" matters, and so they will have to be defended against disapproving public or political forces. This defense is essential, for freedom to challenge old as well as new ideas is the very lifeblood of the institution.

(c) A serious restudy and restructuring of the examination system. Good evaluation of academic achievement is very necessary and examinations certainly play a useful part, but they should not be the end in themselves. As presently practiced, examinations are perhaps the greatest deterrent to creative educational change.

Finally, there are administrative obstacles to consider. Where support is limited, rivalries between institutions or faculties have to be resolved into cooperation based upon acceptance of reasonable priorities and a commitment to objectives that all can accept. Where a strong but possibly unwieldy and traditional organizational pattern exists, leadership must be found with vision and strength enough to adopt new policies as needed to provide really good selection and evaluation procedures, to create and sustain high standards of quality, to limit the development to a pace that does not sacrifice this quality, and to deal effectively with the competition for visible material results. A good graduate school must be built patiently over some decades of time; therefore, the project must be sufficiently insulated from short-range economic or political fluctuations to provide continuity and confidence of growth. This too may prove hard to manage, yet is necessary.

With all these obstacles to progress (not to mention others perhaps equally serious that may have occurred to you), it becomes obvious that the proposed objective of self-sufficiency at the graduate level calls for full and careful study as well as a variety of experimental approaches. Clearly, this is too large a topic to treat satisfactorily within the bounds of this paper. I will not pretend otherwise, but I want nevertheless to offer a few suggestions that might lead to useful discussion.

First let me suggest that nations wishing to move in the directions suggested above should establish a national commission for graduate study (or for university development). It should be created with full political and administrative backing and then vested with real power. Its director should be the best man obtainable, who can command the respect and win the support of the entire academic community. This commission must, of course, be accountable to the nation, but it must not be politically vulnerable in any short-term sense, and it must not be subservient to the university administrations presently existing. It may seem to some that such placement of power is too centralized, giving too little room for private or individual initiative and development. However, the hard fact is that nearly every one of the developing nations controls and administers its educational system centrally. Without the concurrence and participation of the central authorities very little is likely to happen.

As a second suggestion, let me turn to the establishment of centers for scientific research. This is a matter that concerns industry as well as education, and it may be of concern to several branches of government. It is not uncommon, as a result, that research institutes are established which are physically and administratively closer to centers of industry than to centers of learning. The research they undertake may be no less fundamental because of this, and, in any case, some applied research may be very necessary. However, it then becomes much more difficult for these research institutes or national laboratories to participate actively in the work of the graduate schools, and thereby to strengthen them with experienced research staff and research opportunities. Instead, they may find themselves competing with the universities for scientists as well as for money and equipment. A result in some countries is a local brain drain within the country itself, which can have serious consequences. My suggestion, then, is that research institutions be carefully and closely integrated with graduate teaching institutions.

Finally, let me suggest that better use can be made of the foreign assistances that are, and presumably will continue to be, available through such means as the Colombo Plan, the Fulbright grants, and a host of other government or private assistance programs. Much of this assistance could be better used, to create the conditions and atmosphere of a good graduate school, than is now the practice. Good research programs could be developed which would encourage graduate students who study abroad for a while to return tò their own country for the research and dissertation that will complete their degree. Research grants given jointly to a native graduate student and a foreign visiting scholar could be used to strengthen this effort. Scientific societies could be strengthened and supported in establishing first-class journals that offer publication facilities reaching a worldwide scientific readership. Research grants could be offered to young scientists just returning from a doctoral study program abroad for research to be conducted in their country, but with the collaboration of their thesis adviser abroad. This would enhance their status at a time when they need it, and it would free part of their time from the very heavy teaching loads that tend to stifle research or real inquiry. It would also help to provide a growing tradition of research at the graduate universities. One could mention other possibilities, and without doubt some of them, like some of these, are already in practice in some countries. But too often they are in practice as a result of a partial plan or simply by accident of the granting agency, without any really coherent integrated planning by the country itself, such as might be done, for example, by a national commission concerned with graduate education. The country receiving aid could get more value by doing more of the planning itself.

[1] F. E. Dart, *Foreign Affairs* (1963) 41, 360.

[2] Francis E. Dart and Panna Lal Pradham, *Science* (1967) 155: 649.

[3] R. M. Gagne, *Science* (1966) 151: 49; see also "Science—a Process Approach," AAAS Commission on Science Education Publication, 1965.

CHAPTER 11

R. *Murray Thomas*   **Indonesian Science Education and National Development**

To some degree science education has been cast as the servant of national development by each of the governments controlling the Indonesian archipelago during the twentieth century—the Dutch until 1942, the Japanese in 1942–1945, the clashing Dutch and Indonesians during the revolution of 1945–1949, and the Indonesians alone since 1950. However, at no time during the century was science education assigned such a major role as in the 1960s, when the Republic launched its eight-year plan intended to produce a "just and prosperous" life for all. President Sukarno's guided-democracy regime was ended in the violent aftermath to the inept Communist *coup d'état* of late 1965, but the strong emphasis on science education for the nation's socioeconomic growth continued.

The purpose of this chapter is to assess the state of Indonesian science education and to hazard an estimate about what solutions might profitably be attempted to solve the serious problems faced in the latter 1960s by the country's science-education establishment in furthering national development.

SCOPE AND GOALS OF SCIENCE EDUCATION

The conduct of science education in the Indonesian archipelago, both in the prewar Netherlands East Indies and in the postwar Republic, can be divided into three interlinked categories: (1) science as an aspect of the general education of the citizenry, (2) science as the direct servant of socioeconomic development, and (3) science for its own sake.

Science as General Education

During Dutch times a relatively small amount of science was included in the upper grades of the elementary school. Geography was taught one or two hours a week, beginning in the fourth or sometimes the fifth grade.[1] Following the war and revolution (1942–1949), Indonesian elementary schools continued to offer geography in the same amount as before the war, and they divided physical-science instruction into biology and physics, which began in either the fourth or sixth grade for one to three hours a week. (Schools using the local dialect as the medium of instruction in the lower grades had less time for science in the upper grades than did schools which used only the Indonesian language throughout.) Biology consisted of botany and zoology, including the care of animals and of a school garden. The physics syllabus called for discussion of natural phenomena and instruction in the use and repair of instruments and simple machines.[2]

The postwar inclusion of science in the elementary schools was not simply a blind imitation by Indonesians of the earlier Dutch pattern. Science was included, even expanded, because Indonesian educational leaders were convinced that it was an essential element of everyone's preparation for life.

Throughout the 1950s and into the 1960s the science aspect of general education was gradually given additional stress. The new nation-wide curriculum design for the "basic school" in 1964 required the teaching of natural science from the kindergarten through the six elementary grades. Although no exact amount of time for science instruction was specified for the kindergarten, one hour a week was required in grades one and two, and two hours a week from grades three through six.[3]

The course of study defined the purpose of elementary-school science to be threefold: teaching children to study natural phenomena (such as rain, thunder, living things) and their uses in promoting human welfare, to think critically about the what, why, and how of the relationships between natural phenomena and people's lives, and to realize more fully the existence of God and the fact that He is powerful and wise in guiding the conduct of the natural world.[4]

Secondary schools in the prewar Netherlands Indies were of two major varieties: general high schools offering college preparation and vocational high schools offering terminal training for specific occupations. Although Indonesian educators retained this same basic pattern in the 1950s and 1960s, they periodically modified the system so that general education (all students taking a common curriculum) extended higher into the student's school career. Consequently, specialization was postponed until students were older.

We may conclude that in the 1950s the curriculums for elementary and secondary schools furnished pupils common learnings in natural and social sciences from about grade four of the elementary school through the second year of the junior high and hardly any in the senior high. However, new curriculums introduced early in the 1960s extended general education in science to include the entire grade range from kindergarten through the first year of the senior high school. These changes clearly reflected the increased importance the nation's political and educational leaders placed on the value of science for the entire population.

Science Education in Direct Service of National Development

Throughout this chapter, the distinction we are making between general and specialized science education is the following:

1. General science education is provided for everyone, on the assumption that scientific knowledge enhances an individual's life and increases his contribution to the society no matter what occupation he follows.

2. Specialized science education is designed to prepare individuals to assume direct, unique roles in implementing the nation's development plans.

During Dutch colonial times the principal development plans had as their end the primary goals which had drawn Netherlanders to the islands in the first place: to make Dutchmen wealthy. The science education which was in a small amount during the last half of the nineteenth century and in growing amounts in the twentieth was designed to make its contribution to this aim. More specifically, science education was the handmaiden of technical and professional training.

For example, in 1851 an advanced school for training native doctors in Western medical practice was founded in Djakarta (then called Batavia). More than a half-century later, in 1913, a parallel institution was opened at Surabaja. The major purpose of these institutions was to furnish physicians for the public health service and for plantations which did not wish to continue to pay the high fees necessary to import physicians from Europe. In 1927 the Djakarta school became a medical college, the ancestor of today's Faculty of Medicine at the University of Indonesia. The Surabaja school is now the Faculty of Medicine of Airlangga University. Under the Dutch, these institutions taught the kinds of science necessary to support medical practice in the tropical East Indies.[5]

Technical and technological education, along with the sciences which support them, experienced a similar evolution. The first technical institution in the islands was the Queen Wilhelmina School, a secondary school opened in Djakarta in 1901 to teach technical subjects at a higher theoretical or scientific level than had the lower hand-skills schools begun in the nineteenth century.[6] During the first two decades of the 1900s several other such schools opened at different locations on Java. Then in 1920 a private group of Netherlanders organized a foundation which established an engineering college (Technische Hogeschool) in Bandung, West Java, as the islands' first higher-education institution. The original purpose of the school was to train civil engineers for irrigation and road construction projects, because the supply of experienced engineers from Europe had dwindled during and after the First World War.[7] Over the past forty-eight years the college has evolved into the present-day Bandung Institute of Technology, the nation's most prestigious, highly developed center of technological and scientific education.

Since the income of the Netherlands Indies investors and many of the islands' workers depended so heavily on the export of agricultural items (rubber, tea, sugar, rice, copra), the colony's economic leaders encouraged the development of those aspects of science education that supported improved agricultural practices. Although there were agricultural schools at various locations, the principal development of science education was at Bogor, the city in which the Dutch located their world famous botanical garden in West Java. The secondary agricultural school in Bogor was declared a college in 1940, but in 1941–1942 the Japanese military invasion threw the islands' system of higher education into disarray. Today this school is the Bogor Agricultural University, the best of its kind in the archipelago.

During the early months of Japanese military occupation, most secondary schools and all five of the nation's higher-education institutions remained closed. Over the ensuing years many of these schools reopened. Whether an institution was permitted to operate during the war depended upon the degree to which it would cooperate with the Japanese occupation forces. The Japanese endeavored to expand Indonesia's productive capacity by converting the Dutch academic secondary schools into vocational training institutions that prepared agriculturists, shipbuilders, mechanics, machinists, and the like. In April 1943 the medical college in Djakarta reopened to furnish physicians for the Japanese-occupied territories, and a college of pharmacy was attached to the institution.[8] The secondary medical and dental schools in Surabaja were reopened and elevated to college status. In 1944 the Engineering Institute in Bandung began to operate once more, headed by a professor of chemistry from Japan and staffed by Japanese and Indonesian instructors.[9] The agricultural college in Bogor also reopened.

As the foregoing historical sketch suggests, the phrase "science education for national development" meant science primarily for the welfare of the Dutch regime prior to 1942 and for the Japanese between 1942 and 1945. National development that emphasized the welfare of Indonesians could not receive serious attention until the Republic of Indonesia gained control of its own destiny and was at peace, following the successful revolution against the returning Dutch in 1945–1949.

The Liberal Period, 1950–1958

Not long after Indonesians declared their independence in August 1945, they established a government patterned along the lines of parliamentary democracy. Following the 1945–1949 revolution, the united nation in 1950 continued to be governed according to such a pattern. This period, which President Sukarno described as the time of liberal politics and liberal economy, ended in 1959 with the president's dissolution of the constituent assembly and his decreeing a return to the 1945 constitution, which placed a larger measure of control in the hands of the president.[10]

In the early 1950s most of the nation's educational effort was

directed toward expanding elementary schooling and the literacy program for adults. The purpose of this dual emphasis was to achieve as soon
as possible the new republic's goal of universal basic education for the
populace. The effort proved highly successful. Between 1950 and 1959,
elementary school enrollment had increased 66 percent (from 4,926,370
to 8,330,000) and the number of teachers had grown by 144 percent
(from 83,850 to 205,860).[11] The literacy rate for people over age twelve
increased from about 8 or 10 percent of the population in 1950–1951 to
an estimated 58 percent in 1959.[12] The marked expansion of secondary
schools occurred nearer the middle of the 1950s, as larger numbers of
elementary school graduates became ready for secondary schooling. And
higher education, depending for its growth on a large supply of apt
secondary school graduates, did not spread rapidly until near the end of
the 1950s and the early 1960s.[13]

Science education in support of national development during this
period was encouraged by political, economic, and educational planners
during the 1950s, but not in the form of a coordinated overall program.
Individual schools (like the Faculty of Medicine of the University of
Indonesia) or individual sections of the Ministry of Education (like the
technical-education division) created their own development projects,
often with the aid of foreign governments or foundations. Furthermore,
economic planners made some attempts to predict the nature of future
manpower needs.[14] But in the main, all these efforts were initiated
without much cognizance of what was happening in other segments of
the economy or the educational enterprise.

Some noteworthy examples of progress in science education were
recorded during this "liberal" period. For instance, the University of
Indonesia in 1954 graduated 20 medical doctors, an average graduating
class for the nation's most prominent medical school. In 1959 this same
institution graduated 157 doctors, representing a new average for the
years ahead. And not only was the quantity of graduates increased over
this five-year period, but the quality as well. The Faculty of Medicine,
with the help of a medical education team from the University of
California, had revamped the entire science and medical-practices curriculum as well as the entrance and graduation standards.[15] A second and
perhaps more impressive example is the growth of technical secondary
schools. Between 1950 and 1959 the number of such institutions increased about fourfold, from 126 to 505. The most dramatic expansion
occurred during the 1955–1956 period, when technical junior and senior
high schools grew from 249 to 452. Over this same ten-year period the
number of technical teachers increased about four and one-half times
(1,616 to 7,381). But other types of high schools grew even faster;
teachers in nontechnical secondary schools increased about seven times

during the same era (6,063 to 44,764).[16] In the college-preparatory senior high school's mathematics-science track (Track B of the SMA), the number of graduates increased fourfold during the five-year period 1955–1959 (from 2,809 to 11,201).[17] Therefore, science education for people entering vocational specialties important to national development made remarkable gains on a number of fronts throughout the 1950s.

Guided Democracy, Guided Economy, 1959–1965

President Sukarno was the chief spokesman for the segment of the political leadership which contended that the fighting revolution may have ended in 1949, but the social revolution was still in full swing. After 1959, when the president and his close associates took affairs more into their own hands, they stressed the need for coordinating all facets of Indonesian society to work toward successful completion of the social revolution. The spirit of the times was epitomized in slogans proclaiming "Not art for art's sake, but art for the revolution," "Not sport for sport's sake, but sport for the revolution," and "Not science for science's sake, but science for the revolution."

In August 1959 President Sukarno appointed a seventy-member National Planning Council, charged with the task of creating the practical master design for social, cultural, and economic development. Within a year the Council produced an Eight-Year Overall Development Plan, which was initiated in 1961 and was scheduled for completion in 1968. Science education was given a significant role in the plan, principally in the form of an expansion of technical training schools and of science-and-technology colleges in the university sector.

As noted earlier, the most prestigious secondary school during Dutch times was the college-preparatory high school (SMA), particularly the science-mathematics track which provided graduates an opportunity to enter any variety of institution of higher education. The technical-training secondary schools, which in the past were terminal education programs leading to no higher education institutions, carried much less prestige. And though the Indonesian government by the 1960s established rules permitting technical-school graduates to enroll in certain types of engineering colleges, the old attitudes toward the college-preparatory versus technical high school remained firm in the minds of parents and students. Most capable students did not want to enter a technical school, and even in engineering colleges the SMA graduate of the science-mathematics track was much preferred over the technical-school graduate. In the Eight-Year Plan the government meant to change all this. The existing ratio of seven college-preparatory to three technical high schools was to be reversed, so that the expected future manpower needs for industrial expansion could be fulfilled.[18] That is, economic planners saw the greatest need to be for middle-level technicians, and the technical secondary schools were viewed as the proper source of these workers. Implicit in this new stress on technical education was a new stress on the science education required to support technical training.

The Eight-Year Plan assigned higher education a role similar to that given the secondary schools. In the past, the number of college students in the humanities had outnumbered those in the natural sciences. Therefore, the Eight-Year Plan, with its stress on industrial and techno-logical development, decreed that out of every three new colleges estab-lished (public or private), two would have to be in the science-mathe-matics areas and only one could be in the fields of literature, languages, or social sciences.[19]

The Overall Development Plan, launched with great fanfare and high hope in 1960–1961, sank in the roily waters of accelerating political and social disaster that engulfed the Republic between 1961 and 1966. In late 1966, after the Plan had supposedly been developing for six years, the nation's director general of basic industries, Suhartojo, stated that not one of the projects had succeeded.[20] The program for reversing the existing 7:3 ratio of college-preparatory to vocational (including techni-cal) high schools was no exception. Although the government did not establish many new college-preparatory schools, parents who wanted their children to get the coveted college-prep diplomas organized associations and erected schools themselves. Hence, general high schools directed at college preparation continued to multiply. At the same time the govern-ment found itself financially unable to erect many vocational schools. Thus the ratio continued to be just the inverse of the government's plan, or even deteriorated. In Djakarta in early 1965 the relationship was reported to be about seven general to one vocational high school.[21] At a national planning conference in April 1965, delegates from outer islands reported that college-preparatory schools continued to overshadow voca-tional schools 7:2 or 7:3.[22]

The amount of progress achieved in carrying out the higher-educa-tion part of the Plan cannot be appraised accurately, because figures describing numbers of colleges and their enrollments for the humanities versus the mathematics-sciences institutions[23] were frequently not reported to the Ministry of Education during the 1960–1967 period. Data on private colleges were particularly inadequate.

Nevertheless, some impression of trends can be gained from availa-ble statistics on public, and in some cases private, institutions between 1959 and 1967.

In 1959 the seven public universities and one institute contained 26 colleges (called *faculties*) in the science-math-technology (s-m-t) cate-gory, enrolling 47 percent of the total 32,194 students, and 18 colleges in the humanities-social-science (h-s-s) category, enrolling 53 percent of the students. Six teachers colleges, enrolling 5,304, had a much larger percentage of students in the h-s-s departments than in the s-m-t. Therefore, the ratio of s-m-t to h-s-s colleges was about 4:3, but since humanities-social-science departments were much larger, more than half of the university students were enrolled in them.[24]

Vigorous efforts were exerted beginning in 1962 to expand higher education and, in the process, to achieve the 2:1 ratio of science-math to humanities-social-science colleges that had been urged in the Eight-Year Plan. At the beginning of 1962 the number of colleges had reached 46 s-m-t and 34 h-s-s in the public sector, or a ratio near 4:3. By the end of 1962 there were 52 s-m-t and 45 h-s-s colleges, or nearly a 6:5 ratio. By October 1963 the number had reached 76 s-m-t and 52 h-s-s schools, or about a 3:2 ratio. In effect, some headway was being made in expanding the number of science-math-technology schools at a faster rate than humanities-social-science colleges. However, the private institutions were quite another matter. Of the 240 private colleges registered with the Ministry of Education, 28 were s-m-t and 212 h-s-s, or a ratio of 1:8.5 in favor of the humanities-social-science schools.[25]

By early 1967 among public universities and institutes, 46.5 percent were science-math-technology, 28.7 percent humanities-social-science, and 24.8 percent teacher-education. This means that the ratio of science-math to humanities-social-science had reached about 5:3, slightly better than in 1963 but still well below the 2:1 of the Eight-Year Plan. Among the 124 private institutions registered with the Ministry of Education, only 17.9 percent were in s-m-t, 68.6 percent in h-s-s, and 13.5 percent in teacher-education. Thus the s-m-t to h-s-s ratio of 1:4 was an improvement over the 1:8.5 of 1963 (though the 1967 report was on a considerably smaller number of schools). Among the 92 academies offering two or three-year special courses under different departments of the government (the postal service, the police, the civil aviation board, and others), the s-m-t to h-s-s ratio was about 1:2, just the reverse of the Plan's recommendation.[26] Consequently, over the 1959–1967 period, progress toward achieving a 2:1 balance between science-math-technology and humanities-social-science institutions had not been very great. And when the numbers of students enrolled in various curriculums in public institutions are compared, it becomes clear that the balance in 1967 was almost the same as in 1959. Whereas in 1959 there were 53 percent of public university and institute students in humanities-social-science departments, in 1967 there were still 51.5 percent in these curriculums (primarily in law and economics colleges).[27] Not yet half of the nation's public university students were in the science-math-technology sector. And in the private schools the situation was much worse.

Though not much headway was made during the guided-democracy period toward achieving what national planners considered better balance in numbers of students following math-science and humanities-social-science curriculums, significant improvement was made in the actual quantities of students in the math-science-technology stream. In 1959 there were 17,080 students in the math-science-technology departments of public institutions. By 1967 this had more than doubled to an estimated 37,019, a gain that might be considered remarkable if it is assumed that the quality of instruction was not diluted over the eight-year period of growth.[28]

Finally, the question arises: If planners had been able to expand college enrollments so rapidly, why had they failed to achieve the 2:1 balance called for in the Eight-Year Plan? The reasons for this are several.

First, science and technological courses were forced to limit enrollments to the numbers of students that could be accommodated by the short supply of laboratories and equipment like microscopes and chemicals. In contrast, departments of economics and law (which in 1967 enrolled 80 percent of the humanities-social-science students) needed only a larger lecture hall or extra lecture sessions in the same hall in order to expand enrollments, since lecturing—frequently without the assignment of parallel study in library sources—was the dominant mode of instruction. The average enrollment in a typical science-math-technology department in 1967 was 454, or less than one-third the enrollment of the typical humanities-social-science department (1,459).[29]

Second, it was not only the science-math-technology professions which carried the prestige that attracted quantities of applicants; certain humanities-social-science departments were equally desirable. A high level of status has traditionally been accorded degrees earned from colleges of law and economics and, to a lesser extent, from ones of social-and-political science (*sospol*). Graduates with such degrees usually have found employment in the government or, in the case of economics, in business. The law degree, *Sardjana Hukum*, has been particular prized. Some critics of the educational scene have observed that those who write the treasured SH behind their names feel that the degree entitles them to speak authoritatively on any topic. Consequently, large numbers of high school graduates who desired the advantages of these particular degrees —and those graduates who could not secure admission to the more selective science-math-technology departments—sought admission to law, economics, and social-political colleges. And since only an instructor and a lecture hall were needed to accommodate the applicants, these departments proliferated despite the desires of national planners.

A further factor influencing the pattern of growth in university enrollments was the requirement that only students from the math-science track of the college-preparatory high school could apply for a science-math-technology college. (In a few cases, a graduate from a technical secondary school could be admitted.) Consequently, students from the other and more populous tracks of the high school had no choice but to apply to a humanities-social-science department or to a teachers college.

This, then, was the 1959–1965 period of guided democracy as it affected science education for national development. In summary, we can say that the period found no substantial gains in the vocational (technical) schools which the framers of the Eight-Year Plan had hoped would supply the middle-level technicians for a major move toward a more industralized society. The college-preparatory high schools, on the other hand, continued to increase, contrary to the wishes of planning bodies. This increase, however, produced more science-mathematics high school graduates who were prepared to seek entrance to science and technology departments of colleges. At the university level, the numbers of students in the science-math-technology departments more than doubled between 1959 and 1967, but the ratio of science-math-technology students to humanities-social-science students stayed about the same: around 48 to 52.

The Post-Coup Period, 1965–1967

From the viewpoint of progress in science education, the period between October 1965 and Summer 1967 is properly scored a loss. Between the attempted *coup d'état* of October 1, 1965, and the beginning of the student strike on January 10, 1966, instructional programs in colleges were constantly upset by the bloody political and social disorders that disturbed the entire society. Instruction stopped entirely in most higher-education institutions when the students declared a general strike in January. They cast themselves in the role of the nation's social conscience and left the classrooms to engage in mass demonstrations designed to force Communist elements out of the government and, finally, to remove Sukarno as the head of state. With few exceptions, instruction did not resume in any serious way the rest of the year. By the late spring and early summer of 1967, instruction was being conducted in a more or less regular manner in many schools. But a large number of institutions still were not operating with efficiency. Entranced with their new political power, students continued to give considerable attention to public affairs, and their scientific and technological studies suffered.

Thus the unproductivity of higher education during 1966–1967 earned itself a prominent place on the debit side of the national-development ledger. But the new, constructive approach that national planners adopted in late 1966 and throughout 1967 gave promise of credit entries in the future. The years leading up to the coup had been marked by fanciful thinking on the part of government leaders under Sukarno. However, the New Order that took over in 1966 demonstrated a willingness to face economic and social facts with an encouraging frankness. In 1967 a new coordination among government departments to form an overall national development plan was being implemented. Whether this attempt at planning would eventuate in effective action was not yet clear by the end of the year. And the place of science education in the new plan had yet to be spelled out. But at least the tack which officials are taking gives cause for hope that this approach will be considerably more effective than was the Eight-Year Plan.

Before leaving our survey of science-education's role in national development, it is appropriate to look briefly at Indonesians' conception of the proper scope of science in national planning. Up to this point in our discussion we have focused exclusively on education in the natural sciences (including geography) and in the professions they support, such as medicine, engineering, and agriculture. In the main, these are the same fields utilized in most national development schemes. However, in the latter 1950s and in the 1960s some consideration was being accorded certain social sciences, principally economics and political science. To a much smaller degree, attention was directed at sociology, cultural anthropology, and social psychology. But the roles assigned to these disciplines during the guided-democracy period and the preceding liberal period were either slight or were "unscientific." Political and economic planners were often much stronger in debating theory (mostly Marxist versus Western-democratic notions) than in collecting and analyzing data that could support development designs. It was quite apparent that in the era of guided democracy and guided economy President Sukarno and his top aides manipulated or fabricated demographic statistics to suit their political acts.[30] However, during this same period the best of higher-education institutions were teaching scientific approaches in economics, political science, sociology, anthropology, and, to a much more limited extent, social psychology. After the control of national affairs passed into new hands in 1966–1967, the moves made by planners suggested that more of the country's expertise in the social sciences would be brought to bear in national development. A variety of major statistical surveys concerning affairs in the social-science realms were launched so that realistic data would be available for sound planning.[31] Thus, it appeared possible by the end of 1967 that the scope of the sciences serving national development might well be broadened beyond the physical sciences and allied professions to encompass more of the social sciences.

Science for Science's Sake

The third category of science education—the study of pure science or science for science's sake—had distinguished beginnings in the Netherlands Indies colony during the nineteenth and twentieth centuries. Although most science research and instruction aimed at solving practical problems important to Dutch economic and social interests (tin mining, rubber and tea production, cattle production, treating tropical diseases, and the like), a substantial amount of study was also directed at phenomena interesting in their own right: tropical flora (the world-renowned botanic gardens at Buitenzorg [Bogor] in West Java was started in 1817), tropical fauna (the zoological museum opened at Buitenzorg in 1901), volcanoes and earthquakes (with Krakatau the most famous of nearly 100 active volcanoes), the equatorial seas, the equatorial skies (Bosscha observatory was erected in the mid-1920s near Bandung, West Java), ancient man (*pithecantropus erectus* was discovered in Central Java in 1891–1892), and modern man's variety of cultures and social systems (throughout the 350-year Dutch presence in the islands, treatises on the archipelago's many tribes were compiled).[32]

The hundreds of studies in pure natural and social sciences conducted during Dutch times were in most cases the products of men who pursued such scholarly work only as a pastime. Their real purpose for coming to the Indies had been to take posts in the colonial service or to operate plantations and exporting firms. But since so many of them brought to the islands sound academic training from universities in Holland, they were prepared in their spare time to apply scholarly talents to the study of the curiosities of their new environment.

During the Japanese military occupation of 1942–1945 there was little opportunity for the study of science for its own sake. But when the Dutch were released from internment camps in the islands after the war, or when they returned from Holland or Australia during the revolutionary period of 1945–1949, some studies in the prewar tradition were resumed. In 1948 the Dutch, in the territories they controlled, created an Organization for Natural Science Research (*Organisatie voor Natuurwetenschappelijk Onderzoek*), but the attempts of this body to coordinate and stimulate scientific investigation were not very successful in the revolutionary setting. Within the territories held by the beleaguered Republic of Indonesia government, only a slight amount of medical research could be pursued.[33]

In prewar Dutch times pure research found its way into science education by means of textbooks from Holland and research journals or monographs published by research societies. Lecturers in the Netherlands

Indies colleges incorporated such information in their instruction, and advanced students aided with research projects.

During the early 1950s the two public universities from revolutionary times, University of Indonesia and Gadjah Mada University, continued the general Dutch pattern, even to the extent of employing numbers of Dutch professors on their faculties. Thus an amount of science for science's sake continued to be included in the curriculum.

In the final years of the 1950s and through the mid-1960s the numbers of colleges and their enrollments expanded rapidly, so that more and more graduate students were conducting research for their master's or doctor's theses, and in numbers of cases this was pure science, in the sense that it was not directed at solving practical problems related to national development. However, the educational enterprise faced the problem of distributing these research findings throughout the nation's instructional system so they would add to science education in general. Several universities and institutes established journals or monograph series for publishing studies by faculty members and, in some cases, by advanced students. But these journals cared for only a small segment of the publishing needs. In the late 1950s the Department of National Research began issuing *Indonesian Abstracts,* a bulletin containing summaries of scientific articles appearing in Indonesia but not abstracts of theses. This periodical continued publication somewhat irregularly through the mid-1960s. The Department also started a scientific journal, *Medan Ilmu Pengetahuan* (Field of Science), but it, like most of the universities' scholarly publications, succumbed in the mid-1960s for lack of financial support. However valiant the foregoing publishing efforts, they did not suffice to disseminate research findings among academicians who could profit from inserting the findings into their teaching.

In brief, some science for science's sake, both in the areas of natural and social sciences, was being pursued in the forms of research and instruction in the 1950s and 1960s. Most of the research emanated from the institutions of higher education. However, the system for disseminating research findings to instructors and other research workers was quite inadequate. Most of the teaching of pure science continued to be based upon textbooks and journals imported from abroad rather than upon indigenous research and theory.[34]

FOUR PROBLEMS AND POTENTIAL SOLUTIONS

The preceding survey of Indonesian science education has touched on a variety of problems which affect national development. Of these, the four which seem to demand the greatest attention are: (1) determining a reasonable role for science and technical education in a national development program, (2) securing dedicated, well-prepared teaching personnel, (3) providing enough suitable reading materials, and (4) furnishing the equipment and supplies necessary for efficient science education. To close this chapter, we shall inspect each of these problems briefly and consider some steps which might aid toward their solution.

A realistic role for science and technical education in a national development program

Among the shortcomings of the 1960–1968 development plan, the most serious one in the field of education was the gross recommendation that the ratio of vocational technical schools to general college-preparatory schools be changed from 3:7 to 7:3. In making such a suggestion, educational planners appeared to be ignoring several salient facts.

First, the equipment in currently established technical schools was either nonexistent or in such poor condition that it would have been sufficiently ambitious to aim at properly equipping these institutions, much less to aim at opening more than twice as many new ones.

Second, we have already noted that the nation's cultural tradition always placed vocational secondary schools on a much lower status level than general, college-preparatory high schools. Students who completed the general curriculum were accorded greater rewards in prestigious employment than those who went to vocational schools. And the Eight-Year Development Plan included no clear scheme to produce incentives for the vocational student so that a sufficient supply of candidates for technical schools could be ensured.

Third, and most serious, there was no assurance that the intended growth of vocational education would be coordinated with the ability of the economy to absorb the graduates of technical schools at the rate they might be produced. As Foster has illustrated in the case of Ghana, gross manpower-need estimates that are central elements of development schemes in many of today's new nations are apt to contain large measures of unforeseen error.

> There is a tendency to talk of the "needs" for development as if they were quite independent of the actual structure of job opportunities in the economy. This is daring planning, but . . . the production of large numbers of specially trained individuals does not, at the same time, create employment opportunities for them.
> Furthermore, the calculation of varying shortfalls for different types of specific skill is a hazardous endeavor, particularly in areas where there is an absence of any really satisfactory or meaningful data to make such projections realistic. Cumulative errors in the projection of a whole range of manpower needs can ultimately add up to an alarming misallocation of scarce resources, particularly when

these are invested in the establishment of highly expensive vocational institutions. . . .

It might be more fruitful to encourage small-scale vocational
training schemes closely associated with actual ongoing developments
and quite divorced from the formal educational system. This implies
a strategy that relates specific vocational training to other necessary
changes in the institutional framework.[35]

For a variety of reasons, it would appear wise for Indonesia to
employ a vocational-education scheme that incorporates Foster's suggestion of depending on nonschool facilities for vocational training, particularly in the technical areas. One reason is that the nation's planners have
not been sure about which sectors of the economy should be given
greatest emphasis. For instance, those in charge of economic planning in
the 1966–1968 period stressed agricultural over large-scale industrial
development, whereas the Eight-Year Plan of 1960 placed greater emphasis on industry. Therefore, until economic planners see how their
schemes are working out in practice, it appears unwise for Indonesia to
invest large sums in a formal education system dedicated solely to one of
these untested schemes. It might well be practical for Indonesia to adopt
a compromise plan. That is, efforts could be exerted to equip existing
vocational schools with machinery, supplies, and able instructors, but no
new schools would be started. At the same time, on-the-job or apprenticeship training programs could be greatly expanded. The on-the-job plan
offers several immediate advantages. It adjusts the numbers of trainees
more closely to the economy's absorption rate for each specific type of
skilled worker. It ensures that the trainees receive practical experience in
using machines and solving realistic problems, which is often not possible
today in so many vocational schools that are without proper equipment. It
has the incentive value of providing the trainee a small wage while he
learns. To be most effective, such a plan would require effective supervision by the Department of Education and a widespread inservice program
for instructing foremen in industrial plants and supervisors in offices in
the most helpful ways for them to teach the apprentices assigned to their
sectors. The plan would also require the publication of a wide variety of
training guides for specific occupations, including handbooks illustrating
the practical application of scientific principles to the job at hand.

A broad expansion of on-the-job training would not eliminate the
role of the regular secondary school. Rather, most students could attend
junior or senior secondary school part-time to study natural science,
mathematics, language, and social studies of a general-education variety. In this way a broad knowledge of scientific phenomena and methods
could be learned in school, but the application of science to specific
vocational skills would be learned on the job. The student would also be

receiving, at a slower pace, the general-secondary schooling which traditionally has been accorded higher prestige.

In short, existing vocational schools which could be equipped properly would not be abolished, since they are providing a useful service and the economy appears able to absorb their relatively small number of graduates. But the bulk of new workers could come from the combined on-the-job and part-time secondary-schooling sector.

Securing dedicated, well-prepared teaching personnel

By the mid-1960s the problems of attracting and educating capable science and technical teachers had become extremely difficult to solve. Science teaching was not financially attractive enough to draw suitable candidates into teacher-education programs or, for ones who did earn teaching credentials, to retain them in the profession.

In the late 1950s and during the 1960s, educators had fallen into a distressing financial condition. To feed their families, teachers were either having to leave the profession entirely or else spend long hours in part-time occupations outside the classroom, thus reducing the hours they might devote to preparing lessons, correcting papers, and conferring with students. Several college professors told the writer in 1966 that their monthly salaries paid only five days' living costs (not including the purchase of clothing), even when they lived in government housing and were given a rice allotment for each member of their household. The salaries of elementary and secondary school teachers were even less adequate.

The most obvious suggestion for improving the financial appeal of the teaching profession was to raise teachers' pay by several hundred percent. Then there might once again be plenty of teacher-education candidates, as had been true during Dutch times when educators enjoyed a secure standard of living. Indeed, the government in the late 1950s and in the 1960s did raise salaries of civil servants periodically, but economic inflation accelerated at such a rapid pace that living costs consistently outstripped wage increases. Although future attempts to raise salaries to an adequate level are still needed, the problem of attracting and retaining teachers will not be solved by such measures in the next few years, since the Indonesian economy can hardly be expected to recover its footing for some time to come. Other steps must be taken to staff science and technical teaching posts during the period when full-time teaching cannot be expected to provide an adequate wage. For example, in the case of technical education, some relief from the shortage of instructors could come from the apprenticeship plan suggested above. In addition, more efficient use of outside scientists as part-time teachers in secondary schools and universities appears desirable. The large numbers of part-timers now serving in the schools might improve their effectiveness if given inservice education in the form of three- to five-day teaching workshops at which modern science-education methods are demonstrated. Descriptions of improved methods can be distributed widely throughout the archipelago in the form of teachers' guidebooks to accompany the newer texts and pamphlets now being planned for science education at all levels.

In addition to better utilization of part-timers, the government can profitably intensify the program of utilizing the more established universities as the suppliers of personnel for the newer institutions. According to the government's 1967 plan, facilities for advanced graduate work will be concentrated in the older institutions rather than distributed throughout the islands, as was the tendency during the early 1960s.[36] In addition, advanced students are once again being sent to graduate schools in the Western nations to enhance their skills as professors in Indonesian institutions. These two programs, one national and the other international, appear to be the most promising ones for staffing Indonesia's colleges in the latter 1960s and early 1970s.

In a similar manner, the most mature teachers colleges in Bandung, Djakarta, Jogjakarta, and Malang on Java are expected to provide instructors for the newer institutes throughout the islands.[37] In addition, they are expected to expand their extension classes (the former B-1 and B-2 courses given in the late afternoon and evening hours) to upgrade inservice teachers.

The success of the teacher-education programs depends, however, on the success of the government's efforts to make teaching financially appealing. Unless sufficient quantities of able students are willing to enter the teachers colleges, there obviously will be few science teachers graduated, no matter how high the quality of science-education might become in the colleges.

Providing enough suitable reading materials

To solve the great shortage of science and technical books, educational leaders in 1967 planned extensive Indonesian-language writing and publishing efforts for the coming years.

In the mid-1960s approximately 90 percent of texts and reference books in universities were from foreign sources, most often English-language imports from the United States. However, a variety of factors (students' difficulties in reading English, lack of foreign-exchange currencies to buy books abroad, high cost of imported books, transportation difficulties, problems of selecting suitable books from abroad, and Indonesian nationalistic feelings) convinced the leaders in the Directorate General of Higher Education in late 1967 to establish a ten-year scheme, beginning in 1969, aimed at reversing the import-local ratio. By 1979 the

Directorate General hoped that locally produced titles would represent 90 percent of university-level books.[38]

According to the ten-year plan, professors would be given stipends by the government to write text materials, thus eliminating the necessity for them to accept other outside employment in order to live. The subject-matter areas to be treated by the texts would not be assigned by the Directorate General nor would there be much, if any, coordination of efforts among authors or institutions. It would be free, not guided, enterprise. Each author would produce what he felt was needed in his own school. If other colleges then wished to adopt his book, they might do so. But they would also be free to produce their own books in the same field.

The potential effectiveness of the foregoing plan is somewhat in question. Certainly, in light of the continuing dislocation of the economy in 1967–1968, it is highly unlikely that the 1979 goal can be reached. The chief obstacle will be financial. The nation's publishing industry in 1967 was still badly in need of spare parts, new typesetting equipment and printing presses, and imported paper. Foreign-exchange currencies to purchase these commodities would continue to be hard to come by. There is also a serious question about the Directorate of Higher Education's ability to provide adequate stipends for authors. And even if the Directorate General's traditionally meager budget could be extended to furnish a substantial quantity of author support, such support does not at all guarantee that adequate manuscripts will be forthcoming. As publishers in other countries well know, college professors are much better at planning books than they are at completing manuscripts to meet publishing deadlines, or for that matter, at completing manuscripts at all. In other words, the Directorate General should not count on receiving adequate manuscripts from all the authors who might be given stipends.

To solve at least part of the printing problem, the Directorate General of Higher Education in 1967–1968 planned to provide mimeograph machines and some paper to individual institutions so they might issue their manuscripts on their own initiative, without having to depend on commercial publishers. A scheme of this type, which operated with equipment and paper provided by foreign agencies, had already proved of worth during the early 1960s at the Faculty of Economics of the University of Indonesia, the Agricultural Institute at Bogor, and the Teacher Education Institute at Bandung.[39]

The ten-year publishing plan could probably achieve more success in the humanities and social sciences than in the natural sciences and technology, because books in the former areas usually do not require the illustrative material needed in many scientific and technical publications. Some Indonesian educators have suggested that priority be given to the local production of the most widely used, introductory texts in a field like biology and chemistry and books whose contents would be unique to Indonesia or Southeast Asia (titles treating botany or geology of the archipelago). Other science books, in their opinion, should be English-language texts and reference books, because scientific knowledge advances at such a rapid pace today that Indonesian authors or translators and Indonesian publishers could not keep up with the requirements. By the time a scientific tome had been written or translated in a specialized field, its contents would often be out of date.[40]

In view of the foregoing, it would appear wise for the Directorate General of Higher Education to provide some coordination of efforts rather than leave textbook writing entirely undirected. As recommended by the March 1967 survey of Indonesian publishing:

> A study could be conducted by the Directorate . . . with the aim of:
> (1) Preparing a priority list of the kinds of textbooks and supplementary books written in Indonesian that are most immediately needed and those which will be needed in the foreseeable future.
> (2) Determining which titles (in Indonesian) are already in print, those which are in manuscript form, and others which still need to be written or translated and adapted from other languages.
> (3) Preparing a priority list of the kinds of textbooks and supplementary books written in English that are most immediately needed and those which will be needed in the foreseeable future.[41]

Besides furnishing the above types of information to individual institutions and authors, the Directorate General might also provide welcome aid to new authors in the form of:

(a) A guidebook for authors, either written in the Indonesian language specifically for Indonesian authors, or imported from abroad.

(b) Short-term (two weeks to two months) workshops for writers, conducted . . . by experienced Indonesian and/or foreign authors.

(c) Long-term (six months to two years) writing projects to which potential authors are assigned full time under the supervision of, or with the assistance of, experienced Indonesian and/or foreign writers.[42]

The same recommendations regarding a survey of existing books and those that are most needed has been made for the elementary and secondary schools. Likewise, the guidebooks for workshops for writers suggested for higher education would appear desirable for producing authors of science materials for elementary and secondary schools. Since imported books are less practical at elementary and secondary levels than in universities, a high priority for producing science and technical booklets for the lower schools appears necessary. Again, the principal problem is economic. A substantial number of good-quality science books (mostly paperbacks ranging in length from 50 to 120 pages) are currently available from private Indonesian publishers, but they are not distributed nearly so widely among the schools because students and teachers cannot usually afford them. Therefore, some form of subsidy to place these books in classrooms, or at least in school libraries, would seem to be more important even than subsidizing authors to produce new titles.

Obviously there is no single route to solving the problems of furnishing large quantities of high-quality science and technical reading materials to Indonesian schools. Efforts are needed in a variety of sectors, including the revitalized importation of foreign books through foreign aid sources for universities and a vigorous program of writing and publishing of materials in the Indonesian language for all levels of the school system.

Furnishing equipment and supplies for science education

The problem of securing the equipment needed for giving students direct science experiences can evidently be best attacked through a heightened emphasis on three existing programs.

First, projects aimed at instructing teachers in the use of easy-to-secure materials for building simple science equipment can profitably be expanded. The chief programs that would appear to warrant stronger support are the inservice courses conducted by the Science Teaching Centers and the preservice courses in the teachers colleges and the high schools which prepare elementary-school teachers. Traveling teams of science educators could conduct short-term workshops throughout the islands to furnish teachers in rural areas more guidance in preparing simple experiments and equipment. The publication of teachers' guides on simple experiments and field trips could also hasten the spread of improved teaching methods.

Second, the further development and expanded local production of portable chemistry, physics, biology, and earth-science kits for high school teachers might furnish thousands of students in smaller cities with demonstrations of scientific phenomena which otherwise they would never witness.

Third, an expanded program of foreign aid appears necessary to provide the instruments, machines, and supplies which cannot be manufactured locally. Since the government is not likely to have much foreign-exchange money to invest in such items during these years of economic distress, educational leaders will apparently need to seek the help of foreign governments and foundations or else go without the equipment. For assistance to higher education, a renewal of at least the commodity-procurement portions of the major foreign aid projects of the 1960s would appear wise. In addition, other foreign universities and foundations could be solicited to furnish limited amounts of specified items, such as microscopes and electronic equipment.

In establishing a program for procuring equipment and supplies

from overseas, Indonesian education officials face two longstanding problems: (1) deciding to which schools they should allocate available funds
or should assign foreign donors of commodities and (2) establishing who
should determine what equipment and supplies should be ordered. In the
early 1960s, as institutions of higher education multiplied at a rapid rate,
universities in smaller cities and on the islands outside of Java sought
substantial allocations of equipment which would bring them closer to
the rather high standard which the old, established institutions in Djakarta, Bandung, Bogor, and Jogjakarta had reached. On the other hand,
the older, more mature schools stated that, if equipment were dispersed
thinly throughout the nation, there would be no institutions sufficiently
developed to conduct high-quality graduate programs that would produce
able scientists and technological experts. In this competition, the older
institutions, with their foreign-aid ties to universities and foundations
abroad, usually came out best. The major questions appear to be: How
should equipment funds be distributed among institutions? Should it be
equal amounts to all? A lion's share to the best developed ones? Or a
lion's share to the least developed ones? A further question has been:
Should the distribution of foreign aid be determined by the central
authorities in Djakarta, or should each institution be relatively free to
seek connections abroad for securing donations of equipment and supplies? The answers to these questions appeared to be that the government
would first stress the development of the most mature colleges, utilizing
these schools for producing doctorate degrees and for furnishing guidance
in the development of newer schools. So the strong apparently were to be
made stronger, on the theory that in the long run this would be in the
best interests of the newer institutions that would benefit in the future.
The Directorate General of Higher Education would evidently supervise
all connections between Indonesian public colleges and governments or
foundations abroad. But apparently more leeway than in the past is to be
allowed individual schools for seeking suitable donors overseas.

The problem of who should be authorized to determine what
equipment is most needed had arisen in the 1950s, when expensive
scientific equipment had been shipped to colleges which could not make
proper use of the imported items. As a result, the instruments and
supplies sat unused, either in their original shipping crates or on science
department shelves. In some instances, these items had been ordered by
visionaries in a central-department post rather than the instructors who
were prepared to use them. It appeared in 1967 that more local authority
was being given to individual institutions to select textbooks and equipment to buy abroad, rather than having such decisions made in the
Directorate General of Higher Education.[43]

Despite the encouraging signs in 1967 that more foreign agencies
would be willing to donate equipment and supplies, it seems clear that

with the disordered state of the economy the nation's schools and universities can look forward to further serious problems in providing students direct science experiences that require manufactured or imported commodities.

EPILOGUE

To close this survey of the relation of Indonesian science education to national development, we may turn back more than a quarter century to a statement written in 1945 by two Dutchmen who served as editors of a volume entitled *Science and Scientists in the Netherlands Indies.* In the preface to their book, Honig and Verdoorn wrote:

> At the present time, when the right of peoples to self-government is being so much discussed, we may be permitted to ask whether scientific studies should be pursued in the same way as in the past—in a part of the world where nature and custom do not inevitably impel the rational recognition and application of facts established by the pure and applied sciences. To the implied question —namely, whether or not the occidental has the right and duty to continue his work as in the past—this book may offer a partial reply.
>
> Only modern research can answer today's demand for a higher level of material well-being, for "freedom from want," that now basic governmental principle in every country where living standards are diverse. Only modern research seems able to help eradicate the poverty and privation among large groups of the population in many countries—a poverty and privation which would seem fundamentally unnecessary in this twentieth century. Science and its exponents will doubtless continue to have a great mission in the Far East.[44]

By 1968 Indonesian leaders clearly agreed that occidental science and technology would be essential instruments for producing the just and prosperous society to which they aspired. But they did not agree that foreigners from the West would be the scientists and technologists who would produce this happy state. Rather, Indonesia's own science-education establishment would produce the needed experts. Though aid from the West might be needed a while longer to hasten the development of the establishment, it continued to be clear in 1967–1968 that Indonesians intended soon to be, as ex-President Sukarno had urged, *berdiri atas kaki sendiri,* independently standing on their own. The question remains, how soon is "soon"?

[1] M. Hutasoit, *Compulsory Education in Indonesia* (Paris: UNESCO, 1954), pp. 51–52.
[2] *Ibid.,* pp. 47–48.

[3] *Rentjana Pendidikan Taman Kanak*[2] *dan Sekolah Dasar* (Djakarta: Departemen Pendidikan Dasar dan Kebudajaan, 1964), pp. 29, 60–63.

[4] *Ibid.*, p. 252.

[5] *Laporan: Perkembangan Pendidikan Dokter pada Fakultas Kedokteran, Universitas Indonesia* (Djakarta: Fakultas Kedokteran, Universitas Indonesia, 1960), p. 1.

[6] William J. Micheels and Warren E. Phillips, *The Current Structure, Status, and Facilities of Technical Education* (Djakarta: Department of Education, Republic of Indonesia, 1960), p. 11.

[7] Sardjito, *The Development of the Universitas Gadjah Mada* (Jogjakarta: Universitas Gadjah Mada, 1956), p. 3.

[8] *Ibid.*

[9] Interview with S. Yokoyama (Tokyo, 1965), civil administrator of education for Java under the Japanese military government 1944–1945.

[10] Sukarno, *Toward Freedom and the Dignity of Man* (Djakarta: Department of Foreign Affairs, Republic of Indonesia, 1961), p. 44.

[11] Statistics Division, Department of Basic Education and Culture, Republic of Indonesia, Djakarta, 1964.

[12] R. Murray Thomas, "Literacy by Decree in Indonesia," *School and Society* (Summer 1966), p. 279.

[13] *Perguruan Tinggi di Indonesia* (Djakarta: Departemen Perguruan Tinggi dan Ilmu Pengetahuan, 1965), pp. 12–15.

[14] Douglas S. Paauw, "From Colonial to Guided Economy," in *Indonesia,* ed. Ruth McVey (New Haven, Conn.: Hraf Press, 1963), pp. 218–20.

[15] R. Murray Thomas, "Guided Study in Indonesian Universities," *Journal of Higher Education,* Vol. 34, No. 5 (May 1963).

[16] William J. Micheels and Warren E. Phillips, *The Current Structure,* p. iv.

[17] Statistics Division, Department of Basic Education and Culture, Republic of Indonesia, Djakarta, 1967.

[18] *Ringkasan Ketetapan Madjelis Permusjawaratan Rakjat Sementara— Republik Indonesia* (Djakarta: MPRS dan Departemen Penerangan, 1961), p. 99.

[19] *Ibid.*, p. 68.

[20] "Tak Ada Satupun Projek Semesta Berentjana Jang Menghasilkan," *Suara Rakjat* (September 14, 1966), p. 1.

[21] Interview (Djakarta, February 1965) with officials of the secondary-education division, Department of Basic Education and Culture.

[22] Interview (Bandung, April 1965) with delegate to National Planning Conference.

[23] *Report of the Statistics Team on Higher Education in Indonesia* (Djakarta: Directorate General of Higher Education, Department of Education and Culture, Government of Indonesia, May 1967, mimeographed), p. 2. In Indonesian higher-education parlance the science-mathematics cluster is termed the exact-technical (*eksakta-tehnik*) group and includes medicine, pharmacy, biology, physics, chemistry, mathematics, engineering, agriculture, geology, and geography. The humanities-social-science cluster, called nonexact studies, includes law, economics, political science, psychology, sociology, public administration, public relations, languages, and literature. Teacher-education colleges are usually placed in a separate category; typically, their largest numbers of students are in humanities-social-science curriculums.

[24] *Rantjangan Dasar Undang-Undang Pembangunan Nasional Semesta Berentjana Delapan Tahun 1961–1968* (Djakarta: Depernas, 1960, sub-section 950).

[25] *Usaha Merobah Bandingan Djumlah Fakultas Ilmu Eksakta Tehnik: Ilmu Sosial Mendjadi 2:1* (Djakarta: Departemen Perguruan Tinggi dan Ilmu Pengetahuan, November 10, 1963, mimeographed), p. 1.

[26] *Report of the Statistics Team on Higher Education in Indonesia,* Annex I, p. 1.

[27] *Ibid.,* p. 3.

[28] *Ibid.,* Annex I, p. 1.

[29] *Ibid.,* Annex I, p. 2.

[30] For an example of the fabrication of literacy data see R. Murray Thomas, "Literacy by Decree in Indonesia," *School and Society* (Summer 1966), p. 279.

[31] Two such studies conducted during the spring of 1967 were: *Report of the Statistics Team on Higher Education in Indonesia;* Stanley A. Barnett et al., *Developmental Book Activities and Needs in Indonesia* (Washington, D.C.: Agency for International Development, June 1967).

[32] For a survey of work in the natural sciences of the Dutch Indies, see Pieter Honig and Frans Verdoorn, eds., *Science and Scientists in the Netherlands Indies* (New York: Board for the Netherlands Indies, Surinam, and Curacao, 1945). For sample sociological work, see B. Schrieke, *Indonesian Sociological Studies* (The Hague: W. Van Hoeve, 1955), Part 1, and 1957, Part 2. For a summary of studies of social class, both during Dutch times as well as during the early years of the Republic, see M. A. Jaspan, *Social Stratification and Social Mobility in Indonesia* (Djakarta: Gunung Agung, 1961).

[33] M. Makagiansar and R. M. Soemantri, eds., *Research di Indonesia 1945–1965 (II)* (Djakarta: Departemen Urusan Research Nasional, 1965), p. 2.

[34] The most comprehensive summary of research in Indonesia over the first two decades of the Republic, 1945–1965, is contained in the four-volume work *Research di Indonesia 1945–1965,* published by the Department of National Research. The fields covered by the volumes are: Vol. 1, medical and health sciences; Vol. 2, technological and industrial research; Vol. 3, agriculture; Vol. 4, economic, social, and cultural research. These volumes also describe educational trends in the areas covered.

[35] Philip J. Foster, "The Vocational School Fallacy in Development Planning."

[36] Report by Stanley A. Barnett (Wolf Management Services) of interview (Djakarta, January 24, 1968) with Drs. Kandou, representative of the Directorate General of Higher Education for the Republic of Indonesia.

[37] *Ibid.*

[38] Visits by the writer in July 1966 and March 1967.

[39] Stanley A. Barnett et al., *Developmental Book Activities and Needs in Indonesia,* pp. 79–80.

[40] *Ibid.,* pp. 80–81.

[41] *Ibid.,* p. 83.

[42] *Ibid.*

[43] Report by Stanley A. Barnett of interview (Djakarta, January 24, 1968) with Drs. Kandou, representative of the Directorate General of Higher Education for the Republic of Indonesia.

[44] Honig and Verdoorn, *Science and Scientists.*

CHAPTER 12

Lily K. Soemadikarta **The Development of Library Services in Indonesia**

Beyond doubt, Indonesian authorities recognize that education is fundamental in the nation's potential for development, and the government has adhered to a consistent policy of providing schools for every level of education. The number of schools and students have increased very rapidly since the proclamation of independence. Along with this development has come a pressing need for expansion of library services.

Books, journals, and other reading materials are indispensable tools at all levels of education. A program to eradicate illiteracy must be accompanied by a greater availability of suitable reading materials if the newly literate are to keep their skill. Universities must be able to supply the past and current literature of importance to their students, teachers, and research workers. Scientists and engineers require reference materials and the literature of their respective fields.

Libraries are among the most effective and economical means of making information available to all people. A strong, well-supported library system can, therefore, make an effective contribution to education and thus to development. One may say that a measure of any country's progress is the state of its libraries.

When UNESCO started to assist Indonesia in promoting its library services in 1953, there existed already a number of libraries. The development of these libraries, however, had not been proceeding through any central organization. The first national library survey conducted by the UNESCO expert and the former head of the Jogjakarta Provincial Library made clear that there needed to be developed a coordinated library system which would minimize duplication of efforts. Pending the establishment of a national library, the formation of a Library Bureau in the Ministry of Education was then recommended. This bureau was organized and was given the task of establishing provincial libraries. It also has responsibility for further development of the Library School. This school, the only one in Indonesia, has now become part of the University of Indonesia. By 1968 there were still less than 3,000 libraries, with a total of about five million books. From 1962 to 1967 the Library School of the University of Indonesia produced 104 professional librarians and 200 graduates with library certificates.

The following essay will review the various efforts undertaken to develop library services in Indonesia. Brief remarks on the local publishing industry and the local book trade will be included because their progress is also influenced by the presence of a functioning network of libraries which can provide a market for the reading materials that people need and want.

National Library Service and National Bibliography

The national library and the national bibliography of any country are vital for the development of its cultural life. A national library should collect and preserve the nation's literature, and its listings should be published as the national bibliography. The growth and expansion of today's knowledge results in an ever-increasing volume of literature, and this expands the function of the national library and broadens its responsibility to include collecting and preserving microprints of little-used materials for future research needs. Modern duplicating machines and modern telecommunication can make such material accessible to libraries throughout the country.

Although the establishment of the national library in Indonesia is entrusted to the Ministry of Education, it has not yet become a reality. Before 1945 the Museum Library (*Perpustakaan Lembaga Kebudajaan*) in Djakarta, founded in 1778 by a private society, could be called a national library, in recognition of its collection. For many years in the past publishers sent their publications to this library as a courtesy. This museum was thus able to preserve a large collection of Indonesian imprints, including files of Indonesian periodicals and newspapers. No other library, for example, has so comprehensive a collection of materials printed during the Japanese occupation. A complete collection of publications from the revolutionary period of 1945–1949 is preserved in the Jogjakarta Provincial Library.

The National Bibliographical Center (Kantor Bibliografi Nasional) in Djakarta, which was established in 1953, organizes the compiling of a national bibliography and publishes current monthly listings in the *Berita Bulanan Kantor Bibliografi Nasional.* However, it faces great difficulties in securing publications because there does not exist a legal provision for copyright deposit in Indonesia. It is therefore not possible to make these listings broad and all-inclusive.

One of the private firms, the publisher and bookdealer P. T. (*Perseroan Terbatas,* the Indonesian equivalent of Ltd.) Gunung Agung, also compiles a current national bibliography. Since 1955 P. T. Gunung Agung has published listings in its *Berita Bibliografi.* It is likely that publishers are more eager to send their publications to this firm, rather than to *Berita Bulanan Kantor Bibliografi Nasional,* since P. T. Gunung Agung has been able to publish its listings more rapidly.

The Ministry of Education has published a cumulative bibliography[1] which covers the years 1945–1963 and is arranged alphabetically by authors' names. Contributing to this compilation were bibliographies

published by Ockeloen,[2] by the National Bibliographical Center, and by
the publisher P. T. Gunung Agung. Another cumulative bibliography[3]
has been produced by the Association of Indonesian Publishers in com-
memoration of the twentieth anniversary of Indonesia's proclamation of
independence. This accumulation, arranged in subject-order, covers the
years 1945–1965.

The first union list of serials was published in 1953 with the
assistance of the UNESCO. This union list covers the holdings at that
time of six important science libraries in Djakarta, Bogor, and Bandung.
In 1963 the National Bibliographical Center published a national check-
list of serials. It contains reference to about 1,800 Indonesian and about
5,000 foreign periodicals received during the years 1956–1960 by the
principal libraries.

Public, School, and Provincial Libraries

In connection with its literacy program, the Section for Mass Education of the Ministry of Education developed a public library system, and
this program may be looked upon as an important achievement in
Indonesian librarianship, although it did not develop as it should because
of poor planning. By 1953 the Central Public Library (Pusat Perpustakaan Rakjat) in Djakarta reached a service load of supplying 15,000
villages, but because of overconcentration on village services, no funds
were left for the maintenance of public libraries in the cities. Even the
village services, however, could not be maintained permanently. Besides
the acute problem of providing money that was needed to finance this
program on such a large scale, government support in the form of a
strong publishing program was lacking. Publication of Indonesian books
by commercial publishers was then inadequate. Material containing easy
reading for the adult reader was most needed, but could not be provided.

With the progress of science and technology and the growing
demand for education, the careers of more people will depend on access
to new ideas in various fields. A library for children (as a section of a
public library or as a school library) has, therefore, a special responsibility for showing the children how to use written records and where to find
information. In the library, they gain impressions about the vast amount
of information and recreation one can get from written records. Acquiring these values gives them a background for continued library use in
self-education after leaving the schools.

In 1953, the Ministry of Education started to establish a school
library system, with a distribution of books to junior and senior high
schools. By 1956, however, this program had to be discontinued because
no more funds were available. School libraries are therefore generally
nonexistent in Indonesia except for a few model schools.

Almost all the provinces in Indonesia have Provincial Libraries, the largest being in Jogjakarta, Semarang, Bandung, and Makasar. Provincial Libraries at the present time are not trying to build up complete collections. They will rather stress their activities in extending technical assistance to other libraries in the area, and in coordinating library activities and library collections to achieve the most effective and efficient service.

Research and Academic Libraries

Scholars, scientists, and students have central roles to play in the development of the country. As science and technology have an increasing influence on social and economic life, the need will arise for more scientific and technical information. To avoid duplication of earlier works, scientific research should be preceded by a literature-search. Enormous waste of effort may occur when there is no library that can offer this service to a research worker.

The colonial government in Indonesia left a number of research libraries that were to serve the various institutions, and small but effective libraries had been supplied to the professional schools. In the past decade, foreign aid and library exchange programs were helpful in the further development of these types of libraries and in the training of library personnel abroad.

Since 1965 the documentation section of the Council for Sciences of Indonesia (MIPI—*Madjelis Ilmu Pengetahuan Indonesia*) has become the Indonesian National Scientific Documentation Center (PDIN—*Pusat Dokumentasi Ilmiah Nasional*). Equipment and staff training were made available by the UNESCO. This center publishes the bibliographical *Index to Indonesian Learned Periodicals* as a continuation of the *Postwar Scientific Bibliography* which was published by the Organization for Scientific Research (OSR). It also assists the publication of *Indonesian Abstracts,* which since 1958 has issued English summaries of scientific writing published in Indonesia. This Center is now administrating the U.S. AID-NAS (National Academy of Sciences) Science Book Program, which has been in operation since 1964. This program is designed to make American scientific books available to Indonesian scientists, research workers, teachers, and students. The first allocation granted under this program was limited to orders of the research institutions under the Council. During 1966, with a second allocation under this program, other research institutions were allowed to participate. Universities were invited to join only in the placement of orders for 1966.

Plans are being made for the development of a documentation center in the field of tropical agriculture and biology, which is to become part of the Bibliotheca Bogoriensis in Bogor. This library, founded in 1842, is regarded as Indonesia's reference library in the field of tropical agriculture and biology. Originally, the library was intended to serve only research workers of the Bogor Botanical Gardens. It later became the central library also for the General Agricultural Research Station and its various constituent institutions: The Forestry Experiment Station, the Veterinary Institute, the Laboratory for Chemical Research, and the Bureau for Land Utilization. This library is now an autonomous institution, directly under the Minister of Agriculture. In its present situation the Bibliotheca Bogoriensis serves the research institutions of the Ministry of Agriculture as well as those of the National Biological Institute (*Lembaga Biologi Nasional*). Students of agricultural colleges from all over Indonesia come to this library for study, as it has a long run of agricultural periodicals in its collection. Many of the periodicals are received by the library from an extensive exchange program with scientific institutions and scientists from all over the world. The publications used as exchange material are *Annales Bogoriensis, Treubia, Reinwardtia, Marine Research in Indonesia,* all four published by the National Biological Institute, and *Warta Pertanian,* which is issued by the General Agricultural Research Station.

The agro-economic survey, now being conducted by the Ministry of Agriculture, has established a documentation section. This section may be referred to as a forerunner of the proposed documentation center which is to become part of the Bibliotheca Bogoriensis. A directory of Indonesian institutions related to agriculture and its allied sciences is now being prepared by this documentation section. It has also given a start to the indexing of the master's theses of the Faculty of Agriculture in Bogor, and abstracts have been compiled of the theses from the Faculty's Department of Economics and Social Sciences.

A union list of serials covering holdings of all research and academic libraries in the Bogor area is now being completed by the Bibliotheca Bogoriensis with funds provided by the Council for Sciences of Indonesia.

Indonesian scientists are more and more aware of the importance of union lists. Jajasan Pustakatama, a private society established in Bandung by nonlibrarians, has published a printed list of the periodical holdings of seventeen research institutions in Bandung.

The establishment and maintenance of a university library become more and more important if a university is to offer its students a specialized knowledge orientated in a wide and reasoned understanding of human ideas and culture. Universities in Indonesia are generally formed by the grouping of existing professional schools, each school called a faculty. In many cases faculties are widely scattered and are served by independent faculty libraries.

In 1962, a decree of the Department of Higher Education ordered the establishment of a university library in each of the state universities as a means for coordinating the existing separated libraries. It is generally impossible, though, to develop a central university library in its true sense, because in most cases universities do not offer a program of general studies to provide a basic background to all students. Because of the tradition of autonomous faculty libraries, the University of Indonesia, for example, is not yet able to set up a university library. When the Bogor Agricultural University was established in 1963, the Faculty of Agriculture and the Faculty of Veterinary Sciences of the University of Indonesia became faculties of this new university. It was an opportune moment to merge the faculty libraries to become the University Central Library, which now is the central library for the six faculties of this university. Basic studies for all students are being provided by the Bogor Agricultural University, so that with proper accommodation, equipment, and staff, a functioning university library could be expected in the future.

Almost all materials used in teaching and research, particularly in science and technology, have had to be imported. Limited foreign currency and the formalities set for book and journal imports hamper the flow of material. It is generally easier to get an order through for textbooks than for research material of which only one or two copies are needed. Almost none of the importers accept subscriptions to foreign scientific periodicals. Some foreign embassies have accepted a limited amount of periodical subscriptions from their countries, which is very helpful. For most of the libraries, foreign aid has been the only means of getting additions to their book and journal collections. The Bogor Agricultural University, for instance, has been able to build up its textbook and reference collection primarily because of its affiliation with the University of Kentucky. From this affiliation there are holdings of mostly American journals to 1966, when they stop. Other periodicals are received by the library from an exchange program using as exchange materials a publication of the Faculty of Veterinary Sciences: *Communicationes Veterinariae*.

Many faculties are now beginning to give instruction in the uses of a library. This is necessary because for most students it is the first time that they come in contact with a library and it is important to acquaint them with the bibliographies of their specialized subjects, and the task of finding information becomes more and more complex. But it is the teachers who must encourage students to use libraries. Fines and library regulations are being introduced to limit losses in library materials.

Publishing Industry and Booktrade

In Indonesia there were fewer than twenty publishers in 1950. Now there are about three hundred, and almost all of them are members of the

Association of Indonesian Publishers. This association and the Association of Indonesian Booksellers (*Persatuan Toko Buku Indonesia*) have been active in organizing book exhibits to develop the love for books and reading and to promote book production.

Among the state enterprises of Indonesian publishers there are P. N. (*Perusahaan Negara*) Pradnja-paramita, P. N. Balai Pustaka, P. N. Fadjar Bhakti, and P. N. Sumur Bandung. P. N. Balai Pustaka was owned by the former colonial government and was used for publishing popular readings in the various regional languages. Pertjetakan Negara is the central governments' official printer and is under the administration of the Ministry of Information. It mostly prints the publications of this ministry.

Most of the private firms with a good publishing reputation are located in Djakarta; among them are P. T. Djambatan, P. T. Gunung Agung, P. T. Pembangunan, and P. T. Pembimbing Masa. In their early days, some of these publishers had been affiliated with publishers in Holland. P. T. Djambatan published the first world atlas in the Indonesian language about 1954. This atlas has not since then been brought up to date. As previously mentioned, P. T. Gunung Agung has a bibliographical department that publishes the current national bibliography. They have the ambition to make this publication the *Publisher's Weekly* of Indonesia, since *Suara Penerbit Indonesia,* which is published by the Association of Indonesian Publishers, does not contain current listings. P. T. Pembangunan is known for its scholarly books, published in a series entitled *Pustaka Sardjana,* and also for its pocketbook editions of fiction for adults and teenagers. P. T. Pembimbing Masa specializes in publishing military books. Many publishers run bookshops with branches in other cities, and some of them are also book importers.

Correct information on the numbers of books published is lacking. The chairman of the Association of Indonesian Publishers (IKAPI) has reported that 80 percent of the publishers are producing textbooks for elementary and secondary schools. There is a good market for such books because the number of students is increasing rapidly. Books on general subjects have a very slow market. This is primarily because of the lack of a functioning network of libraries. The bibliographical department of P. T. Gunung Agung estimated that 2,000 titles were published in 1962, but this includes reprints. Probably this annual production could be brought up to 5,000 titles with the authors and scholars available now, and primarily if publishers could get the facilities they badly need, such as paper, ink, and printing machines. The price of the Indonesian book does not depend on the number of editions printed, but rather on how the publisher gets his facilities. A book will be much more expensive if the publisher has to buy paper from the free market, rather than to get it through the Literature Bureau (*Jajasan Lektur*).

Publishers are not eager to produce scholarly books. Most of the scholarly books published are in the social sciences and law; very few are in science and technology. For this reason the former Department of National Research and the Department of Higher Education provided grants to scholars who were able to publish texts for the use of university students. Most of Indonesian learned periodicals are subsidized also by those departments.

Almost all the books needed for higher education and research have to be imported. Among the well-known book importers are those already mentioned as publishers. Besides these are P. T. Filia in Bogor, known for its American imports, P. T. Indira, known for its imports of American popular magazines, publications from Europe, and also publications from the World Health Organization. For publications of the FAO and the U.N., the sole agent is P. T. Pembangunan.

Book-importers accept orders mostly for multiple copies of textbooks because of the complex import procedures required by the government, ignoring, therefore, orders for one or two copies of a research title. All book imports are controlled by the Literature Bureau. Imports are divided into scholarly and popular publications. The difference is in the rupiah exchange rate of the dollar. It is low for the scholarly books. About 1959, when foreign currency could be acquired by book importers from the Information Media Guarantee Program, the dollar rate for the American scholarly book was set for US$1.00 = Rp. 30.00; the official rate at that time was US$1.00 = Rp. 45.00. The price of the American book was then comparatively lower than that of the Indonesian book, but it was still high for the general public. Those who took profit advantage of the low-priced American books were mostly foreigners. To aid students of higher education, the government had been granting book coupons to subsidize their purchases. Book coupons were made available also to scholars associated with institutions of higher education. These coupons enabled students to buy their required and recommended books for half-price. Scholars could buy any book they wanted for half-price, except for dictionaries and encyclopedias. This aid was later discontinued, primarily because of the various misuses of the book coupon. The U.S. AID–NAS Science Book Program that is now in operation under the administration of the Indonesian Scientific Documentation Center is primarily intended for securing research material needed by scientists and students. Since no commercial channels are involved here, it can offer some assurance on the arrival of material in the libraries. This program permitted the purchase of published American scientific books against a dollar rate of US$1.00 = Rp. 315.00 in 1964–1965 and Rp. 10.00 in 1966. Only 10 percent is paid for each book.

Books are sold in bookshops, on stands in marketplaces or along the streets, and also by streetvendors. Transportation is a problem, limiting the distribution of books throughout the country. Books published in a certain area tend, therefore, to stay in that area, except for the books published by the bona fide publishers in Djakarta. Their books usually do reach representative bookshops in the big cities. The price of every book sold, imported or not, includes transportation costs. Because most of the publishers and book importers are located in Djakarta, book prices are always lower there than in any other city.

Future Needs in Library Services

Indonesia is in great need of well-supported libraries. For the establishment of a nationwide library system, government support is vital. National library legislation is needed for the development of a national library service that includes a copyright depository as a resource for a national bibliography. Without a depository law it is impossible for the National Bibliographical Center to publish an all-inclusive national bibliography. It is not impossible that the collection of Indonesian imprints acquired by the U.S. Library of Congress (Public Law 480 Program) might exceed the collection owned by the National Bibliographical Center, if no action is taken for immediate enactment of a law now being drafted by the Library Bureau of the Ministry of Education. The establishment of a national library might also solve the problems of a depository for government publications.

In many of the developing countries library development proves to be most successful when started from above, that is by starting with library projects in the big cities. If one notices the crowds that use the libraries of foreign information services, it is evident that a public library project started in Djakarta and other big cities would be more justified. Leadership for this project could be given both by and to the provincial libraries. Provincial libraries are vital in Indonesia's national library system. Their organization and administration badly need to be improved. They should serve as clearinghouses in all the provinces, and they should be made depositories for publications of the provincial governments.

Foreign aid has proved useful in strengthening research and academic libraries. However, it cannot guarantee the continuous flow of foreign journals and other serial publications. Stability in the provision of funds, particularly of foreign currency by the government, is, therefore, quite essential for keeping current files of the journals needed. So far, it always has been the policy to divide among individual libraries the available funds, whether these come from government sources or foreign aid. This created small overlapping collections in individual libraries. With the limited funds that are available, it might be better to establish specialized subject-centers by assigning responsibility to the now leading libraries and dividing the funds among them only. One specialized subject center that is able to acquire an extensive collection of foreign journals and thereby fulfill the demands of scholars throughout the country is better than having several small overlapping collections in individual libraries. These proposed centers should operate on a national basis. The Bibliotheca Bogoriensis, for example, could be made a center for the journals and serials in the agricultural sciences and biology; the National Documentation Center for those in science and technology; other leading libraries could be made centers for other branches of knowledge. When funds could be extended for distribution to other libraries, these centers can then carry out a program for cooperative acquisition of journals.

These national subject centers could also develop a collection of micro records. They could start with ordering microprints of the little-used material that might be needed for future research. The purchase of microprints makes possible a more extensive use of available funds, is less expensive in its shipping and handling, and microprints require minimum storage space. Back files of journals for filling in gaps could be acquired in microform. The U.S. AID–NAS Science Book Program, which excludes in its operation the purchase of journals, might consider a grant for this purpose. With microprints, these centers should be equipped with micro-readers and duplicating machines to enable the dissemination of their material throughout the country. An easy way to announce what is received by the center is to mimeograph the table of contents of every current journal and distribute this to other libraries in the country. Copies of articles needed could be provided for small fees.

Specialized subject centers should be staffed with subject specialists whose task would be to evaluate information, making it digestible and ready for dissemination to people interested in the specialized subject field.

Conclusion
In this age of science and technology, libraries do not exist only for reasons of tradition, prestige, or national pride, but because libraries are important if education is to achieve its objectives. The extent of the problems that face Indonesia, including its deteriorated economic situation, has made the establishment of library services a problem that challenges Indonesian librarianship. For future library development, Indonesian librarians will need increased recognition and support in order to realize the potential that libraries have for the social and economic development of the country.

REFERENCES

Bogor scientific centre. *Organization for Scientific Research,* bulletin no. 12, July 1952, p. 8.

Dunningham, A. G. W. 1957. Indonesian libraries. *New Zealand Libraries,* 20 (7): 153–63.

Esheim, Lester E. 1965. University libraries in developing countries. *ALA Bulletin,* 87 (9): 795–802.

Gardner, Frank M. 1960. Public libraries in perspective; a candid commentary on a tour of South Asia. *UNESCO Bulletin for Libraries,* 14 (4): 145–50.

Hoetaoeroek, M. 1965. *Publishing Industry in Indonesia, 1945–65.* Djakarta: IKAPI–OPS Penerbitan, 1965. 20 p.

Indonesian library development, 1955–1960. 1960 *UNESCO Bulletin for Libraries,* 14 (1): 17–20.

Partaningrat, Winarti. 1962. Indonesia: an eight-year plan. *Library Journal,* 87 (20): 4143–47.

————. The U.S. AID–NAS Science Book Program in Indonesia. Progress Report until this date, March 1, 1967.

[1] *Bibliografi Nasional Indonesia;* kumulasi 1945–1963. Diusahakan oleh Projek Perpustakaan Nasional & Biro Perpustakaan Departemen Pendidikan Dasar dan Kebudajaan. Djakarta: Balai Pustaka, 1965.

[2] *Catalogus dari buku[2] jang diterbitkan di Indonesia:* 1870–1937–1954. Bandung: Gedung Buku Nasional. 6 v. in 7 (Vol. for 1942–1944 was not published).

[3] Ikatan Penerbit Indonesia. *Daftar buku 20 tahun penerbitan Indonesia,* 1945–1965. Djakarta: IKAPI–OPS Penerbitan, 1966. xii, 416 p.

Discussion

[*The discussion was opened by Dr. Bayard McConnaughey.*] The problem of supplying adequate books is indeed a very serious one anywhere, and particularly in developing countries. There are scattered facilities; there tend to be duplications, not only of holdings but also of omissions through the shortage of funds, lack of trained personnel, as well as difficulty in cataloging and spacing. Cataloging, keeping, and maintaining libraries are fully as important as acquiring the materials, because a book that cannot be located is useless. The problems of the Indonesian librarian are further complicated by the fact that most of the literature is in foreign languages. This, of course, adds to the difficulties of the library staff and of the students who wish to use the material.

There is always, in any library in the United States as well as in Indonesia, a tug of war between the instincts of the librarian to maintain the collection intact and his desire to make it easily available and useful to the public. The problem can be clarified if we keep in mind the distinction between two types of library materials. Mrs. Soemadikarta brought this out, but we should emphasize again that there are, on the one hand, materials which need to be used frequently and which are needed in multiple copies, including most literature (the indigenous literature), textbooks for students, and books for school children. The second kind of material is that which constitutes a repository of the worlds' knowledge. These are primarily reference materials. They are a real problem because of their frequently extreme bulk, their diverse origin, the great expense of getting them, and the fact that many items are out of print and unobtainable. Any particular item of these materials may be used only very rarely, but when needed, it is needed badly. If it is lost or deteriorates, it is usually irreplaceable.

With reference to this second category of material, Dr. McConnaughey expanded on Mrs. Soemadikarta's comment about the use of microfilm and microcards. He viewed the situation as a great opportunity for support and sponsorship by institutions such as AID or UNESCO. Dr. McConnaughey's suggestion was directed to American or international institutions rather than to the libraries in Indonesia because of his feeling that the biggest breakthrough in service can come at these levels rather than in efforts to meet requests by individual libraries abroad. He proposed that microfilms of specialized collections be prepared in many duplicates by some international or national agency, with enough copies to send to any library which requested one. This, he said, could be done very cheaply. Duplicating equipment and reading equipment could be sent with this kind of material at much less cost than that of acquiring the collections themselves. The total cost of shipping the collections would also be saved; the cost of housing and preservation would be largely saved, and a minimum number of librarians would be needed to maintain them. The ease of reproduction from microfilm or from microcards is such that a central library could easily make multiple copies of any item requested and distribute them as subsets to other libraries or to individual scholars. Such an arrangement would avoid the risk of loss, because the original item would still be in the central library. Dr. McConnaughey envisaged great advantages and opportunities in such a scheme. He advocated that the savings involved should not be regarded as an economy in the library system, permitting diversion of funds to nonlibrary uses, but that the money be used to train more library staff to help establish branch libraries, to increase the collections of books which are needed in multiple copies, and to provide more textbooks and more school children's books. By microduplication, reference sets and subsets on different subjects could be shipped promptly and with a minimum of cost to any library in the world requesting them. This might be a great breakthrough for the entire system.

Dr. Robert Sheeks followed Dr. McConnaughey's proposal by describing the program to which Mrs. Soemadikarta had alluded which the National Academy of Sciences has continued to sponsor in Indonesia with AID. In 1959 the Indonesian government instituted very drastic measures to reduce foreign exchange expenditures and it became economically very unprofitable for book dealers in Indonesia to import anything that wasn't really in bulk quantity. Two hundred copies seemed to become pretty much the absolute minimum. For research scientists it was almost impossible to obtain through any normal channels the material needed for research, and such need is usually for only a limited number of copies. There were hardly any resources for occasional book purchases until a contract was concluded in April 1964 which provided for this AID-National Academy of Sciences book program in cooperation with MIPI (Council for Sciences in Indonesia).

This is administered by MIPI, and more specifically by the documentation center. It is designed to make available the latest American scientific books to Indonesian scientists, research workers, technicians, professors, and students. Payment is made in Indonesia in rupiah at very nominal exchange rates. American and other scientific books are selected from publishers' lists. The rupiah fund is supervised by AID in Djakarta; rupiah accumulate from payments made there and they are used to defray the expenses of operating the program in Indonesia (the costs of purchasing, ordering, and performing clerical functions). The documentation center has these responsibilities. The first allocation under this contract (for 1964 and 1965) was small, only $35,000, but this did provide for about 2,300 book titles. Ordering was done for the research institutes under MIPI; in 1966 the number involved had grown to thirty-two, including all the major institutes. Among those receiving orders at a cost of $1,500 or more, for example, are the National Chemical Research Institute and the Institutes of Metallurgy and Electrical Research. The National Biological Research Institute received about $13,000 worth of books. The documentation center itself cost a couple of thousand dollars; also included is the Directorate of Meteorology and Geophysics. The universities in Indonesia ordered approximately five copies each of nearly four hundred titles, distributed among the fields of medicine, electronics, chemical engineering, education, chemical biology, architecture, and pharmacy. The field of medicine is by far the largest beneficiary, its purchases running to something over $13,000. Next is chemical engineering, at about $5,000, and then architecture and pharmacy. The results of the program are necessarily limited by its small scale, but the program has made possible the acquisition of much-needed books in practically every facet of science, and has allowed the MIPI to concentrate on the purchase of periodical subscriptions. Because the program can provide only a limited number of copies, it has encouraged better organization and cooperation among the Indonesian science libraries by union-cataloging and sharing of the volumes. Prices of the books thus provided are in sharp contrast to the prices in local bookshops. For instance, a certain international dictionary of physics and electronics, which otherwise would have cost 1,114 rupiahs, cost only 27 under this program; a book on differential equations, priced at 110 rupiahs in the store, cost only 7¼ rupiahs.

In 1965, more than 5,800 scientific and technical books were published in the United States in such fields as agriculture, medicine, various sciences, and technology. It was estimated by the documentation center in Djakarta that Indonesia should have approximately 3,000 of these. At an estimate of $15 per volume for one copy each, the cost would be $45,000. In addition, if the social sciences and humanities are to be included as formerly they have been, only to a limited extent, the need in 1967 would be for about a thousand titles or $15,000.

One of the more important desiderata is that Indonesia receive the reproduction equipment which has been on order and which UNESCO has been indicating that it will probably help to provide; it is to be hoped that there will be no further delay in obtaining this equipment. Dr. McConnaughey's reference to the potential use of microfilms suggests, though the idea needs further "spelling out," that the technique might be adapted to this book program, not as a substitute, but as a device for including a much larger number of titles, and these more widely distributed.

In order to be most effective, this idea of microfilms, particularly of continuing journals, should not wait upon the request of individual countries and individual libraries. Rather, the agency which makes the microfilm should, on a continuing basis, take the most important selected journals and reproduce them completely, ready to send to anybody in the world who needs them. They could then be furnished either in entire sets or subsets, according to need, with considerable savings in production costs and volume of correspondence.

Dr. Tojib explained a plan under which, in 1963, the policy of the government of Indonesia with respect to textbooks needed in universities shifted from fostering purchase by students to a system of lending. The government bought the books and distributed them to the colleges, which then loaned them to students. This policy remained in force for only a year or so, however, and books for students are still a serious lack.

There was extensive discussion of how to break old patterns, promote use of libraries by students, keep libraries open evenings for student use, and finance supplemental library staff to keep library resources accessible.

At the end of the discussion, a plea was repeated (in Dr. Ralph Allee's words) "for consideration of the nonacademic uses of the world's intellectual output." In addition to concern for "people like us" who live in a world of books and students and seminars, there must be concern for the person "on the firing line." He may be an extension agent, a supervisor of the extension agent, a minor administrator, or, at the other end of the scale, a policymaker. For the most part, these are people who do not frequent libraries a lot, nor are they accustomed to digging specific items out of lengthy abstracts. They need material that is readily available and easily digested. Dr. Allee reported: "We are trying now in Indonesia and in the Philippines to cut articles and pull out the material that these busy, practical people need, and to mimeograph it and send it to them. In both countries, this rather small effort has had rather encouraging results. The problem is one of upgrading, for example, personnel in agriculture, keeping them informed on the things they ought to know from developments elsewhere in the world. Plans are being considered for mimeographed abstracts from journals, some of which would be translated into Indonesian, others of which might be used just as well in the original language. This would not be an expensive type of service, but it would require access to the source-publications. It would require one or two people full time and access to others who have judgment as to what the people in the field really need. Dr. Allee viewed this as a very promising activity, and one that would reach a group that is, in a way, the "proof of the pudding" in discussions such as this. These are the people who are out there doing the work in agricultural development, and they are the ones who up to now are reading almost nothing of these things that we think are necessary.

Dr. Earl Slone then cited the U.S. example of a regional institution, the Midwest Library Center. This is a storage and retrieval facility for volumes which are needed only occasionally but which are too valuable to throw away; these would otherwise occupy urgently needed space in the individual libraries. The cooperating libraries in the central states deposit materials with this Midwest Library Center, and there is an interlibrary loan system by which any of the cooperating libraries can borrow a particular volume or have portions reproduced.

It was recalled also that at the ITB in Bandung, the Kentucky contract team had established a rental textbook library from which textbooks were rented to students for a very nominal sum. There had been in 1965 some study of the possibility of the use of microtapes, microcards, and films. The central library and three departmental libraries were going to cooperate and, had there not been the intervening period of disturbance in Indonesia, those libraries would be using that equipment today.

There was extensive discussion of the centralization-decentralization operations, with proponents for each view. The idea of a central library at Bogor for agriculture and biology in Indonesia was endorsed, with the suggestion that its base and nucleus, presently the strongest library available, is that of the Bibliotheque Bogoriensis. Problems explored by discussants included staffing, elimination of overlapping, and problems of strategy in overcoming the old systems by which book-hungry professors kept access for themselves to the few available volumes. A "small-but-large" problem in centralization was recalled in the effort to merge the catalogs of the agricultural and veterinary libraries in Bogor; there was a differently sized card in each catalog, and no money available for making them uniform. "It sounds so easy, but the money and labor involved . . . we still have to use boxes instead of drawers."

Promise is found in the upgrading of librarianship in Indonesia, as library education is now becoming a department of the University of Indonesia, and is thus recognized as academic education. Previously it was provided in a separate three-year school. Now librarians will earn the degree of *Sardjana Muda in Perpustakaan* (Bachelor of Library Science). A start is also being made toward an M.A. (*doktorandus*) degree in library science. There are now about four or five graduates from the library school in Djakarta, and there are a few graduates from foreign schools.

The discussion ended with another reference to the microfilm system previously suggested by Dr. McConnaughey, and cited again in the consideration of centralization. Dr. McConnaughey said it is certainly vital that the material be available where needed, as possible, for example at Medan, Makasar, and other outlying areas, but the main problem there is the lack of money. In the face of limited funds and the impossibility, at the moment, of supplying a good library in each province, Indonesia could probably "get more from the money" by having a good, complete collection in Bogor or Djakarta and by availing itself of foreign reproductions of any desired item on request from there. It is rather essential that if this should be done and if there are any substantial savings involved, that these savings should be retained in the library system and not diverted to other uses. It should be used for training more staff and for acquiring more of the books which are needed in multiple copies and which are vital to have at Medan and at other places.

CHAPTER 13

Stephen A. Douglas Science and Technology
and the Political Culture

We have been considering the prospects for application of science and technology to specific problems of economic and social development in Indonesia. Let us now consider another dimension of development, the political. There is a linkage between the two, perhaps best appreciated by the would-be agents of scientific and technological change. The foreign technical adviser participating in the construction of a fertilizer plant soon learns, as does the indigenous agricultural extension worker, that the success of his mission depends very largely upon the political climate. The lesson is manifold—in Indonesia and in every other country where men have tried to manage their economic and social fate—yet it is seldom adequately comprehended.

This is not to say that we are concerned here only, or even mainly, with the ways in which politics "interferes" with scientific progress and application. Political activity can and often does play a positive role. It is difficult to conceive of a particular application of technology which could completely bypass the political process, and the two are interactive. Not only do political institutions and processes influence the role of science and technology in a nation's overall development; it is equally clear that science and technology may impede or contribute to processes of political and social change, and the scientist and engineer may well bear this in mind.

This general concern has been expressed by others in a variety of contexts. Political novelists of our time have expressed it as a cosmic question: what will be the "outcome" of the continuous and reciprocal interaction of the scientific-technological and political dimensions? The question has a remote and artificial ring, though the novelists serve a useful if troubling function in alerting us to the possibility of a brave new world in which science has conquered man, or of a world devastated through man's misapplication of his technological sophistication. It seems unlikely that we shall be able to guess the final human condition as it will be shaped by the interplay of science and politics. There are, however, more immediate questions arising out of the tension between science and politics. The immediacy of these questions is largely a consequence of the fact that the rapid extension and application of science has not been matched by equivalent progress in understanding political responsibility. This discrepancy is greatest, of course, and the attendant problems are therefore more urgent, in those parts of the world where, for most of the population, the scientific-technological revolution is just beginning.

The Clash of Cultures in Indonesia

The image of Western man as an inquisitive, scientific thinker is an exaggerated one,[1] as is the stereotype of the "prescientific" mentality attributed to the peasantry of Asia and Africa.[2] Still, the mix of scientific and traditional presuppositions with which men confront their environments does vary from one society to another. In Indonesia technological practices of certain kinds—in wet-rice farming, fishing, and batik production, for example—have long coexisted with the characteristics commonly attributed to traditional societies. The level of technology is not high in these and most other spheres of activity, however. In the case of Indonesia the cultural mix is clearly biased in a nontechnological, traditional direction. It is important to emphasize that the specific content of the traditional culture in Indonesia varies from one area and from one ethnic group to another. This, of course, is one of the major points of difference between the traditional and the modern values and patterns of behavior. The former are particularistic and parochial; the latter are more general.

By employing a high level of generalization, however, it is possible to speak of typical systems of traditional behavior and belief, and we may speak of Indonesia as a whole. For example, ascriptive standards of recruitment prevail among the Atjehnese as well as the Javanese and every other ethnic community. Similarly, religious authority, whether it be of the folk variety, Islam, or a mixture of the two, is not sharply differentiated from political authority.[3] Status is extremely important, in that the prerogatives and obligations of various social ranks are rather narrowly prescribed, and for most people, social mobility is not possible. Perhaps most important as an indicator of political culture is the tendency of most Indonesians to regard government (to the extent that they do see it as a sphere of authority separate from religion) as something remote and largely arbitrary. One way of dealing with the potential discomforts of such social characteristics is through the maintenance of a belief in the propriety of thoroughgoing deference to and respect for authority. Respect is closely related to two other social values which have been reported by most observers of Javanese society—social harmony (perhaps better expressed as avoidance of conflict) and tolerance of diversity.

Such a broad picture of traditional society in Indonesia is useful, but it does injustice to the realities of social change in addition to those of ethnic and geographical diversity. For example, many communities which superficially are traditional (inasmuch as they are not "modern") are better regarded as "post-traditional." This is especially true in those parts of Java where the older forms of social organization and standards of social conduct have broken down and have not yet been supplanted by widely shared and integrative patterns of thought and behavior.[4] In these post-traditional sectors of Indonesian society, a variety of factors have begun to stimulate change in the form of rejection of established ways of doing things.

One source of socio-cultural change and of values quite different from those which we have just considered is the world culture—the style of life that has developed in the West and is generally associated with the concepts of modernization or development. Lucian Pye has defined the world culture as being "based upon modern science and technology, modern practices of organization, and modern standards of governmental performance."[5] The mechanics of the process whereby the world culture is being diffused are far from clear, but the fact of its diffusion is beyond dispute. Even if there were no intellectuals, businessmen, governmental officials, missionaries, peace corpsmen, and others in the West actively engaged in "pushing" the world culture, one suspects that the "pull"—in the form of an intense interest in modern things, especially on the part of young people—would still exist in the non-Western world.

The evidences of the world culture are quite manifest in Indonesia. In the educational system modern science is valued. In the economic system, the fruits of modern technology are visible as railroads, currency, and the other features of modern economic life. There are business enterprises, political parties, trade unions, youth organizations—the whole range of organizations characteristic of Western culture and society. Even the formal structure of government at the national level since independence has been based on principles and institutions derived from Western Europe.

These traces of the world culture have not, however, had a deep impact on the lives of most Indonesians. It is probably true, as Palmier has contended, that a new, national (as opposed to ethnic or otherwise subnational) status system has emerged, and that it is based largely on familiarity with Western ideas and practices.[6] Within this status system, knowledge of the political philosophers of eighteenth-century Europe is a possible source of prestige, as is skill in the game of golf or in operating a motorcycle. But this is a status system limited largely to the younger people of certain social classes in certain urban areas. Most of the population participate in more parochial status systems.

On the other hand, and this is a crucial point, it appears that most of the population is aware of the "new" technology and its accompanying set of norms, and of the ascendant popularity of what we have called the world culture. All but the most isolated Indonesians have had glimpses of the material and cultural products of the West through movies, newspapers, radio, word-of-mouth accounts, and visits to cities. This means that in the individual life of most Indonesians, as well as in the society as a whole, a conflict is in the making if not already raging. At the individual level this clash of cultural standards is a major component of what has been called a crisis of identity.

> The problem is that, in the period of transition when old value systems are breaking down and new ones are not yet sufficiently crystallized, no such wider structure of meaning presents itself. The progressive breakdown of traditional social structures, with their established customs, and the difficulties of relating to emerging new ones have left many in our traditional societies with great uncertainty and anxiety, leading in some cases to a genuine crisis of identity. The image of one's self, the answer to "who am I, and who do I want to be?" has become blurred and fragmented. Questions like to whom or to what to be loyal? after whom to model oneself? which patterns of behavior to adopt or adjust to? have all lost their obvious answers, and no satisfactory new ones are readily available.[7]

Such are the likely psychological consequences whenever far-reaching social, economic, and cultural changes are compressed into a relatively short period of time. The role of science in this confrontation of cultures is pervasive; the world culture can probably be traced to the Enlightenment, with its emphasis on faith in science and scientific man's capability to manipulate his environment, more than to any other historical event or set of ideas. The role of technology is obvious, especially in the area of economic change. As for the political consequences, Soedjatmoko's comment on the uncertainty surrounding the question of "to whom or to what to be loyal?" provides a hint of the fundamental nature of the political problems arising out of cultural conflict and change.

The central element in the concept of culture as we have employed it to this point is the set of values and attitudes which characterizes any integrated social system. Following this usage, it is convenient to use the concept "political culture" in seeking to outline the political effects of scientific-technological progress, or, more generally, of acculturation to the world culture in Indonesia. Political culture refers to the systemwide distribution of knowledge, feelings, and judgments about political ideas and institutions and actors. Description of the political culture thus entails direct analysis of orientations toward the political world at various levels of society.[8]

Of course there is little available data bearing on the range and content of political orientations among Indonesian citizens. It happens, however, that the detailed and reliable observations of one of the leading students of Indonesian politics have been reported in a framework which lends itself easily to an interpretation in terms of political culture and which highlights the reflection of the clash of cultures in the political sphere. The reference, of course, is to Herbert Feith's treatment of politics

in Indonesia during the early and mid-1950s in *The Decline of Constitutional Democracy in Indonesia.*[9]

Without reviewing Feith's argument in detail, it is clear that his
view of the underlying causes of the political trend reflected in the title of
his study centers on the uneven impact of the world culture. The "skill-
group" which he labels "problem-solvers" is identified by its acceptance
of "modern-type technical skills." Their political style is one of pragmatism and calculating confrontation of short-term problems. In the years
leading up to the "guided democracy" period, these political actors were
competing with a second group, a group which Feith calls "solidarity-
makers." The solidarity-makers were less willing to embrace modern
ideas and norms, and their style was more traditional in that they
emphasized their identity with the people and the nation. Their claim to
political office was based on ability to provide symbolic gratification to
"the people" rather than competence in dealing with problems of development through knowledge of economics and other sciences.

Every polity probably includes leading political actors who can fit
into one of these two categories, but in most countries where the role of
science and technology has evolved more gradually there are also large
numbers of people who are neither problem-solvers nor solidarity-makers
—or, more properly, who are both. The crisis in Indonesia has lain in the
degree of polarization in this dimension of political life. When the
problem-solvers held the upper hand they were unable to evoke suppor-
tive responses from those Indonesians who felt a need for symbolic
reassurances about the prestige of their nation and the glory of its future
as well as its past, about the legitimacy and security of their own political
interests, and about their belief systems in general. These things the
Sukarno regime—the solidarity-making clique which emerged victorious
out of the political instability of the 1950s—strived to do well, but at the
expense of dealing skillfully and rationally with the mundane problems
of developing a viable economic structure.

This conflict of political cultures exists not only within the political
elite. It cuts through the ranks of all the politically aware and interested
people in Indonesian society, and it does so in a particularly destructive
way. One of the major problems of nation-building in Indonesia is the
population's ethnic diversity. It happens that the cleavage between solidarity-maker and problem-solver styles coincides in some degree with the
cleavage between the Javanese on the one hand and other ethnic groups
on the other. A related differentiation, that of specialized economic role,
produces another cleavage which tends to be superimposed upon and
therefore to further exacerbate this cleavage in Indonesian culture and
society. To oversimplify this factor, it centers on the fact that most
Javanese, to the extent that they are engaged in national economic

activity, are directly or indirectly involved in importing. It seems consistent with their greater acceptance of the world culture and technology that the outer island ethnic groups are more committed to exporting. In terms of political positions and policies, this meant that the non-Javanese had more compelling economic reasons to resent inflationary governmental actions during, say, 1959–1965, than did the Javanese.[10]

Discontinuity in Political Socialization

If political instability in Indonesia's recent past and present can be understood in terms of a divided and changing political culture which is partly the result of the impact of science and modern technology, any assessment of the future of the political system must give some weight to the problem of diffusion of the accompanying new values and the world view they support. Both at the individual and societal level, the challenge is to adopt the world culture in its constructive aspects in such a way that it blends rather than collides with the traditional, parochial ways of life. The problem is most severe for young people who, given the diversity and high rate of change in Indonesian society, are asked to learn their values from social institutions—families, schools, mass media, and others —which transmit variable and conflicting messages about the world and the individual's proper relationship to it.

This process by which values are transmitted through social structures and adopted by individuals, can be termed the process of socialization, and the transmission of political orientations or the political culture occurs through political socialization. The critical role of political socialization in the development of an effective political system can be seen in a phenomenon apparently confronting Indonesia and certain other new nations: fragmentation and rapid change in political systems give rise to variations and contradictions within the political socialization process, and a variable and inconsistent pattern of political socialization produces a fragmented and unstable political culture. Much of the recent theoretical literature on political development, in recognition of the fundamental importance of this situation and of the role of political socialization in maintaining or possibly breaking out of it, has focused on the structure and content of the political socialization process. Sidney Verba, for example, has stated: "There are many discontinuities in the socialization process that make the lessons of early socialization inapplicable to later political performance. And, indeed, there are few political systems in which a smooth transition is the desired goal of most people. Therefore the comparative study of political socialization might best be focused on the questions of the source of these discontinuities, their nature, the implications they have for the political system and, not least important, the way they can be manipulated to create desired changes in a political system."[11] In the light of the theoretical importance of the notion of discontinuity as well as the practical importance of youth in contemporary Indonesian politics, an examination of the extent to which a cultural clash has produced discontinuity in political socialization should contribute to our understanding of the political culture of Indonesia and its possible course of transformation.

Unfortunately, concepts which appear neat and manageable in the abstract often turn out to be complex and elusive in operational application, and so it is with continuity. The process of political training may be more continuous for some individuals than for others in the same social and political environment. Most of our generalizations here will be derived from data pertaining to a class of Indonesians who have experienced relatively little continuity—urban high school and university students, especially as represented in a sample interviewed in Djakarta in 1964 and the first half of 1965.[12] Furthermore, socialization may be continuous where some dimensions of political orientations and action are concerned, but quite discontinuous with respect to other aspects of political life. Our analysis of the degree of congruence among values transmitted by families, schools, and mass media, as elaborated below, provides some basis for hypothesizing that orientations toward broad and diffuse political objects are more likely to evolve through continuous socialization than are orientations toward specific political objects. For example, all major agencies of political socialization transmit favorable messages about the most fundamental symbol of politics, the concept of Indonesia as a meaningful political unit.

This is not to say that the family promotes the idea of an Indonesian nation as thoroughly as the primary school. Since political socialization in the family is subtle and latent rather than manifest, and Indonesian family structure is generally quite weak and unstable,[13] the family appears to have a limited role in the formation of knowledge and sentiments about the nation. To the extent that it does have a role here at all, however, it is consistent with agencies of instruction with which Indonesian children interact in later years. The high value which parents place on education is indirect endorsement of the nation-state which government-operated educational institutions have come to represent, and it surely encourages young children to be receptive to the patriotic content of early primary education. This sort of experience may be a more significant and frequent means by which Indonesian families influence their younger members than direct transmission of information and values about politics, but the latter does occur. Student interviews brought out the fact that although many university and all high school students were too young at the time of the revolt against Dutch colonial rule to grasp its full significance, a number of students had been brought to an appreciation of the dramatic birth of the Republic of Indonesia through parents' accounts of personal experiences during the years 1945–1949.

In the educational system, basic national symbols are presented in the first years of elementary schools, and, although more sophisticated and particular political concepts continue to be added during the student's career, even university students are repeatedly exposed to the flag, the nation, and the myth of the Revolution. The mass media are equally nationalistic. Radio and television transmit pro-Indonesian messages in much the same indoctrinational style as the public schools. Newspapers present a less harmonious image of politics. The disharmony, however, is cushioned by a common assumption which is consistent with what has been learned in family and school—that each argument is made with the objective of supporting the idea of Indonesia and advancing the interests of that political entity and the people living in it.

The central political questions since independence have been concerned not with the appropriateness and desirability of an Indonesian nation but with the suitability of various forms of organization. Perhaps the most determinative factor shaping the general pattern of relationships among and between the public, the organized and unorganized political interests, and the various parts of the government is the distribution of orientations toward authority. This aspect of political thought and behavior, bolstered by the assumptions that "beliefs about authority . . . structure the political interactions in a society" and "belief that one ought to defer to authority serves as a guide even if the authority figure changes and the subject on which authority is being exercised changes," receives more emphasis than any other in the literature on political socialization.[14]

The evidence, however, does not conform to the expectation that beliefs about authority will be well-defined and consistent. The principal agencies of political socialization all seem to present ambivalent values with respect to authority relationships. Socialization affecting beliefs about authority is characterized by extensive discontinuity—within specific agencies of political socialization as well as among them.

Authority within the family, for example, is not clearly related to sex roles. In some areas historical circumstances have caused patriarchal norms to be superimposed on matriarchal societies. At the present time fathers have much formal status, but rarely exercise power in family affairs. This discrepancy between formal and applied authority does not support the main lesson of family life, respect and deference toward authority, because it leaves unclear the location and definition of authority. The child's picture of authority is confused further by the great flexibility of family structure and processes in Indonesia. Older siblings or, in wealthy families, servants may assume parental functions; divorces and economic problems frequently cause children to be moved from one household to another; fathers, perhaps as a means of protecting their formal status within the family, tend to withdraw from daily family life.

However ambiguous these factors render the hierarchy of prestige within the family, they do not entirely nullify the family's ability to teach its younger members that respect for authority is virtuous. Children are noticeably subdued in the presence of their elders, strikingly so on formal occasions. The term *bapakism* expresses the belief of Indonesians that proper family relationships are based on obedience to the father (*bapak*) and that these relationships are carried over into behavior within social and political organizations. Surely a general inclination to respect and defer to authority would be included in any attempted portrayal of the "national character" of Indonesia.

Thus, although the family is very heavily involved in conveying an image of authority relationships, the pictures it provides for its younger members are inconsistent and unclear. Depending upon which of the aspects of family structure or child training practices they are rooted in, impressions which the child receives about authority are likely to be quite different, even contradictory. This appears to be a case of something not anticipated in the literature on political socialization—discontinuity in the political content of values and attitudes expressed through a single social institution.

Schools probably present a less confusing picture. Teachers are the normative and actual repositories of authority, and, with the important exceptions of historical uprisings against colonialism and the final struggle for independence, classroom lessons tend to advocate deference and respect. By successfully bringing together persons with diverse social, religious, and ethnic backgrounds, schools promote social harmony and tolerance, values which generally reinforce deference to authority. At higher levels of education this latent integrative function is especially effective.[15] Nevertheless, postprimary educational experiences are in some ways incongruent with a positive outlook toward authority.

One of the most typical characteristics of teachers during the period of guided democracy, and especially during 1964 and early 1965 when the data upon which this discussion is based were collected, was their cautious avoidance of political issues and involvement. Students appeared to be aware of the low political efficacy of their teachers, and this awareness undermined teachers' prestige in the eyes of their students. Nor were teachers very impressive in fulfilling their professional roles, a condition which persists. Their training generally is deficient, and their dress and deportment are more appropriate to the low salaries they receive than to the position of authority they are supposed to occupy. Students are sensitive to these features of the teaching profession, as reflected in the fact that only one of the 116 young Indonesians interviewed in Djakarta expressed an interest in attending a teacher training institution. It is not surprising, therefore, that student indiscipline is a common problem in secondary schools. The ineffective performance of an authoritative role by teachers contravenes the norm of student deference and submission in much the same way that abdication of day-to-day leadership and decision-making by most Indonesian fathers makes the center of authority within the family uncertain.

Of course, under guided democracy, educational institutions and mass media alike presented information favorable to the maintenance of existing political authority. This aspect of orientation toward authority had less impact in educational institutions than more salient authority relationships, such as those of teachers and students. In the mass media, however, controlled indoctrination and favorable news about the government are not subject to competition of this sort. The mass media, however, unlike the family with its hierarchical arrangement of roles and the school with the sharp differentiation between student and teacher, do not confront the individual with built-in norms and roles relating to the distribution of authority. True, radio and television may be regarded as more or less official extensions of the Indonesian government, but their impersonal character and vulnerability to inattention provide little basis for exacting respect and deference from their audience.

At least two categories of information transmitted through the mass media conflicted with the values broadcast in the framework of *indoktrinasi*. First, all the media gave some attention to conditions which reflected poor governmental performance, especially in the area of financial management and economic development. News of this kind only reinforced what people already knew, but the fact that they received it from a source which simultaneously was urging loyalty and respect to the groups responsible for mismanagement furnishes another example of incongruent messages about authority coming from the same agency of political indoctrination. Second, the open and intense political conflict among Indonesian newspapers throughout 1964 and 1965 was in forceful opposition to the general prescriptions that social harmony is paramount, differences should be tolerated, and conflict should be avoided. Admittedly, these ideals are not identical with those pertaining to authority relationships. Nevertheless, when a person is told implicitly that expression of conflict is permissible and that almost no precepts are beyond challenge, he is less likely to pay uncritical obeisance to all supposedly authoritative persons and projects. This is not to say that the more sacred symbols of the supreme political authority ensconced in the Indonesian state and government under Sukarno were openly attacked in the course of journalistic political warfare. They were used, however, in such a way that their ultimate correctness was called into question. In its implicit recognition of the existence and function of political competition in a quantity and intensity much greater than would be appropriate in a political system based on relationships of thoroughgoing respect and social harmony, the political content of the press was discontinuous with that of the family and educational system.

From the foregoing analysis, one might expect a comparably confused pattern of social indoctrination relating to political participation, for attitudes toward political authority and political participation would appear to be closely associated. All the evidence, however, points toward a fair degree of consistency among the three agencies of socialization being considered here; none of them openly encourages participation. Children in both the family and school environments participate only in the sense that they belong to these social structures, without having any effective voice in the conscious determination of standards and patterns of action which families and schools maintain and adapt. The mass media inherently provide for participation only in a limited sense. Indonesian students, as a matter of fact, make extensive use of the mass media, and this was true in the months and years prior to the sudden emergence of intense political activism of students and youth in October 1965.

Although this exposure to the mass media cannot be construed as actual and direct political participation, it may represent a significant discontinuity in the process of political indoctrination, in that it clearly provokes what must be a prerequisite to political participation—interest in politics. In contrast, most parents, to avoid controversies, do not encourage political discussions and other activities in the home which might stimulate interest in politics. During the "guided democracy" years, teachers generally followed a similarly apolitical path. At all levels, teachers tended to adhere closely to the political content prescribed by indoctrinational programs and materials. The official ideology as presented in the classroom rarely promoted the value of widespread participation, and when participation was advocated it was on the order of personal sacrifice and loyal conduct rather than envisioning a positive role for the average citizen in determining public policy and the composition of government.[16] With respect to the development of interest in politics, the dull and unrealistic content of indoctrinational messages stood in marked contrast to the exciting and vital political information conveyed by newspapers.

Views of the nation, of authority, and of participation are basic aspects of the political culture in any country. We could examine other aspects of political orientations. For example, the solidarity-maker vs. problem-solver dichotomy appears to be reinforced by the fact that some

experiences of political preparation favor an expressive, ideological political style; others promote an instrumental, pragmatic approach to politics.
Or, some agencies of political preparation do not encourage the formation
of particularistic political sympathies; others may advocate the virtues of
certain movements or parties or politicians. Except for nationalism, there
is hardly any aspect of politics that is treated in a congruent fashion at all
levels of political indoctrination.

Politics, Technology, and Problems of Development

Cultural clash and inconsistency in political socialization represent
the broadest manifestations of the impact of science and the scientific
world view on the Indonesian polity. There can be little doubt about the
practical political importance of the pervasive and divisive effects of
uneven exposure to an acceptance of the values of the world culture. The
task of making the political socialization process less discontinuous is of
an order to discourage even the most optimistic and energetic social
engineer. Instead, our attention is more profitably directed to the more
specific level of a whole series of issues which are components of the
broader problem of the interaction of science and politics in Indonesia.
Many of these issues involve technology, and some of them have already
been introduced in the above discussion.

Most conspicuous among these is the expansion of mass media as
made possible by technological advances in the field of communications.
The question of interest here is what are the political effects of such a
development in Indonesia?

On the one hand, the role of radio, television, and newspapers is one
of great potential in the overall nation-building process, for it is through
these media that the citizens of this island nation can maintain continuing
awareness of the form and content of politics at the national level. From
this perspective, the role of the media is in political preparation—the
transmission of information and values to the public. Of course this
function is important from the point of view of the governmental elite as
well as the mass of the population. The extent to which the output of the
government can be effective and meaningful throughout the nation is
limited by the state of the communications system.

Another way of putting this is to suggest that one of the key
variables upon which national integration depends is the structure of
mass communications. At first glance, Indonesia's problem would appear
to be the relatively underdeveloped state of its communications industries.
One study of the role of mass communications in overall development
places Indonesia 100th out of 109 countries ranked according to 54
indices, 12 of which directly measure mass media development.[17] Newspaper circulation figures are subject to a wide latitude of interpretation,

but in no case do they approach the "UNESCO minimum" of one copy for every ten inhabitants.[18] As for radios, there were fewer than one million sets in Indonesia in 1963, and many of these were probably inoperable.[19] Television, although its potential impact in the political sphere is incalculable, is not yet very significant.

On the other hand, increased utilization of communications technology hardly would be a political panacea. Extension of newspaper, radio, and television facilities surely would promote national political integration in the long run, but the short-term effect of development of these media could be to fragment rather than unite the political culture if the media develop unevenly. For example, of the approximately 1,300,000 newspapers distributed in Indonesia in 1963, more than 40 percent were marketed in Djakarta,[20] yielding the population of the capital city a ratio of better than one newspaper for every six people. Exposure of university students to mass media in Djakarta, as reported by a sample interviewed in 1964 and 1965 and shown in Table 13:1, obviously is much higher than that of many other sectors of the population in Djakarta and elsewhere in the country.

TABLE 13:1   Student Exposure to Mass Media

Frequency of Exposure	News-papers	Radio	Tele-vision	Movies	Maga-zines
Daily exposure	91%	94%	8%	1%	4%
Once a week	5	1	64	12	28
Occasionally	3	2	17	69	56
Never	1	3	11	18	12
Totals	100	100	100	100	100

The point is not simply that exposure to mass media is uneven throughout the population and thus is both a vehicle for and manifestation of the clash of cultures in Indonesian society. There is this additional consideration: the suddenness and intensity with which substantial numbers of people in Indonesia and the other new states of Asia and Africa are being exposed to the impersonal and nation-oriented messages of the press and radio is producing a crisis of political participation. Whether the pattern of participation will be one of constructive, civil awareness and involvement or one of ritualistic obeisance to doctrine coupled with denunciation of ideas and people "outside" the doctrine—this is the critical question with respect to democratic political development.

The impetus to political participation can be seen in the content of the Indonesian press. Politics is not just one of several topics receiving journalistic attention; it is far and away the dominant category of daily newspaper content. An analysis of Djakarta newspapers during the five-month period ending in March 1965 revealed that nonadvertising subject matter occurred in the frequencies shown in Table 13:2.[21]

TABLE 13:2   Types of News Items and Frequencies with Which They Occur

Political affairs in Djakarta	9%
Domestic government and politics	20
Foreign affairs	19
Opinion on government and foreign affairs	3
All governmental and foreign affairs	51%
Crime, vice, accidents	5
Social events and items about people	5
Sports	6
Business and financial	11
Miscellaneous	22
Total	100%

It is conceivable that for one reason or another readers of newspapers pay little or no attention to political items; however, a 1964 survey conducted by the Institute for Press and Public Opinion in Djakarta found that the contrary is true. Of the total of 2,801 respondents, 41.3 percent reported that they were much interested in politics and foreign affairs; 53.3 percent were much interested in editorials (most of which related to some level of political activity). The third most frequently mentioned category, Djakarta news, evoked "very interested" responses from only 19.4 percent of the sample. In its interpretation of these data, the Institute's report concluded that "the Indonesian public is very 'political minded.' "[22]

All these data were obtained during the guided democracy period. The fact that the power structure in Indonesia has been transformed over the past two years means at least that an opportunity exists to set a new pattern or style of political participation which is different from the negative participation the Sukarno regime appeared to be promoting. This is not cause for unqualified optimism about the prospects for the construction of representative institutions and the extension of civil liberties, however. For one thing, the means whereby the best-intentioned elites can use their skills and resources in support of a positive style of political participation are difficult to specify. For another, some writers have suggested that under certain conditions the dynamics of the developmental process render what we have called positive political participation impossible or inappropriate. Marshall McLuhan's analysis of the force of modern communication in Asia and Africa, for example, emphasizes the tendency of mass media to create hyperintense communal (nationalistic) loyalties best expressed through structured, ritualistic participation in an authoritarian political system. In McLuhan's view, it is not the content of the media which produces this result; it is in the nature of mass media of communications, regardless of the content of the messages being transmitted, to integrate the society. In those societies where the gradual historical phases of exposure to cities, books, and industrial life have been skipped or greatly compressed, this process of integration is a volatile one.[23]

Similarly, although from quite different theoretical and empirical bases, Phillips Cutright has predicted that Indonesia will not be able to maintain competitive and participative political institutions and norms for some time. Working with data pertaining to the years 1940 to 1960, Cutright found that Indonesia's political system was "too developed" (compared with other countries of the world) given its relatively underdeveloped mass communications. On the basis of this evidence, he argued that the "decline" of representative institutions in the late 1950s was to be expected. While this line of reasoning is logically incompatible with that of McLuhan's, the two approaches share an underlying conviction in the prime importance of mass communications in the political development process.[24]

Our approach to communications has been a relatively narrow one in that we have not—in contrast to McLuhan, for example—included railroads and the transportation system in general. Technological advancement in transportation has its political implications too: greater mobility of bureaucrats enables a higher degree of centralization of legislative and administrative activity; transportation facilities bring traditional people to the cities and into contact with the world culture; railroads and trucks and highways facilitate the integration of the economy, a process bound to have some political consequences, including that of greater governmental attention to problems of regulation. For the most part, however, transportation development is best regarded as just one, albeit an important one, of the many components of industrialization.

Industrialization, or economic development in the direction of industrialization, is a process of such scope and complexity that we can do little more than suggest some of the general effects that a trend toward industrialization could have in the political sphere in Indonesia. Industrialization would undoubtedly lead to the formation or reinvigoration of groups (potentially political) with a shared interest based mainly on economic specialization. Industrialization would also bring large numbers of people into contact with the world culture, or at least that part of it represented by impersonal and rationalized modes of production. Industrialization might cause a restructuring of socio-economic status accruing to various categories of skill-groups, and this in turn would probably produce change in patterns of political recruitment. Implicit in this last point is the likelihood that there will be some elite groups whose status would be threatened by industrialization and who therefore could be expected to oppose it.[25]

There are any number of other possible political consequences of industrialization, but most of them come back to a problem so fundamental to Indonesian development that it provides a compelling framework for a final overview of the connection between science and technology and political development. We are speaking of Indonesia's population problem. Its political ramifications are rooted in the brutal fact that an increasing number of people are making increasing demands for values that are scarce. Nathan Keyfitz has spelled out the demographic dynamics of one aspect of the problem very nicely by focusing on the disparity in the birth rate after 1950 as compared with previous years.[26] The marked increase in births in the decade following the Japanese occupation and the struggle for independence is just beginning to be reflected in an increase in the number of persons reaching adolescence and the point where they must think about and seek suitable adult roles. Their ideas of what is suitable will be determined partly by the fact that more than three-fourths of them have had or will have had some education at the high school level. In 1966 the employment market for the unskilled as well as the university-educated was not good; yet in 1971 there will be about twice as many seventeen-year-olds in Indonesia (a total of about three million) as there were five years previously. Surely the political orientations of these youth—and one suspects that this is true of the self-styled *"generasi '66"* as well—will be shaped not only by incongruities of indoctrination and the ensuing crisis of identity, but also by their perception of the capability of the socio-economic and political systems to gratify their quest for employment, status, and self-realization.

Virtually every category of technology would be of potential value in meeting this challenge. To return to transportation, for example, efficient movement of large numbers of people represents one approach, that of interisland migration, to alleviation of the population problem. This is so because, looking at the country as a whole, it is not absolute overpopulation but a maldistribution of the 116 million or so inhabitants of Indonesia which needs to be corrected. Demographic experts are of mixed opinion with respect to the adequacy of interisland migration as a solution or partial solution to the problem of overcrowded conditions on

Java and Madura,[27] but the two points of most relevance to our topic are clear: first, the high density of the population is a source of political strain and potential instability; second, one of the key variables in any migration effort necessarily is the technology required physically to move large numbers of people.

A second category of technology which could be exploited in an effort to cope with Java's overpopulation is that of birth control. Obviously birth control is a potential solution only in the long range, and therefore it is complementary to interisland migration. Of all the types of technology mentioned in this analysis, birth control has been most directly retarded by political factors. For years President Sukarno's position was that Indonesia's large population was one of its greatest blessings, that the nation could support an additional 150 million people, and that in general birth control was unnecessary. The technological dimension of this topic has witnessed considerable progress, and it seems likely that pills and intrauterine devices will be improved upon further in the not-too-distant future. Until recently, however, political factors prevented exploitation of the technology.[28]

Birth control represents merely one aspect of the broader category of technology arising out of biological science, medical technology. Of course, with respect to the population problem and its political consequences, the application of medical technology through expanded public health facilities and programs is not altogether constructive. For some time, gains made in terms of voluntary family planning probably will be more than offset by increased longevity and reduced infant mortality resulting from public health advances. On the other hand, one can at least speculate that there may be a positive correlation between development of public health services and the extent to which the nation includes a substantial proportion of loyal, participating citizens.

The speculation seems less tenuous with respect to the application of technology in agriculture. As the developing communications system makes rural people more aware of their relative deprivation and of the existence of a central government with some degree of responsibility to them, their reaction to chronic food shortages predictably will change from passivity to protest. Thus, one additional approach to the population problem is to seek to increase food production through modern farming methods.

Various efforts at agricultural development have been underway in Indonesia for some time, of course, and the record here illustrates two features of directed socio-economic change which have obvious implications for the shaping of the political culture. The first of these is the fact that technology alone is unlikely to generate far-reaching changes very quickly.[29] This is strikingly the case in the agricultural sector, where very traditional socio-cultural and psychological patterns tend to prevent technological innovations from having much impact. It is true in other fields as well, however; the search for "easier" birth control techniques, for example, is a response, not to the inadequacy of present contraceptive technology *per se,* but to the cultural and psychological barriers to the utilization of this technique. The point is that the effects, including the political effects, of technological means and practices are closely intermeshed with social, psychological, and cultural considerations.

The second point of which efforts at agricultural development remind us is that the technology being promoted is a foreign one. Somewhere in the process of introducing and applying this technology in Indonesia foreigners will be involved. To some extent, this applies to all fields of development, not just agriculture, and it probably will continue to be the case. There can be little question that the mere fact of receiving foreign assistance, much less the visible presence of foreign technicians, advisers, and equipment and commodities, will have an impact on Indonesians' orientations toward other countries and toward their own government. Just what that impact will be is not at all clear, however.

As might be gathered from the bafflement expressed in this last statement, there is little basis in the foregoing remarks for very specific prescriptions concerning the optimum use of technology. The relationship between technology and the political culture is complex and broad-gauged. It does seem clear, at least, that the burdens on the political system would be reduced if the economy's performance were improved,[30] and of course the contribution of science and technology to such an improvement can be great. At more specific levels of analysis, however, the political influence of science and technology is not easily perceived. From the point of view of the national leadership of Indonesia, the problem is not just to use and control science and technology. A number of other governments have found that taking charge of science, at least in a structural sense, is quite feasible. The real need of the Indonesian elite is an awareness of the full implications of the clash of cultures an imported technology may bring to their nation. They might well examine the experiences of other nations, as well as their own, as a basis for evaluating specific science and technology policy alternatives in terms of their probable political consequences.

[1] Indeed, if modern man were as rational as this image suggests, political scientists might cope with their subject more effectively. As Harold Lasswell and, more recently, Murray Edelman have shown, political thought and behavior are pervaded by nonrational, affective elements. See Harold Lasswell, *Power and Personality* (New York: Norton, 1948) and *Psychopathology and Politics*

(Chicago: University of Chicago Press, 1930); and Murray Edelman, *The Symbolic Uses of Politics* (Urbana: University of Illinois Press, 1964).

[2] A more realistic and very vivid portrayal of the Southeast Asian peasant is presented in Manning Nash, *The Golden Road to Modernity: Village Life in Contemporary Burma* (New York: Wiley, 1965).

[3] This, of course, is an oversimplification. The subject is treated most thoroughly in Clifford Geertz, *The Religion of Java* (Glencoe, Ill.: Free Press, 1960).

[4] The notion of "post-traditional" society in Indonesia is developed in Clifford Geertz, "The Javanese Village," in *Local, Ethnic, and National Loyalties in Village Indonesia: A Symposium,* ed. G. William Skinner (New Haven, Conn.: Yale University, Southeast Asia Studies, Cultural Report Series, 1959).

[5] Lucian W. Pye, *Politics, Personality, and Nation Building: Burma's Search for Identity* (New Haven, Conn.: Yale University Press, 1962), p. 10.

[6] Leslie Palmier, *Social Status and Power in Java* (London: Athlone Press, 1960).

[7] Soedjatmoko, "The Identity Crisis," in *Religion and Progress in Modern Asia,* ed. Robert N. Bellah (New York: Free Press, 1965), p. 2. For a more theoretical treatment of this topic see Lucian W. Pye, "Personal Identity and Political Ideology," in *Political Decision-Makers,* ed. Dwaine Marvick (Glencoe, Ill.: The Free Press, 1960).

[8] This conception of political culture is taken from Gabriel A. Almond and Sidney Verba, *The Civic Culture: Political Attitudes and Democracy in Five Nations* (Princeton, N.J.: Princeton University Press, 1963). Needless to say, this is a specialized and relatively narrow usage of the term culture.

[9] Herbert Feith, *The Decline of Constitutional Democracy in Indonesia* (Ithaca, N.Y.: Cornell University Press, 1962).

[10] This point is based on the assumption that inflation generally hurts exporters far more than importers. The most vigorous advocate of the primacy of this economic factor as a determinant of political attitudes in Indonesia is Hans O. Schmitt. See his "Post-Colonial Politics: A Suggested Interpretation of the Indonesian Experience, 1950–58," *The Australian Journal of Politics and History* 9 (November 1963): 176–83.

[11] Sidney Verba, "The Comparative Study of Political Socialization," paper delivered at the 1964 Annual Meeting of the American Political Science Association, Chicago, Illinois, p. 4.

[12] It is important to emphasize that this section is based on data collected in the field during the last year and a half of the "guided democracy" period, and changes which may have occurred in the political socialization process since October 1, 1965, therefore are not reflected in this analysis.

[13] Hildred Geertz's description of the Javanese family emphasizes its "loose" structural character; kinship ties are weak and flexible, and the usually large nuclear family is augmented by secondary relatives and close friends from the immediate community. See Hildred Geertz, *The Javanese Family: A Study of Kinship and Socialization* (New York: The Free Press of Glencoe, Inc., 1961). Familial instability is reflected in the report of the Central Bureau of Statistics that the ratio of "repudiations" to marriages-plus-reconciliations was 55 percent for the entire "Moslem community" in Indonesia in 1962. *Statistical Pocketbook of Indonesia 1963* (Djakarta: Biro Pusat Statistik, 1963), p. 25. This instability of the family, in combination with problems of family finance, results in large numbers of children living away from home, being with their parents only inter-

mittently if at all, and generally experiencing "irregular" childhoods during which the influence of the family is probably less—or at least less regular and determinative—than it otherwise would be.

[14] The quotations are from Sidney Verba, "The Comparative Study of Political Socialization," p. 4. The general significance of socialization into attitudes toward authority is stressed in Talcott Parsons and Edward Shils, eds., *Toward a General Theory of Social Action* (Cambridge, Mass.: Harvard University Press, 1951), pp. 150–51.

[15] On the diversity of the student bodies of Indonesian universities and especially of Gadjah Mada University see Joseph Fischer, "Indonesia," in *Education and Political Development,* ed. James S. Coleman (Princeton, N.J.: Princeton University Press, 1965), pp. 115–21.

[16] Consider the advice found in the workbook supplementing *Manusia dan Masjarakat Baru Indonesia (Man and the New Indonesian Society)* :

"What should our attitude be?
Answer: In order to comply with the ideals of the Proclamation of 1945, realize the Message of the People's Suffering, and avoid disgracing the Heroes of our Fatherland who sacrificed their blood and souls and passed away before us, our attitude must be:
a. Loyalty to the Revolution and the Great Leader of the Revolution, Bung Karno;
b. Highest respect for the Constitution;
c. Conformity in spirit and behavior with the goals of *Sosialisme Indonesia;*
d. Complete abandonment of democracy based on 'Free Fight Liberalism' and full acceptance of Guided Democracy and all its consequences;
e. Support of Guided Economy;
f. Return to Indonesian Personality in the spirit of *Gotong Rojong* mutual assistance and cooperation."

Sjofjan Hasan and Mawardi Djalins, *305 Tanja-Djawab: Civics (305 Questions and Answers: Civics)* (Djakarta: C.V.P.P. "Miswar," 1963), pp. 45–46.

[17] Vincent R. Farace, "A Study of Mass Communication and National Development," *Journalism Quarterly* 43 (Summer 1966): 305–13.

[18] UNESCO, *Mass Media in the Developing Countries* (Paris, 1961), p. 16. Combined circulation of dailies in all of Indonesia in 1963 was reported to be 1,300,000 copies. Lembaga Pers dan Pendapat Umum (Institute for Press and Public Opinion), *Petundjuk Pers, 1963 (1963 Press Directory)* (Djakarta, 1965). This figure, however, is based on permits issued for the purchase of newsprint. The most important source of variability is the fact that single copies of newspapers are likely to be read by several people.

[19] *Statistical Pocketbook of Indonesia 1963*, p. 211. These figures are based on licenses issued for radios, and probably date back to pre-independence days.

[20] Lembaga Pers dan Pendapat Umum, *Petundjuk Pers, 1963.*

[21] The sample consisted of copies of various newspapers collected on four days randomly selected each month. Percentages refer to proportions of items appearing, not proportions of total space. The effect of counting frequencies of categories rather than, say, column inches, is to underemphasize long and prominently displayed articles. It happens that most such articles in Indonesian newspapers are concerned with political issues.

[22] Unpublished "readership survey," Institute for Press and Public Opinion, Djakarta, 1964, p. 15.

[23] Marshall McLuhan, *Understanding Media: The Extensions of Man*

(New York: McGraw-Hill, 1965). McLuhan's term for the integrative process stimulated by newspapers and radio is "retribalization."

[24] See also Wilbur Schramm, *Mass Media and National Development: The Role of Information in the Developing Countries* (Stanford, Calif., Stanford University Press, 1964), and Lucian W. Pye, ed., *Communications and Political Development* (Princeton, N.J.: Princeton University Press, 1963), for discussions of the crucial role of mass media in political development.

[25] The importance of such groups and their resistance to change is argued in S. N. Eisenstadt, *Modernization: Protest and Change* (Englewood Cliffs, N.Y.: Prentice-Hall, Inc., 1966).

[26] Nathan Keyfitz, "Age Distribution as a Challenge to Development," *American Journal of Sociology* 70 (May 1965): 659–68.

[27] Compare Irene Taeuber's view of the futility of transmigration in Indonesia with the cautious optimism of Nathan Keyfitz and Widjojo Nitisastro. Irene Taeuber, "Population: Dilemma of Modernization in Southeast Asia," *Asia* 1 (Spring 1964); and Nathan Keyfitz and Widjojo Nitisastro, *Soal Penduduk dan Pembangunan Indonesia* (Djakarta: P. T. Pembangunan, 1964), esp. chap. 17.

[28] For indications of renewed interest and efforts in family planning see the *New York Times,* April 10, 1967, p. 22.

[29] A forceful statement of the inadequacy of technology alone as an agent of change may be found in G. Balandier, "Comparative Study of Economic Motivation and Incentives in a Traditional and in a Modern Environment," International Social Science *Bulletin* 6 (1954): 372–87.

[30] A striking example of economic performance facilitating political change is presented in Sidney Verba, "Germany: The Remaking of Political Culture," in *Political Culture and Political Development,* ed. Lucian W. Pye and Sidney Verba (Princeton, N.J.: Princeton University Press, 1965).

CHAPTER 14

David H. Penny and J. Price Gittinger **Economics and Indonesian Agricultural Development**

Economics has a critical role to play in the formulation and execution of effective programs to further agricultural development in Indonesia. The static nature of much Indonesian agriculture calls for a more aggressive economic policy.

Unfortunately, there the clichés end, and the determining of just what role economics can play in the social, political, and economic life of present-day Indonesia presents unexpected difficulties. This paper, based on firsthand knowledge of Indonesian agricultural programs, examines possible contributions of economics in a very practical context—one which, we hope, can lead to more "economic" use of economic research talent for agricultural development.

The Place of Agricultural Economists

Economists, particularly good agricultural economists, are a scarce resource in Indonesia today.[1] General economists in Indonesia rarely study agriculture, even though agriculture occupies 80 percent of the population and produces some 55 percent of the national income. Of the thirty-four-man Economic Stabilization Board, a critical body at the present juncture, only one is an agricultural economist.

We feel that the valuable resource represented by good research agricultural economists is best used for the present primarily to determine relationships between variables and to a much less extent to estimate aggregates. Indonesian policymakers need to know the shape of the economic and other processes at work in the agricultural sector; only later will it be necessary for them to know in some detail about totals and other quantities. They already know something about the totals—total production, total areas, total exports, total imports, and the like. But knowing these things has given them little upon which to base programs to increase production. For example, to some economists it might seem worthwhile to calculate the price elasticity of supply of smallholder rubber. Yet if it is easy—as we believe it is—to increase the supply of smallholder rubber by means of an imaginative program modeled after the BIMAS[2] program, using agriculture college students or perhaps plantation laborers as extension workers, then there is little use in making a conventional study.

To us, this means ranking economic analysis efforts in the following order of priority: (1) formulation of effective agricultural development policies firmly rooted in economic realities; (2) research using the minimum of resources necessary to provide "directional" answers—that is, answers that point the way to program formulation without the much greater research effort needed to supply the elegant details so dear to the heart of professionals; and (3) only in last place worry about such items as careful quantification of large samples yielding highly significant data which lead to quite precise quantitative statements as a basis for policy formulation.

Economic analysis of the agricultural situation in Indonesia indicates first of all the magnitude of the problem. It should also indicate in a general way what should be done if development is to occur. It should outline alternative economic policies in a form which can readily be used by policymakers and which will increase their awareness of the opportunity to use economic policy more effectively. Many policymakers lack a clear idea of the economic processes in agriculture at the micro level. In Indonesia, this persists in large part because there is not yet the "social control" which in other countries comes through farmers' organizations and lobbying activities. One result is that Indonesian policy still does not pay enough attention to creating the environment which will give farmers and others the opportunity to work to make themselves more prosperous. How many policymakers have ever met, talked with, and understood a farmer or a small trader? It is here that agricultural economists can make a substantial contribution.

Examples abound of how rather simple economic analysis can indicate policy directions. For instance, the ratio between the price of rice and the price of fertilizer remains today so unfavorable that few farmers can afford to use fertilizer, even when they are aware of what it can do and know how to use it. Yet it can be readily demonstrated that it would be cheaper for the nation as a whole to import fertilizer than to import rice, as Sie demonstrated as long ago as 1954 (Sie 1954) and others have done since. Unfortunately, the agricultural economists allowed a number of wrong conclusions to be drawn from this calculation. One was that simply because importing fertilizer could be more profitable than importing rice it could likewise be assumed that the actual profits would be the same as those calculated. It was not sufficiently realized that it costs money and requires effective administration to create demand for fertilizer and to make its use profitable in practice. A second wrong conclusion was that fertilizer should be imported for rice because that was profitable when it was evident that it was even more profitable to use fertilizer on other crops. The quota system devised—based on areas under wet-rice cultivation rather than on market or farmer demand— led to black markets, corruption, and a decline in farmers' confidence in government promises. Fortunately, this system of allocation has now come to an end.

With the evidence that fertilizer is profitable from the standpoint of the national account on the one hand and on the other the ample evidence of black markets and bare warehouses that there is substantial demand, a clear policy implication can be drawn. Indonesia would benefit were it to import fertilizer up to the amount of effective demand when offered for sale in the ports at a price to the farmer that would bear the same ratio to the artificially low domestic price for rice as imported fertilizer bears to imported rice. The "subsidy" this would involve would be profitable from the national standpoint, the brake on rising rice prices would be maintained, and farmers would have economic incentive to use fertilizer but only up to the point where it ceased to be profitable from the national standpoint. How much fertilizer this might involve is not easy to estimate, but the limits of such a policy can be identified. The largest amount of fertilizer Indonesia ever imported was 472,000 tons in 1961. In 1966, only 90,000 tons were imported. On the other hand, the amount of money budgeted for rice imports in 1967[3] is enough to purchase somewhere in the neighborhood of 700,000 tons of fertilizer. Hence, the policy prescription would be valid were the effective demand to lie somewhere in the range between the low of 90,000 tons of 1966 and the high limited by the value of the projected 1967 rice imports. "Leaks" in the system caused by using fertilizer on other crops do not affect this analysis, provided they do not drive total demand beyond about 600,000 tons.

A second example of how simple agricultural economics analysis can be used to point the direction to effective policy may be drawn from rubber cultivation in Sumatra. As long as a decade ago, policymakers were saying that replanting rubber would not be profitable because of the cleverness of synthetic rubber producers. At the same time, rupiah prices were depressed relative to world (dollar) prices due to the government's exchange rate policy. It was therefore not surprising that estate managers concluded that new methods such as new tapping techniques—long proved worthwhile in Malaya—would be quite unprofitable.

Such were the reasons that led policy makers to conclude that rubber was not profitable and would be even less profitable in the future. The same story is being told today, even though rubber remains a highly profitable crop for Indonesia. In 1958 the average full cost price for rubber on estates on the east coast of Sumatra was in the neighborhood of Rp. 12 per kilogram, with a range of some Rp. 6 per kilogram. The domestic price for rubber at the time was about Rp. 20 per kilogram, so that the average gross margin actually received by the estates was about 66 percent, even in the absence of the higher-yielding varieties and better cultivation techniques used across the Strait of Malacca in Malaya. Indeed, had the black market price for the rupiah been used for the calculation, the price would have been about three times as high and the profitability of the estates much greater. Today, a decade later, even though rubber prices on the world market have dropped by nearly half, rubber still remains extremely profitable in east Sumatra which has better soils, lower real wages, and higher labor productivity than Malaysia. Yet the price policy of the nation still is structured in such a manner as to discourage rubber production. In December 1966 the ratio between the world price for rubber and that of rice worked out to about 3.3 while the rubber-rice price ratio in Indonesia was 1.2, even though the rupiah price of rice was 25 percent below the world price.

Agricultural economists through clearly stated, cogent analysis—which need not necessarily rely on complex or highly sophisticated techniques—have an opportunity to illustrate convincingly to policymakers such relationships as these and to outline the policy implications which flow from them. Properly done, such analysis can serve as a guide for action in other fields. Careful farm management analysis, for instance, not only can point the way to increased agricultural productivity through better resource allocation on individual farms but can also serve as a useful base for knowing more about farmers themselves, about social life in rural areas, and for learning about the interrelationships between agriculture and the other sectors of the economy. At this stage, the main contribution of economic analysis is to indicate the scope of the problem and to show what could be done to achieve certain economic goals. The "solution," the effort of will needed, depends on the national leadership, and the people of Indonesia.

Economics in a Unique Cultural Environment

So much has been written about the impact of culture on the form taken by economic activity in Indonesia (e.g., Geertz 1963) that it may seem unnecessary to return to this topic. Yet we contend it is quite important to understand the cultural environment more clearly. What is needed is to see the application of economic tools and, more important, an economic way of thinking about Indonesian problems in a much broader context than is necessary in the well-understood cultural environment of the West.[4]

Agricultural development in Indonesia, as elsewhere, is a many-sided process. One of its core elements is economic. If what is done is not "economic" then there will be no development. Economists have a responsibility to point to where the economic opportunities lie (and there are many more than is generally realized). Agricultural development in Indonesia is not possible without taking into account the economic aspects of introducing new technology and more scientific methods. Often new methods are suggested without proper consideration being given to profit and loss as seen by the peasant farmer. Economists must wrestle with the extent to which successful development depends on proper application of science and technology in a peasant farming environment, and, thus, must come to grips more realistically with the problem of creating incentive patterns that will lead to economic change and that will shape the "other factors" that we all agree are important in Indonesia. It is clear from the BIMAS program and other instances of response to economic incentive that one can realize economic improvement even though the land tenure system, the social structure in the village, the inefficient marketing structure, and even the tools and equipment used remain unchanged.

The social sciences, the physical and biological sciences, and the technologies—each category has a critical role to play in agricultural development. Even so, it is more the responsibility of the economists than of the anthropologists, sociologists, or physical and biological scientists to ascertain just what these roles are. The problem of agricultural policy formulation in Indonesia is to work from the standpoint of "economics and . . ." not "economics in . . ." This comes down to a responsibility for economists—and through them the economic policymakers—to determine, based on what is already known in Indonesia and elsewhere about the economics of innovation in agriculture, what is best to be done in Indonesia to achieve a more rapid rate of development through the introduction of science and technology and through induced institutional changes. Coupled with this is a heavy responsibility for economists to outline what needs to be known about the economics of innovation and institutional change in Indonesia.

The importance of the cultural context in Indonesian economics is illustrated by some unconventional economic questions which would be well worth studying. As an example, the government will doubtlessly in the future put much more emphasis on *gotong-rojong,* or mutual help, in order to accelerate progress in such areas as maintenance of irrigation systems. What are the economics of *gotong-rojong?* Initial assessment indicates it may be rather efficient in mobilizing labor, but more needs to be understood about the scale at which *gotong-rojong* projects start to become less efficient than other institutional approaches. What are the economics of land reform in Indonesia? What are the economics of cooperatives versus privately owned and managed enterprises for the distribution of agricultural inputs? What are the economics of agricultural credit for the shopkeeper, the village moneylender, the government-sponsored program, and for the peasant farmer? What are the economics of *transmigrasi?* Of induced settlement programs? What are the economics of the cost in terms of failure-to-succeed versus low-outside-investment for those settlers who do succeed in spontaneous settlement programs?

Another subject about which too little is known is that of house gardens. In 1961, a farm management study made in connection with the Tjiawi agricultural development seminar estimated the income in cash and prerequisites from the house-garden, dry land, and wet rice land for a group of farms. The returns came out in that order. The seminar group, all senior civil servants, had estimated previously that it would be the reverse—that is, the wet rice land would return more than the dry land and both would be more productive than the house plot. The figures for gross returns per unit of area indicated, moreover, that if the families studied had put all their rice land into house plots and dry land they could have bought more rice than they were raising. (No more investment would have been needed, either, since investment per acre is highest for wet rice land.) Paradoxically, Javan farmers spend almost no time or thought on house-gardens, even though these are more profitable than either wet rice land or dry land sown to food crops. But the potential is great: there are over 1.5 million hectares of house-gardens on Java.

One might even go a step further in applying conventional economics unconventionally. Farm management studies usually assume area as fixed and optimize by changing variables of labor and nonagricultural inputs. In contrast, in the tropical environment of Java, farmers have over the years devised a cultivation system on house plots which takes advantage of the intense sunlight by planting coconut trees which mature to heights of 15 to 20 meters; coffee, citrus, or other small trees which mature at heights of 5 to 7 meters, and herbs and vegetables which grow to heights of only half a meter, and there are other combinations. In this context, sunlight (and hence area) becomes a variable, and some very interesting problems of practical importance for Javan peasants center on optimization of this use of sunlight.

Innovation versus Subsistence-mindedness

One of the authors of this paper has proposed a theory of Indonesian peasant behavior which is summed up in the term "subsistence-mindedness" (Penny 1964). Peasant farmers tend to pass up opportunities to increase their incomes even when that involves nothing more than rearranging their present capital, labor, and land inputs. Farm management analysis of village economies in Indonesia indicates that income in most could be increased merely by a change in resource use patterns. The incomes of farmers could be further increased if they were more willing to invest; many have capital but prefer not to use it for productive investment. In the village of Suka Damai in North Sumatra, for example, a small transfer of labor from crop production to repair work on the irrigation system would increase total production considerably. Similarly, spending a little less money on fertilizer and more on animal vaccines would raise net income. In the Depok area of West Java, growing papaya and other fruits for the Djakarta market is much more profitable than growing food crops for sale, yet only a few farmers engage in the trade. In most parts of Indonesia there are one or more crops which if grown, or grown more widely, would result in higher incomes. All these opportunities, and many more, could be grasped without farmers having to work harder or without making more than minimal demands on their capital resources (Penny 1964).

In many parts of Indonesia, moreover, farmers could afford to buy and use fertilizer, pesticides, improved seeds, vaccines, and the like, even though they rarely do. Many of these innovations will give very high returns, sometimes even 1,000 percent or more. One such is the use of selected rubber seed on rubber smallholdings (Penny 1965). Capital invested in any one of a number of new ways would yield much higher returns than it now earns, but few farmers are willing to take the plunge. As long as this situation persists, agricultural development will be limited.

Yet, given their context, these seemingly perverse activities are quite rational for the Indonesian farmer. The context involves subjective risk and uncertainty. It is this which lies at the heart of subsistence-mindedness, backward-bending supply curves, "agricultural involution," and a number of other seemingly obstinate, noneconomic responses. It strains conventional tools of economic analysis to tackle this problem, which offers one of the greatest challenges to the agricultural economist interested in development.

Most peasant farmers in Indonesia attach extremely high discounts to risk and uncertainty, particularly the latter.[5] The risk discount may usefully be divided onto a "real" or "objective" component and a "subjective" component. In the case of uncertainty, the distinction tends to disappear. Once the real or objective risk is determined, the firm that is not pressed for time and money need not—and does or would not—apply any subjective risk discount at all; it can simply take the objective risk as its working base in much the same way a life insurance company does. But the Indonesian peasant struggling to support his family on half a hectare or less (and there are many of them) has a very different situation. He suffers from severe capital rationing and has a time horizon extending hardly to the next harvest (indeed, probably only to about the time of the next *patjeklik*[6] season). He has a very small risk base, indeed, yet it is this base which to a large extent determines how much of a chance the rational entrepreneur feels he can afford to take with some change in his farming practices—that is the size of his uncertainty discount. Furthermore, gains and losses are not equally weighted, since the possibility of a small loss which means someone must go hungry is more important than the equal possibility of a larger gain. Under these circumstances, it is hardly surprising to find peasants adopting large subjective discounts.

But it is not only the peasants with small farms who are subsistence-minded and reluctant to adopt innovations that objective calculations have shown to be profitable. In many parts of Indonesia all farmers—those with much land and cash such as landlords as well as those who lack both such as tenants—are subsistence-minded. The differences between the subsistence-minded and the development-minded farmers are most clearly seen in the new settlements in the east coast of Sumatra. In none of these new settlements are there landlords or moneylenders. In some of these settlements the farmers are willing to invest for the future. As a consequence, they have started to grow commercial crops, to use fertilizer, and so forth. In other settlements the farmers continue to believe that the most economic way to farm is for them to continue to use the tools and methods they are accustomed to in order to grow only food crops.

The economic difference between the development-minded and the subsistence-minded farmer lies wholly and solely in the size of the subjective rate of discount each applies to his future income. For the development-minded this rate is low; for the subsistence-minded it is high.

The subsistence-minded small farmer believes that the returns he would realize from new technology, from growing new crops, and the like are much lower than he would in fact receive if he adopted such innovations. He is deeply skeptical about the profitability of all innovation. In other words, the subjective rate of interest he uses to discount future income to be gained from new crops and new methods is very high. Even so, subsistence-minded farmers the world over generally are interested in new opportunities. It is not at all hard to generate interest in a conversation about new technology in an Indonesian village. If a new opportunity seems worthwhile, one or more men will try it experimentally on a small scale. If the experiments work, they, and their neighbors, will soon begin to accept the new innovation. The trouble has been that new economic opportunities have often not turned out to be anywhere near as good as first anticipated. Farmers are keenly aware—as outside advisers may not be—of such things as market price fluctuations, the influence of rainfall variations on profitability of fertilizer applications, and cash liabilities in the face of in-kind income.

Most small peasant farmers, with their narrow risk base, value security highly. It is not surprising, therefore, that they define security in subsistence terms, for they measure their margin of safety according to the size of the marketable surplus of subsistence, or safe, crops they can produce from their minute holdings with their labor intensive, low productivity—but low risk—technology.

In this context, it is clear why subsistence-minded farmers, whether poverty-stricken or more prosperous, are not economically irrational. In a basic sense, they, too, would like to get the same output for less effort, or a higher price for what they sell. Where most of them differ from the development-minded farmer is that they often do not perceive the opportunities inherent in their economic environment. In those cases where they do, they lack the resources or the organization to exploit opportunities, or they discount future income so heavily that they will not even try the new things, even though the rate of profit is apparently very high. In short, they may be classed as acting in an economically irrational way only if their economic behavior is judged by standards other than their own.

A problem which arises in trying to deal explicitly with subjective uncertainty discounts is that the rejection by peasants of new opportunities tends to become automatic—hence, many observers insist they are "tradition-bound." The subsistence-minded farmers who earn well above average incomes have such a high subjective rate of discount or else respond so automatically (no one can be certain which) that they act in a manner just as subsistence-minded as small peasants. The need to react to ceremonial occasions within the community conflicts with and is stronger than the "need" to respond to opportunities to innovate. Roekasah shows that on most occasions both rich and poor farmers in the Krawang region on the coast of Java east of Djakarta show a high preference for consumption—often conspicuous consumption—to investment (Roekasah 1964).

A high subjective discount for innovation may be a characteristic of a group as well as of individuals, and when this happens the difficulties of introducing change are severely compounded. Geertz cites the instance of the progressive farmer who tried to introduce use of a sickle in place of the cutting knife, only to find his fields burned by his neighbors, who attached a much higher subjective uncertainty discount to the implications of labor-saving than the individual (Geertz 1963). But such is not strictly an Indonesian phenomenon or even that of a developing nation; after all, the Luddites were Europeans, and outmoded building codes are buttressed by craft union support in the United States.

The interrelationships of high discount rates with other influences show the complications which arise immediately if serious study is undertaken. But in the past, explicit understanding of the rational aspects of subjective uncertainty have too often been ignored and all resistance ascribed to tradition or culture. If such were the case, then innovation would be very hard to introduce indeed, for tradition and culture are clearly difficult to change. But to the extent that resistance to innovation can be ascribed to rational discounting—and it is our opinion that at least some significant fraction can be—then the problem of modernization of traditional agriculture is to that extent reduced. The result of the BIMAS program is only the latest in a series of incidents which indicate how high individual subjective discount rates can be quite rapidly lowered to where innovation can proceed. The problem, admittedly not easy, is how to lower the discount rates on a much broader scale.

A major contribution of agricultural economics to better policy formulation in Indonesia would be to begin to outline the dimensions of the influence of subjective risk and uncertainty discounts. At first, the need might be less for precise measurements than for orders of magnitude, and whether these differ significantly for various kinds of innovations or for various areas of the country. As the concept becomes more widely understood by policymakers, then new formulations of program approaches which permit farmers to reduce their subjective discounts can be proposed and gain support.

Closely related to the uncertainty introduced by market fluctuations is the influence of price policies on economic incentive. The government of Indonesia has consistently depressed the prices of all agricultural products relative to the prices of goods bought by farmers.[7] From mid-1960 to mid-1966, the ratio of rubber prices to rice prices on a per kilogram basis in the world market was between 4 and 5.5, while in Indonesia it rarely rose over 3 and sometimes fell to 0.5. As a result, far too few farmers turned to commercial crops, the first step to agricultural modernization in many instances. Artificially low prices for rice itself have also discouraged productivity improvements. The elasticity of marketable surplus of rice in Indonesia is admittedly low, but it is positive, as Mubyarto and Fletcher have shown.[8] Without more carefully designed agricultural price policies, however, no advantage can be taken of this. Transportation taxes and restrictions imposed on movement of rice between areas are other examples of disincentives in Indonesian agricultural policy. Agricultural economics can make a signal contribution if it can demonstrate the necessity for a more "economic" solution to these economic problems.

Seeing the Problem in the Proper Perspective

Agricultural economists in Indonesia will make their mark on the agricultural development of the nation as they contribute to a more widespread, more realistic view of the economic problems of innovation and adoption of science and technology by farmers. In doing this job they will probably find that the ideas and the theories developed in the West well need modification, and that new concepts, theories, and so forth appropriate to the Indonesian situation will need to be developed. One way that the agricultural economists might do this is to identify the elements which have contributed to success in programs which have already engendered change in order to draw from them the attributes which they bear in common. Indonesian peasant farmers can and will innovate, despite the high subjective discounts, subsistence-mindedness, and "shared poverty" concepts which seem to be such insuperable barriers to change at the present time.

A current example of a development activity enjoying at least modest success in the face of a very difficult situation is the BIMAS program. Under this approach, university agriculture students take time out to live in a village during an entire rice-growing season. They devote their time to helping farmers adopt more productive cultivation techniques and to teaching them how to use modern inputs. The *Direktorat Pertanian Rakjat* is now trying to design a "systematized BIMAS" to extend this program and to establish it on a continuing basis. Its observers have identified four elements of success in the BIMAS approach:

(1) the *potensi* principle—that is, choosing to concentrate at first in those areas with water control, transportation, and similar favorable advantages.

(2) adequate living allowances for the BIMAS workers, so that they can work without needing to resort to other sources of income.

(3) a leverage on scarce stocks of fertilizer—although departmental supplies are limited, too. The point here is not so much quantity as it is an assurance that whatever does exist and is promised will in fact be available at the time needed.

(4) a quality of "exhilaration" felt by the students participating in the programs.

To this list, some observers would add a fifth item: farmers feel that for once officials really are concerned with their problems, so that the BIMAS program acts as a bridge between city and country.

Clearly, these "elements of success" cannot all be transferred without modification to an ongoing program. The fourth point, particularly— that of initial enthusiasm—cannot be reproduced as it presently exists. The advantage of identifying success elements clearly is not necessarily just in trying to reproduce them. Rather, it is to recognize them so that programs can be designed in their light, and those which cannot be reproduced can be understood and accounted for. It is possible, for instance, that it will be decided that the enthusiasm of young college students is so critical to success and so impossible to replace that no ongoing program with permanent personnel can use the BIMAS approach; hence, additional resources allocated to this type of effort would be wasted. Or, it may be that some device of rotation, promotion, or something else can be used to maintain an atmosphere of enthusiasm over the next several years.

There are other instances of responsiveness and success in Indonesian agriculture which would bear broad-gauged economic and sociological analysis. One can cite the spread of vegetable crop production to supply the Singapore market, the persistence of a black market for government-distributed fertilizer when the ratios between rice prices and other agricultural commodity prices are not allowed to adjust, or a recent Bogor student's study in Tjipaku, about fifteen kilometers from Bogor, that found most farmers bought and used fertilizer even though no extension work had ever been done in the village and no local outlet sold fertilizer. The problem is that these instances of responsiveness are too few, too far between, and too slow in spreading. Economists, among others, must contribute to a better understanding of the mechanics of these success stories so that they can be duplicated elsewhere.

It would help, too, if it were more widely realized in Indonesia that the country is not somehow inherently rich and only some magic button need be pushed for a cornucopia to open up. Most of the soils remaining to be settled in Indonesia are not inherently fertile; cultivating them will take skill and persistence. Indonesian farmers, like farmers everywhere, continue with good reason to regard nature as niggardly. It is the Europeans and the nonfarming people of Indonesia who talk of the untapped agricultural riches of the Indies. They do not understand the resource endowment picture very well, and until agricultural economists and others can convince them that development is chancy at best in Indonesia, requiring the most economic policies possible, then suitable development policies and programs cannot easily emerge.

Agricultural economists themselves will have to develop more objective viewpoints. Many, but certainly not all, believe that farmers are so poor and exploited that only welfare policies are appropriate. Clearly, this is often not true, as is seen in the success of BIMAS. Indonesia is a complex country, and for most topics research must be undertaken in many places. Economists will have to examine what they often accept as given in their studies—the propensity to save, price elasticities of supply and demand, subjective rates of discount. But all these can be changed, perhaps in a short time, if vigorous, inventive policies are carried out. Economists must make themselves equal to the task of analyzing Indonesia's problems within the context of fewer givens without losing their grip on the realities of economics nor losing the valid elements in their economic tools. It is no small task.

Before better policy formulation can be expected, many of the government officials themselves must shake their own "subsistence-mindedness" and embark on much more "economic" programs. The theoretical premises of many past agricultural productivity programs have been weak. For example, government officials note that farmers are poor, and draw the conclusion that they need cheaper credit. When farmers get this credit, they often use it for consumption or to pay off old debts to storekeepers and moneylenders. They know the government is a lenient creditor. What the government has failed to take into account is that subsistence-minded farmers will not use production credit effectively until they feel more secure economically than they do now.

We have tried to indicate that there is much agricultural economists can do now through perceptive economic analysis but without too elaborate use of complex new techniques. The BIMAS program is an example of success where economic elements are incorporated into a development activity. The report by Rangkuty on an extension and education project in North Sumatra discusses an example of an initial step which was highly pragmatic and very useful (Rangkuty 1965). But if agricultural economists are to make their full impact on the development of Indonesia there are several steps—an agenda, if you will—which we feel they will need to undertake. The first is a better inventory of existing information, something that is already being undertaken through the Agro-Economic Survey. Another is to improve utilization of data already collected. There is a tendency to collect lots and analyze little. Agricultural economists need to husband their resources much more carefully so that their efforts will not be lost or dissipated. Research projects should be chosen carefully, in full consultation with decisionmakers and designed always from a policy-oriented standpoint, not a professionally oriented view. They must be continued long enough and personnel maintained continuously enough that something can be realized out of preliminary preparation and pilot projects. Research projects must be kept to a scale that can be coped with in present-day conditions. Nationwide surveys of ambitious scope can be reserved for later; smaller projects which can have a near-term impact on policy formulation will be a greater contribution to the economic advancement of the nation.

Happily, we can report that most of the points we have touched upon are drawn from our conversations with Indonesian agricultural economists and farmers themselves, so that we have reason to know that our comments and suggested directions of work are well known to thoughtful economists in Indonesia. We hope, however, that by bringing them together in the context of improved policymaking we can encourage Indonesian economists and decisionmakers to see the role of agricultural economics in their national development effort more clearly, and, hence, to make better use of its potentials.

REFERENCES

Geertz, C. 1963. *Agricultural Involution*. Berkeley and Los Angeles: University of California Press.

Mubyarto, and Fletcher, Lehman B. 1966. *The Marketable Surplus of Rice in Indonesia: A Study in Java-Madura*. Ames, Iowa: Department of Economics, Iowa State University.

Penny, David H. 1964. *The Transition from Subsistence to Commercial Family Farming in North Sumatra*. Ph.D. dissertation, Cornell University.

———. 1965. "Case Studies in Subsistence and Transition: North Sumatra, Indonesia." A/D/C Seminar on Subsistence and Peasant Economics, Honolulu.

———. 1966. The Economics of Peasant Agriculture: The Indonesian Case. *Bulletin of Indonesian Economic Studies*, No. 5 (October).

———. 1969. "Case Study: Growth of 'Economic Mindedness' among Small Farmers in North Sumatra, Indonesia," in Clifton R. Wharton, Jr., ed., Subsistence Agriculture and Economic Development, Chicago: Aldine Publishing Company, 1969. pp. 152–61.

Rangkuty, R. 1965. *Laporan Suatu Projek Penjuluhan di Kampung Kaju Laut, Tapanuli Selatan*. Mimeographed. Fakultas Pertanian, Universitas Sumatera Utara, Medan.

Roekasah, F. Adiratma, et al. 1964. *Penguasan dan Penggunaan Padi oleh Petani dan Pergaruhnja terhadap Ekonomi Keluarga Tani*. Mimeographed. Institut Pertanian, Bogor.

Sie Kwat Soen. 1954. The Use of Fertilizers in Indonesia. *Ekonomi dan Keuangan Indonesia*, Vol. VII, No. 9.

de Vries, Egbert. 1937. "Rijstpolitik op Java in Vroeger Jaren." *Landbouw*, Diertiende Jaargang, Nos. 7 and 8.

[1] The present tense is retained here to stress the paper's temporal orientation.

[2] BIMAS is an acronym derived from *bimbingan massal* which means mass guidance.

[3] The government budget for rice imports in 1967 was $70 million. The most that has ever been spent in any year to import fertilizer was $23.1 million (1961). In 1966 only $4.5 million were used to import fertilizer.

[4] An early important contribution in this direction was Boeke's theory of dualism (1953).

[5] Economic jargon distinguishes between risk and uncertainty. In general, risk involves a collection of events which we can predict for a group, even though we cannot predict the occurrence of one event for a particular individual. Risk, therefore, is something which can be insured against, and life insurance is the classroom example. Uncertainty applies to those events about which too little is known to predict their occurrence even for a group. Either these events have never

occurred before or else they occur too infrequently to provide the basis for prediction. New technology is an example of the former; agricultural development theory based on historical example is an instance of the latter.

[6] Time of food scarcity just before harvest.

[7] DeVries argues that this has been the case for 300 years (deVries 1937).

[8] (Mubyarto and Fletcher 1966).

Index

AID (Agency for International Development), 5, 6, 55, 168, 170, 225, 229, 233, 234
AMPERA (Amanat Penderitaan Rakjat), 25
Academy of Nutrition, 153. *See also* nutrition
Agency for International Development. *See* AID
agricultural development, 2, 19, 20, 21, 23, 25, 26, 29, 33, 39, 40, 48, 49, 239, 254, 270. *See also* BIMAS S.S.B.M.; rural development
Agricultural Development Council, Inc. (A.D.C.), 5
agricultural economics. *See* economics
agricultural extension service, 51. *See also* BIMAS S.S.B.M.
agricultural production. *See* agricultural development; BIMAS S.S.B.M.
agricultural products: sugar, 1, 21, 33, 34; sweet potatoes, 4; rubber, 10, 19, 21; cacao, 21; coffee, 21; palm oil, 21, 151–53; quinine, 21; tea, 21; tobacco, 21; corn, 22. *See also* rice
Agricultural Research Station, 53, 226
agriculture. *See* agricultural development
agro-economic survey, 226, 271
Anderson, John: writings on Indonesia, 94
animal husbandry. *See* agricultural development
Association of Indonesian Publishers, 224, 228
Atjeh, 239. *See also* ethnic groups
authority: socialization toward, 239, 245, 246, 247, 248

BIMAS S.S.B.M. (Bimbigan Massal Ses Semboda Bahan Makanan), 2–4, 6, 26, 29, 33, 40, 42, 44, 259, 263, 268–71; principles of, 2–4; student role in, 4, 41; fields, 26;

systemized, 29; aspects of, 41; rainy season, 41, 45; area and yield, 42; benefit-cost relationships, 43, 44; alternatives compared, 45, 47; reducing constraints on, 50; elements of success in, 269
Bali: BIMAS in, 42
Bangka. *See* mineral resources
Bapakism. *See* authority
batik production, 239
Behrman, Walter: writings on Indonesia, 96
bibliography, lack of a national, 5, 223, 224. *See also* libraries
Bibliotheca Bogoriensis, 53, 54, 225, 226, 231, 237. *See also* libraries
Bio Farma Institute: Bandung, 176, 177. *See also* health
biological education, 58, 62, 65, 214. *See also* science education
biological research, 3, 55, 58, 61–65. *See also* research
birth control, 4, 27, 177, 254, 255; and birth rate, 253
Blankhart: nutrition studies, 1957–1959, 153–54
Bogor, 63, 65, 66. *See also* IPB; Botanic Gardens; NBI
Botanic Gardens: at Bogor, 53–55, 57, 58, 60, 67, 68, 77, 209, 226; at Eka Karja, Bali, 53; at Gunung Ardjuno, 53; at Purwodadi, 53; at Selya-Mulia, 53; at Sibolangit, 53; at Tjibodas, 53, 56, 63, 68; at Udjung Kulono, 56, 63, 68
Broek, Jan O. M.: writings on Indonesia, 97

Cereals Experiment Station, 30
Chemical Research, laboratory, 53, 226
colonial period, 11, 14, 15, 19, 25, 57, 58, 77, 166, 182, 198–200, 209, 213, 225, 226, 244
copyright: national law needed, 5, 223, 230. *See also* libraries

www.ingramcontent.com/pod-product-compliance
Lightning Source LLC
Chambersburg PA
CBHW031502270326
41930CB00006B/205